T0306138

"Ilene Lefcourt's *When Mothers Talk* is a treasure – an original, creative window into the experiences of mothers, babies, and toddlers. Her first book, *Parenting and Childhood Memories*, was full of parent–infant stories that beautifully illustrate how parents come to have deep empathy for their children and for themselves. Now she invites us into the intimate talk among mothers – the pleasures, the stresses, and the awakening of childhood memories – fairy godmothers, witches, and good enough mothers. This new book reveals solutions that different mothers find to everyday stumbling blocks. Bravo!"

> **Beatrice Beebe**, Ph.D., clinical professor of Psychology in Psychiatry, College of Physicians & Surgeons, Columbia University; Department of Child and Adolescent Psychiatry, New York State Psychiatric Institute. Author, *Mothers, Infants, and Young Children of September 11, 2001: A Primary Prevention Project*; *The Origins of Attachment: Infant Research and Adult Treatment*; *The Mother–Infant Interaction Picture Book: Origins of Attachment*.

"Having a child is an extraordinary opportunity for self-understanding and growth. Ilene Lefcourt guides mothers through the maze of reverberations from the past. There is no single way to answer the myriad questions posed by mothers. The most productive and helpful way for a mother to find answers is to walk with peers and find her own path. For decades, Ilene Lefcourt has offered mothers the opportunity to discuss these issues in a protected and caring environment and for each mother to find her own answers.

Every step in a baby and toddler's development and each difficulty awakens a memory and provides an opportunity to share reflections, learn useful information, and discover explanations of developmental phenomena. What may feel like a failure for a mother may represent for her child a space available for progress, and an opportunity for success. This process may consolidate a child's sense of self and mother–child connectedness.

In this rich journey, the leader's gaze sets the course. Like a good fairy, Ilene Lefcourt wonders and questions with mothers. She accompanies, guides, and supports them with confidence in their ability to wonder and question. *When Mothers Talk* is an opportunity for every mother to take a journey with this exceptional expert leader."

> **Nadia Bruschweiler-Stern**, M.D., pediatrician, child psychiatrist, supervisor at the University Hospital of Geneva; director of the Swiss Brazelton Center. Author, *The Birth of a Mother*.

"*When Mothers Talk* is a rare gem to keep close. Ilene Lefcourt integrates decades of scientific research with her insightful empathic imagination to deeply understand everyday mother–baby and mother–toddler interactions. She is able to imagine a baby's and toddler's emerging thoughts and feelings that accompany a developing sense of self. This insight into a baby's developing mind provides a treasure trove of information.

The relationships among women during early motherhood – mommy-friends – resonate with childhood memories and provide a framework for maternal care. Mothers' personal stories about their friendships add a vital perspective to the challenges mothers encounter and the pleasures they enjoy. 'During the first three years of motherhood, not only do mothers nurture their babies' development, but they themselves change in many ways.' Ilene Lefcourt beautifully describes intricate details of this complex process. The readers' own memories are awakened and lead to new ideas."

Susan Coates, Ph.D., clinical professor, Medical Psychology
Columbia University; faculty, Columbia University Center
for Psychoanalytic Training and Research. Author,
September 11: Trauma and Human Bonds.

"Yes, there is an inner world with fantasies and emotions in babies, toddlers, and their mothers! Ilene Lefcourt gives the readers quite a feast revealing this fact, sharing with us her vivid experience leading mother-baby-toddler groups. Her insights don't come from theory, but from real-life examples, told in a sensitive way. Thus, she can illuminate aspects of the dyadic emotional life that otherwise could pass unnoticed to parents and readers. Ilene Lefcourt stimulates the internal work of mothers to elaborate emotions, offering a unique understanding of each situation, far from protocols. And she doesn't shy away from contradictions, accepting that she is walking on the razor's edge to provide comprehension without being judgmental or dampening maternal spontaneity. The self-reflective questions help the reader to move from a passive stance to a more active identification with the author's thinking mind."

Vera Regina J. R. M. Fonseca, M.D., psychiatrist and
psychoanalyst, training and supervising analyst of the
Brazilian Psychoanalytic Society of São Paulo.

"Ilene Lefcourt has drawn on over 35 years of experience leading mother-baby-toddler groups to cast a light on some of the delights and difficulties many mothers experience as they care for their young children. This book broadens the scope of the already vast literature on early development by focusing primarily on the growth and development of the relationship between mother and child. While acknowledging that early development can be studied from many perspectives, Lefcourt makes it clear that her choice has been to examine early development through the lens of mother–child love and attachment. This perspective may serve as a means to integrate other perspectives.

Central to *When Mothers Talk* is the consideration of the role of memory. Recollection of past events can serve to expand a mother's understanding of the possible meanings of her child's behavior as well as her own reactions to it as she guides her child to negotiate the world in which they are developing. The self-reflective questions can serve as a stimulus to a mother's memories as she deals with the inevitable questions that arise when caring for babies and toddlers. The recollections can often point the way to future action.

The implicit message of this very readable account of mothers and their children during the first three years of life is that while child rearing is often stressful it is also deeply satisfying and pleasurable. While reading I found myself recalling many of my own childhood experiences, as well as interactions with my now middle-aged children. From that perspective, this book is indeed a success."

Margaret Hertzig, M.D., professor of Psychiatry, Weill Cornell Medical College Cornell University.

"Ilene Lefcourt's remarkable book about motherhood must be set apart as the reader considers her own experiences as a child to influence her parenting. Lefcourt's positive outlook on the legacy of Sigmund Freud highlights how unconscious memories, thoughts, and feelings impact mothering.

Lefcourt draws attention to mothers' attunement to children by discussing the inevitable, universal rupture and repair of unattuned interactions as loving bonds grow.

Lefcourt values mothers' insights about the underlying meanings of babies' behavior and interactions. She invites mothers to consider how their own memories influence their mothering, including the impact of a young girl's reflections on whether she wants to become a mother.

Mothers learn how babies think, feel, and communicate their intentions: an accomplishment that enhances the sense of self of both mother and child.

Without reservation, I highly suggest *When Mothers Talk* as a number one choice for mothers. Readers will remember and reflect on their own experiences as they absorb the well-detailed research findings Lefcourt offers. Lefcourt's careful rendering of the life of a mother and her child is bolstered with exemplary examples from enlightening conversations with mothers."

Laurie Hollman, Ph.D., faculty, Society for Psychoanalytic Study and Research, New York University. Author, *Unlocking Parental Intelligence: Finding Meaning in Your Child's Behavior*; *Playing with Baby: Research-Based Play to Bond with Your Baby from Birth to One Year*; *Are You Living with a Narcissist?*

"This book is a moving and intimate portrayal into the wondrous world of motherhood. With deep respect for both what the mother and baby bring to this extraordinary first relationship, Lefcourt helps mothers see the baby's world as well as their own. The book will guide mothers to better understand themselves and become the parent they desire to be with clear reflective questions and suggestions for each stage of the first three years of life."

Tovah P. Klein, Ph.D., director, Barnard College Columbia University Center for Toddler Development; associate professor, Psychology. Author, *How Toddlers Thrive: What Parents Can Do Today for Children Ages 2 to 5 to Plant the Seeds of Lifelong Success.*

"'Your greatest qualification for being a mother is the fact that you were once a child.' With this wonderfully insightful assurance, Ilene Lefcourt becomes our guide on a journey of self-discovery where mothers find rich new meanings in their early memories that emerge during everyday moments with their babies and toddlers. She weaves together crucial information about their developing inner life with questions that evoke the reader's reflections about both being a child and becoming the mother she wants to be. Based on her trailblazing group work with more than 1,000 mothers over 35 years, this marvelous book embodies the wisdom of women coming together in conversations that nurtured their love for themselves and for their child and shows the way for others to follow in that path."

> **Alicia F. Lieberman**, Ph.D., professor and Irving B. Harris endowed chair in Infant Mental Health, University of California San Francisco; director, Child Trauma Research Program. Author, *The Emotional Life of the Toddler*; *Make Room for Baby*; *Don't Hit My Mommy*.

"*When Mothers Talk* is a significant addition to books for mothers in the exciting and transformative yet often fraught terrain of parenthood. Ilene Lefcourt is unusual in her capacity to distill complex developmental concepts and scientific research findings into highly accessible, warm, and engaging language to describe everyday mother–child interactions. Drawing on decades of work leading mother-baby-toddler groups, she provides a unique conceptual framework for understanding the complexity of early parent–child relationships. She intersperses poignant stories from her groups, helpful scholarship about child development, and her own wise reflections.

Lefcourt poses sensitive keenly crafted questions to mothers which direct their attention to their babies' and toddlers' capacities, communications, and inner life. Most notably, the questions direct mothers' attention to their own childhood experiences – remembered, forgotten, and newly activated. Lefcourt encourages the mothers in her groups, and the reader, to reflect on their own memories in relation to what can feel like stumbling blocks in their interactions with their babies and toddlers. Mothers achieve insight into the ways in which their own childhood experiences can shape their perceptions of their babies and toddlers, and their interactions with them. Mothers find new and more satisfying responses to behaviors which might have seemed baffling or intractable. When mothers talk to each other and to Lefcourt, they find solutions that are suited to their families' particular needs and circumstances. They also find the connection and friendship so needed at this transformative time.

Ilene Lefcourt and the mothers in her groups are welcoming, compassionate, and comforting guides for both new and experienced mothers."

> **Sally Moskowitz**, Ph.D., co-director Anni Bergman Parent-Infant Program; faculty and associate dean, Institute for Psychoanalytic Training and Research.

"*When Mothers Talk* is an exceptional book for mothers. Ilene Lefcourt brings her years of experience leading mother-baby-toddler groups together with her deep knowledge of psychoanalytic theory and infant research into one elegant volume.

A pioneer in the field of 0–3, Lefcourt synthesizes a huge body of literature on memory, theory of mind, infant development, and intersubjectivity into a beautifully written and truly inspiring guide to the entwined minds of babies and their mothers as they co-construct and navigate their developing relationship. Lefcourt's voice resonates with gentle authority, tact, and candor as she describes the ways that mothers find meaning in what can feel like an overwhelming landscape of responsibility, passionate feelings, and at times confusion. With vivid examples along the developmental timeline from birth through toddlerhood, Ilene Lefcourt brings alive some of the challenges and successes as mothers come to know and understand their babies' minds, while simultaneously discovering the ways their own early memories can resolve impasses.

Through a myriad of examples, Ilene Lefcourt shows how mother–baby and mother–toddler interactions can unwittingly catapult mothers into inchoate early experiences of their own. By providing a road map that highlights cornerstones of emotional development, Lefcourt lets the voices of real mothers illuminate both the challenges and the magic of early motherhood. She sensitively acknowledges the inevitable ruptures and repairs of loving interactions. Her writing style skillfully toggles between theory and everyday examples in a way that enhances the integration of a tremendous amount of information, triggers memories, and promotes insight. My only regret in reading this book is that I did not have it to guide me when I was embarking on my own parenting journey."

Susan Scheftel, Ph.D., faculty, assistant clinical professor of Medical Psychology in Psychiatry Columbia Psychoanalytic Center for Training and Research; child analyst, program chair Association for Psychoanalytic Medicine; vice president, Margaret Mahler Foundation. Author, *Psychoanalytic Study of the Child: Papers on Childhood and Creativity*.

When Mothers Talk

When Mothers Talk is an intimate book about early child development and motherhood which offers an extraordinary view of the first three years of life and practical information that rarely gets talked about.

Ilene Lefcourt's unique experience leading groups for over 35 years with mothers, their babies, and toddlers informs every page. Lefcourt sensitively links mothers' childhood memories with current mother–child interactions, and exquisitely details mothers' unfolding insights. Vivid examples of mothers' memories, with hidden answers to typical questions and concerns, trigger the reader's own memories, self-reflection, and new ideas. The narrative approach of *When Mothers Talk* speaks directly to the reader and activates an experience similar to being in a supportive mother-baby-toddler group.

Experienced and new mothers, infant mental health students, and experienced professionals will find this original book, grounded in long-established ideas, exceptionally informative and inspiring.

Ilene S. Lefcourt established the Sackler Lefcourt Center for Child Development in 1982. She was the director, led the mother-baby-toddler groups, and provided developmental consultation to parents for over 35 years. She taught child psychiatry residents and parent-infant psychotherapy trainees about her work. She has been a faculty member at the Columbia University Center for Psychoanalytic Training and Research Parent-Infant Program since 1995. Ms. Lefcourt is currently in private practice in New York City. She is the author of *Parenting and Childhood Memories: A Psychoanalytic Approach to Reverberating Ghosts and Magic* and *Mother-Baby-Toddler Group Guide: A Psychodynamic Approach*.

When Mothers Talk

Magical Moments and Everyday Challenges
from Birth to Three Years

Ilene S. Lefcourt

Routledge
Taylor & Francis Group

LONDON AND NEW YORK

First published 2025
by Routledge
4 Park Square, Milton Park, Abingdon, Oxon OX14 4RN

and by Routledge
605 Third Avenue, New York, NY 10158

Routledge is an imprint of the Taylor & Francis Group, an informa business

© 2025 Ilene S. Lefcourt

The right of Ilene S. Lefcourt to be identified as author of this work has been asserted in accordance with sections 77 and 78 of the Copyright, Designs and Patents Act 1988.

All rights reserved. No part of this book may be reprinted or reproduced or utilised in any form or by any electronic, mechanical, or other means, now known or hereafter invented, including photocopying and recording, or in any information storage or retrieval system, without permission in writing from the publishers.

Trademark notice: Product or corporate names may be trademarks or registered trademarks, and are used only for identification and explanation without intent to infringe.

British Library Cataloguing-in-Publication Data
A catalogue record for this book is available from the British Library

ISBN: 9781032403311 (hbk)
ISBN: 9781032399119 (pbk)
ISBN: 9781003352549 (ebk)

DOI: 10.4324/9781003352549

Typeset in Times New Roman
by KnowledgeWorks Global Ltd.

For Jeff and Karen

Contents

Acknowledgements

My earliest memory of an interest in babies was the day my brother was born, and I held him. I was 5 years old and was intrigued. When I was 10 years old and my next door neighbor gave birth, I spent every possible moment with the baby. She was precious and I was eager to learn. One instruction I was given but questioned was: "Put the baby in the crib and prop the bottle." I thought babies needed more. My memory of a little baby perfectly swaddled in a pristine crib with a full bottle, but all alone, is vivid. The image and its meaning to me are easily recalled. Beginning when I was about 17, and increasing over the years, I focused my learning about babies on psychoanalytic theories of the mind, and on research findings about early development. The ideas throughout *When Mothers Talk* rely on their scholarly rigor.

The history of the ideas is important. During the early 1900s, Sigmund Freud observed that human behavior is influenced by memories, thoughts, and feelings that are out of conscious awareness. Donald Winnicott, a pediatrician and psychoanalyst, extended this basic premise to include the importance of early relationships. These fundamental ideas are central to this book. During the 1940s, René Spitz, a psychoanalyst who had been in analysis with Freud, demonstrated that interaction with other humans is essential for children's development. This idea may seem obvious, but at the time was being questioned. During the 1950s and 1960s, John Bowlby showed that mother–baby attachment is a primary motivation and need, and mother–child separation can be traumatic. In 1952, James Robertson's documentary, *A Two Year Old Goes to Hospital*, showed a little girl's distress reaction to separation from primary caretakers, and changed pediatric hospital practices to include parent visitation.

During the 1970s, Mary Ainsworth extended Bowlby's research and identified babies' strategies for maintaining attachment. In 1986, Mary Main developed the Adult Attachment Interview that identified adult internal working models of attachment and intergenerational patterns of attachment. In 1975, *The Psychological Birth of the Human Infant*, written by Margaret Mahler, Fred Pine, and Anni Bergman, described the Separation Individuation Process from birth to 3 years: an important aspect of development. Selma Fraiberg's classic paper, "Ghosts in the Nursery" (1975), described how parents' frightening and in other ways distressing childhood experiences influence their interactions with their own children, and paved the way for approaches to mitigate the intergenerational transfer of trauma. Alicia Lieberman's paper, "Angels in the Nursery" (2005), added the importance of nurturing experiences and their memory to Fraiberg's focus on painful experiences. I am indebted to these innovators and many other infant mental health researchers and clinicians who created the theoretical foundation of my work with mothers, babies, and toddlers, and the core ideas in *When Mothers Talk*.

In 1972 my son was born, and in 1976 my daughter. My interest in babies and toddlers, in addition to being satisfied by books and scientific papers, was now enriched with the experience of being a mother: a vibrant, all-consuming new perspective to be integrated with book knowledge. My children becoming parents, and my five grandchildren, furthered my understanding and my passion.

From 1982 to 2020, I was director of the Sackler Lefcourt Center for Child Development and led the mother-baby-toddler groups. I wish to thank the mothers, babies, and toddlers who participated. They have been my most important teachers; this book would not have been possible without them. In 1989, the Columbia Center for Psychoanalytic Training and Research invited me to be an affiliate scholar. After joining the faculty in 1994, I helped to develop their Parent-Infant Program. I am fortunate to have worked with major thinkers in the fields of psychoanalysis and early development, most notably Daniel Stern.

I thank all the colleagues I have worked with throughout the years, including: the parent-infant psychotherapy trainees and child psychiatry residents who were participant observers at the Sackler Lefcourt Center, Margaret Mahler Child Development Foundation board members, Infant Psychiatry Seminar participants at the Weill Cornell Medical Center department of psychiatry, Watermill Art and Science Workshop participants, and members of various psychoanalytic committees and study groups. Each has contributed to shaping my ideas.

I especially want to thank the following esteemed colleagues: Susan Coates, Ph.D. for her thoughtful critique of the manuscript. Her careful attention to detail based on her wealth of knowledge, extraordinary perceptiveness, and years of experience helped me to sculpt the final version of *When Mothers Talk*. Margaret Hertzig, M.D. whose comprehensive and thoughtful comments brought attention to needed details, and added an important perspective. Robert Michels, M.D. whose incisive comments expanded my understanding and enriched the manuscript. Whenever I stumbled while writing, Meriamne Singer, M.D. and Mark Sorenson, M.D. treasured colleagues, helped me to distill complex ideas and ways to write them. And Myrna Weissman, Ph.D., whose inspirational thinking from vision to publication nurtured me and strengthened the book.

I also wish to thank Gail Davis, Suzanne Dikker, Ph.D., Judith Levitan M.S.W., and Patricia Nachman, Ph.D. for their insightful additions to early drafts of the manuscript. Alyson McCormack, M.S.W. who worked with me at the Sackler Lefcourt Center for many years added a unique perspective. I thank Kate Hawes and the entire Routledge team for their commitment to the wide circulation of psychoanalytic ideas. A special thank you to Betsy Lynn whose technical support, administrative handiwork, and clear editorial thinking were invaluable.

After completing the manuscript and re-reading it several times, I began to realize that remnants of my own childhood memories are embedded in each vignette. This realization highlights the idea that when mothers talk, whether the words are being spoken, heard, read, or written, memories are activated and find expression.

Introduction

Childhood Memories

When mothers talk, important things begin to happen and practical information emerges. Surprisingly, the most valuable information about the first three years of life is sometimes rooted in each mother's own memories; the challenge is to understand the multiple meanings of memories. A mother's childhood memories hold some of the answers to the questions and concerns that typically arise with babies and toddlers and the decisions that need to be made. Mothers' memories also contain the building blocks to create moments of shared delight that can nurture development. Memories can enable mothers to experience the enchantment of early childhood and the deep satisfactions of motherhood. The idea of magical moments captures the feeling that something extraordinary is happening. Love with all its complexities is its essence.

Children, teenagers, and adults, before they have children and long after their own babies have grown, are often charmed by a baby. Mother–baby interactions in other species can intrigue us. Playful puppies and kittens can capture our attention. Whether watching monkeys, elephants, tigers, or kangaroos, caretaking interactions and the emotional bonds of attachment can be alluring. Human babies can engage us. Their joyfulness and vitality are pleasurable; their vulnerability is compelling. Their raw expressions of pain affect us. The wonder we attribute to babies is easily evoked; their curiosity and futures seem endless. Most enthralling, though, out of awareness, may be our own memories that are awakened.

An important part of this book are questions for mothers to ask themselves in groups or quiet self-reflective moments. Answers can lead to the hidden meanings of childhood memories and help to find solutions to everyday typical challenges with babies and toddlers.

The greatest qualification for being a mother is the fact of having been a child: part of a mother–baby and mother–toddler relationship. Elusive and frequently recurring memories about childhood influence ideas about early development and motherhood. The protective and loving memories as well as the angry, rejecting, and frightening ones have an impact. Most mothers have had both kinds of experiences. The remnants of past experiences are intertwined in memories, but remembering is

DOI: 10.4324/9781003352549-1

a current experience. This aspect of memories, an interweaving of past and present, can lead to understanding the meaning of memories.

Children experience moments of safety and terror, care and neglect, approval and disapproval, affection and anger, understanding and intolerance. Contrasting memories reflect the capacity to hold this complexity in mind. The challenge for mothers is to understand the complexity of their own childhood memories and to help their babies and toddlers adapt to the everyday ups and downs of life, as well as to the exceptional ones.

"We relive our childhoods with our children," is an often-repeated adage that captures the intensity of revived feelings and the impact of past experience on current interactions with babies and toddlers. While it is generally recognized as true, we can be unaware when it is happening. In the moment, the past is disguised and the intensity of feelings that originated in childhood is relived rather than remembered. These kinds of experiences are a universal part of being a parent. They sometimes bring joy and sometimes unhappiness. With reflection, the memories that are related to awakened intense feelings can be identified. Parts of memories that are disguised can be clarified. Overwhelming feelings that are reactivated can be transformed into understanding and effective action. Motherhood offers huge potential for adult development.

Mothers Talk

Mothers talk to each other on park benches, on-line, and at home. They talk in mothers' groups that meet regularly and groups that gather by serendipity. They talk over dinner and at work. Mothers talk about their own childhood memories: the things they want to do the same as their own mothers and the things they want to do differently. They envision the future they want for their children and talk about ways to achieve it. They talk about the latest child development research and the nitty-gritty details of everyday life. The range of topics they talk about is vast; from the color and texture of poop to ways of promoting their babies' and toddlers' emotional, social, and cognitive development. They talk about their worries. Mothers are highly motivated to connect with other mothers and to learn from them.

During the early months and years of motherhood, with all its pleasures and stresses, feeling the loss of early nurturing from one's own mother, or wished for mother, may be activated and contribute to the loneliness and isolation typically felt by many mothers. This imagined mother is omnipotent. She provides feelings of safety when threatened and self-worth when criticized. Her approval is rewarding.

These intense feelings, sometimes out of awareness, may motivate women to seek friendships with other mothers – often referred to as mommy-friends. The support that mothers give to each other can help them to be less self-critical and more self-forgiving. In addition, watching a mother lovingly care for her baby and toddler and her child's positive response can be vicariously enjoyed.

For over 35 years I led mother-baby-toddler groups with more than 1,000 mothers at the Sackler Lefcourt Center for Child Development: a neighborhood program in New York City. While babies and toddlers may have other caretakers and important relationships, this book focuses on the mother–baby and mother–toddler relationships. Both the uniqueness of individual mothers and children, and shared aspects of early motherhood and development are discussed. While many of the ideas also apply to fathers, some may be unique to mothers. The stories about friendships among mothers, including the pleasures and pains, are those of women. Mothers' worries and satisfactions are in the actual words of women. To maintain confidentiality, all examples are disguised, fictionalized composites.

The child development information and self-reflective questions that appear in this book were used to generate mothers' group discussion and personal insight. The child development information during each phase highlights the inner experience of babies and toddlers, including theories about their thoughts, feelings, and developing sense of self.

Answers to the self-reflective questions, and the examples that other mothers provide, can awaken memories. A mother's childhood memories can help to understand her child's developing mind, to minimize the inevitable stresses during the first three years of life, to resolve emerging difficulties, and to maximize the magical moments of love and the emotional bonds of attachment when a mother's kiss can make everything feel right. It has been said that every story can be told in different voices: for example, romantic, tragic, ironic, or comic. I have chosen the lens of love and attachment to tell the story of early development and motherhood.

Child Development Research

Child development researchers and experts agree but also disagree about many aspects of early development. For example, it is generally agreed that both nature and nurture play a role in development. That is, both the environment and innate characteristics contribute to each child's development, including personality traits, intelligence, talents, strengths, and vulnerabilities. However, scholars disagree about the exact contribution of nature and of nurture. Mothers choose which research findings and theories fit with their own ideas and experiences, and make decisions about how they want to respond to their babies and toddlers based on how they integrate all the available information.

The child development information here focuses on the developing mind of babies and toddlers – the meanings of their behavior and the thoughts, feelings, and intentions that motivate behavior. When the underlying meanings of a child's behavior cannot be known, what the mother imagines is important because it influences mother–baby and mother–toddler interactions. The information and questions in this book can expand imaginings in ways that enrich interactions.

Life events in parents' pasts, including those that were pleasurable, those that were difficult, and others that were barely noticed, create a potential context for resilience and further development. Becoming a mother is a new context for resilience and emotional growth. Motherhood is a life-defining and transforming experience with many pleasures and stresses. It is my hope that readers of *When Mothers Talk* will become intrigued by their own childhood memories, their self-understanding will expand, and the complexities, pleasures, and personal satisfactions of their mother–baby and mother–toddler love relationships will be profoundly appreciated and deeply satisfying.

1   Becoming a Mother

A Girl Becomes a Woman

From the moment a young girl gets her first period, she has physical evidence of her potential fertility. The cramps and bloody inconvenience that need to be managed accompany the pride of growing up and the possibility of motherhood.

The first image of blood-stained panties may be easily called to mind. It may have been an eagerly awaited event, an alarming surprise, or both. You may remember where you were and who you told. You may remember the congratulations and the warnings that emphasized the fertility potential. A personal body experience with sexual meaning became public and may have aroused a jumble of feelings.

For some women, being a mother became a goal when they were little girls, and continued throughout development. Other women rarely or never thought about having a baby and may have fewer plans or expectations. For some women, the loving mother–baby relationship they envision having is a replacement for the painful relationship they had or continue to have with their own mothers. For others, their pleasurable memories predominate.

Pregnancy, Childbirth, Adoption, and Surrogacy

Ideas about pregnancy and childbirth originate in childhood and evolve. Memories of your own mother's stories, scenes from movies, and images from books may be vivid and may have influenced your expectations and life-plan. Prior pregnancies, miscarriages, and abortions may also influence current thinking.

Some pregnancies are long-planned and include arduous undertakings; others are a total surprise. Some wished-for pregnancies never happen and the evolving recognition of that fact may trigger an onslaught of feelings and a variety of adaptations including adoption, donor-egg or sperm, or surrogacy. The specifics of each baby's conception, gestation, and delivery may continue to influence mother–baby and mother–toddler interactions. A mother's own conception history may have an impact.

DOI: 10.4324/9781003352549-2

Good Enough Mothers, Fairy Godmothers, and Witches

Being a mother occurs in both a cultural and personal context. Many aspects of caring for babies and toddlers are idealized and others are socially, politically, and economically devalued. Many books have been written and efforts have been mounted to make legal changes to support mothers: for example, paid maternity leave.

The fairy godmother is a familiar idealized mother image. A witch epitomizes the mean, scary, mother. These artistic and cultural images of good and evil mothers emerge and are sustained because they resonate, though disguised, with childhood memories of actual mothers, wished-for mothers, and feared mothers.

Most adults have access to combinations of loving and angry, gratifying and frustrating, protective and frightening, idealized and devalued memories of their own mothers. Integrating good and bad mother images into one person with strengths and weaknesses can be a challenge. Toddlers face the same challenge to adaptively assimilate their pleasurable loving experiences and those that are disapproving, rejecting, and frightening.

The wish to be a "good mother" is shared by women in a multitude of settings, with a variety of backgrounds; but a good mother is difficult to define. A good mother in one culture may not be good in another. A protective mother in one family may be overprotective in another. Strict can be viewed as mean, empathic as over-indulgent, and permissive as reckless. A good mother for one child may not be good for others, even in the same family. Furthermore, personal definitions of a good mother may change over time.

For some women, the mother they want to be is unattainable because it is an over-idealized, wished-for fantasy mother left over from childhood, or an ideal fantasy promoted in popular culture. The over-idealized mother is a version of the fairytale mother who is always gratifying and never gets angry, tired, overwhelmed, bored, or busy with things other than her child. She never makes mistakes. She protects her child from all physical and emotional pain. Her child never gets angry at her. An over-idealized mother fantasy can never be an actual mother. And while idealizations may be intellectually recognized as such and rejected, they may still be emotionally real.

Some women believe they will never themselves be as good a mother as their own mother. This can occur for a variety of reasons and play out in different ways. Viewing their own mother as ideal may protect them both from acknowledging deficits. An idealization may seem to be needed to preserve a valued adult mother-daughter relationship. Some grandmothers contribute to this dynamic and implicitly demand the status of "best mother."

The "bad mother" and the "un-natural mother" are images in contrast to the "ideal mother." The wicked stepmother of fairytales embodies the bad mother. She is mean and frightening. Sometimes, childhood memories of an actual mother exude danger or even evil, the essence of a witch. Fear or hate may accompany these memories. Memories of one's own "bad mother" can fuel the desire to be a "good" mother and can be used to maintain "good" mother self-feelings. A mother's dread about being, or appearing to be, a witch-mother can hover and at times intrude into conscious awareness; for example, when a toddler has a temper tantrum in public, especially in a confined space like an airplane, feeling like a bad mother can escalate.

"Unnatural mother" is a designation in contrast to a believed standard of what is "natural." A woman who self-identifies as an "unnatural mother" may be rejecting the attributes that are designated "natural" or may believe she does not inherently have needed maternal traits. A woman who feels like an "unnatural" mother may be warding off memories of her own "bad mother" whom she does not want to be like.

In some ways for all mothers, the personal good-mother-self/bad-mother-self pendulum swings. Integrating the image of the good mother she wishes to be with the mother she thinks she is, is an ongoing process. This process includes recognizing and accepting that she will be a mother whom she views as her best at times and her worst at other times. The notion of a good enough mother becomes a useful concept.

The good enough mother provides sufficient amounts of sensitive maternal care so that the inevitable failures are buffered. And while an equation for sufficient amounts does not exist, an important element is that the universal ruptures in loving interactions are repaired and loving interactions return, predominate, and promote development. A woman who had been in a mother-baby-toddler group explained feeling like a good enough mother, "I often fondly remember what a truly unnatural mother I thought I was. I was exhausted and at times overwhelmed. I got angry, impatient, and bored; and yet I felt assured I was okay and my babies were okay."

2   A Baby Is Born

Mother–Baby Falling in Love

When mothers hold their babies and feel their small, contented bodies cradled gently in their arms, they may feel a rush of tender love. The same mothers in other moments may have a different experience. Impressed by the helplessness and vulnerability of their little babies and the enormous responsibility of being a mother, the changes in roles and identities, the sleepless nights, and inconsolable crying, they may feel helpless themselves and want to escape. The origins of these different feelings may not be obvious as they are occurring, but upon reflection can be traced to memories.

Emerging mother–baby, face-to-face, affectionate playful interactions during the first three months are a complex, intuitively improvised dance. The specifics of mother–baby play interactions are original for each mother–baby pair. Both the mother and the baby contribute to the details. These mutually pleasurable interactions are part of the mother–baby early relationship foundation. The primary elements are mutual gaze, a mother's lilting words, a baby's expressive sounds, facial expressions, and synchronized smiles. These ways of being together are implicitly known, not explicitly taught; they are passed from one generation to the next. The mother's feelings of connectedness might be, "I am your mommy, you are my baby, we go together."

The falling in love experience and the being in love experience are unique for each mother with her baby. They can feel extraordinarily pleasurable and at times stressful, they can emerge gradually or instantaneously, they can be exquisitely subtle, breathtakingly intense, and everything in between.

The mother–baby relationship, the first love experience for the baby, has been studied primarily in terms of attachment. Attachment research highlights the importance of mother–baby attachment for the baby's survival and mental health; feelings of safety are at its core. Feelings of self-worth, for both the mother and the baby, emanate from it. A baby's physical proximity-seeking and readiness for feelings of connectedness with Mommy are part of this robust system. A mother's sensitive caretaking promotes her baby's security of attachment and her own sense of well-being. Mother–baby attachment and mother–baby love overlap and merge; they are the same in some ways and different in others.

DOI: 10.4324/9781003352549-3

Mothers' Expanding Sense of Self

The mother–baby love and attachment relationship initiates a mother's expanding sense of self. When a woman becomes a mother, her mental landscape changes. Feelings of love and anger can be surprisingly intense. Her thoughts about the past, present, and future reverberate. Mothers gain a new perspective on their own childhood memories. A woman's primary intergenerational relationship identity shifts from "I am my mother's daughter" to "I am the mother of my child." A mother's expanding sense of self is set in motion by her growing attachment to her baby, the intensity and complexity of evoked feelings, revived childhood memories, and her mothering goals.

A mother's expanding sense self is sometimes experienced as a blurring of oneness with and separateness from her baby. During a new mother-baby group, as we gathered in a small circle on the floor, the mothers described this experience. One mother mused, "Sometimes I don't know for sure if what I am feeling is my own feeling or my baby's feeling. If I feel hot is my baby hot, if I feel cold is my baby cold?" Another mother who had gone for a walk without her 4-week-old baby for the first time added, "Each time I came to the end of the sidewalk and waited for the green light, I began to slightly sway. I finally realized that swaying was a body memory of rocking the baby carriage. Mentally, my baby was with me." Another mother with a 6-week-old baby had been waking each morning with a swollen upper lip. She explained, "My baby had developed the typical sucking blister on his upper lip that breastfeeding babies often get. I finally realized that I had been sucking my own lip in the middle of the night, just like my baby." Another mother confided, "From the moment my baby was born, I never had my mind to myself again. I'm not sure if he is a constant companion or an intruder."

A mother's feelings of oneness with and separateness from her baby slip and slide. This aspect of a mother's expanding sense of self includes her ability to identify and empathize with her baby and toddler, and gradually fuels her readiness for insight.

3   Childhood Memories

Meanings of Memories

Memories are a fundamental part of mental life. The details of a memory, including those that seem incidental, can have important meanings. Something pleasurable can disguise something painful. A delicious, sugar-coated cookie that seems central to a memory can be an attempt to sugar-coat the painful elements. For example, after her parents' divorce when she was 8 years old, over 30 years ago, Sheila saw her father every Sunday for hot chocolate and cookies. Her memory of the marsh-mallows floating on top of the sweet chocolate and the powdered sugar that she licked off her lips helped to soothe the ongoing pain of her parents' divorce. The pleasurable tastes and textures remained vivid; the pain faded.

Feelings expressed by one person in a memory can represent feelings of the memory's creator. A mother described, "My recurring memory of my sister crying inconsolably whenever my mother went out, and my critical attitude towards her crying changed when my baby was born. I had always thought it was only my sister who missed my mother and cried for her. When I heard my baby cry, I realized that I had been crying silently for my mother my whole life. I now understand how my baby feels when she cries for me."

The new perspective of being a mother can change the meaning of a life-long childhood memory. Memories are ways of coping with stressful events and savoring pleasurable ones. Memories help us to make sense of our lives and to make decisions. An experience that was difficult or impossible to make sense of as a child may be remembered in a phantasmagorical way.

During an excited group discussion about parents' sex lives when they have young children, Claudia recounted a fanciful childhood memory, "When I was about 8 years old, I was alone in the kitchen and there was a knock on the screen door. It was the Easter Bunny. He was standing right there on two legs, like a grown-up, much taller than I was. He was holding a basket with two brightly colored eggs in a nest of brown grass. I know this sounds impossible, but my memory is clear; it feels like it really happened. I ran upstairs to my parents who were still in bed and told them about this amazing thing that I saw."

The women in the group offered possible rational explanations, "A grown-up may have been dressed in a bunny costume. It could have been a toy bunny."

DOI: 10.4324/9781003352549-4

Claudia insisted, "It was real, it was alive. I know it sounds impossible, but the memory feels real." Claudia had repeated this memory to others many times and was always told, "It never happened." Being told it never happened, and believing herself that it sounded unrealistic, had never changed her feelings about the memory being real. Claudia's memory had narrative truth and personal meaning.

Our lively group discussion continued about whether parents close the bedroom door when they have sex, or have sex when their baby or toddler is sleeping in bed with them, or is in the room. Claudia chimed in, "I never thought of this before. My parents always told me that I once walked in on them when they were having sex, but I never remembered it. Maybe the unrealistic Easter Bunny was my way of remembering the unimaginable, incomprehensible sight of my parents having sex."

The excitement Claudia felt during the group discussion about parents, children, and sex may have triggered her recurring Easter Bunny memory. Her experience of being a mother with young children created a new context for the emergence of the new meaning that she attributed to her memory: seeing her parents having sex. Specific images in Claudia's memory supported her sexual interpretation: two brightly colored eggs, the brown grass, her parents in bed, and the size of the bunny that placed his genitals at Claudia's eye level. The details of Claudia's memory were consistent with her new sexual interpretation. She decided to close the bedroom door when she and her husband were having sex.

Explicit and Implicit Memories

Memory is a way the brain responds to lived experience. Explicit memories are constructed narratives that mentally represent an experience in an organized and cohesive way. Explicit memories are portrayals of an event that illuminate personal meanings. The familiar experience of adult siblings having different memories of the same childhood event underscores the personal meaning of memories.

Childhood memories sometimes reveal attempts to incorporate unacceptable feelings into a positive sense of self and a coherent autobiographical history. A mother remembered, "My baby sister was born and was coming home from the hospital. I was 4 years old and my parents left me alone in the hospital lobby to hold her while they went to get the car. I always protected my sister, but how could they have done that? I could have dropped her. I know my parents would have never done that, but that is what I remember."

Emotions and bodily sensations can be implicit memories. Implicit memories are not narrated; they include body procedures such as riding a bike. Ways of being with others including shared smiles, hugs, turn-taking rhythms in conversation, patterns of mutual gaze, and gaze averting can be implicit memories. Tastes, scents, and sounds – shivers, quivers, and swoons can be memories. Sometimes music or terms of endearment are part of an implicit memory. For example, a mother recalled, "From the time Elizabeth was born I called her sweetie. She's now almost 2 and I just realized that my mother always calls me sweetie. I have a warm feeling all over whenever I say sweetie."

Childhood Memories Relived

A mother's activated feelings during interactions with her baby or toddler can be a memory. Interactions can awaken feelings of love and tenderness or anger, fear, and helplessness. Intense feelings in the present moment that are a reliving of the past may replace consciously remembering. When a memory is being relived emotionally, its "pastness" can fade.

Cliff was a thriving 30-month-old little boy in a mother–toddler group. For the past three weeks he had awakened happy every morning in his mother and father's bed. Every morning his mother Sally was surprised. She insisted, "I definitely want Cliff to stay in his own bed, but there is nothing I can do about it; I sleep through it."

Sally believed that "sleeping through it" was happening to her and she could not control it. She felt helpless. The following question that created a connection between a childhood memory and her current interactions with Cliff was the first step towards control: "Who slept through what when you were a little girl?" Sally's memory immediately came to mind. "Every night I had nightmares about our house burning down. I was terrified. I would sneak to my parents' bedroom and sleep on the floor outside their closed door. I didn't want to wake my mother. She slept through it every night."

I suggested a connection between her memory of the past and the present. "The current situation with Cliff is similar to your memory of nightmares and sleeping on the floor outside your parents' bedroom, but there are differences. You are now the parent sleeping through your child's distress, rather than the scared child sleeping alone on the floor. And Cliff is the scared child getting something that you did not get. Despite this, like you, Cliff's distress is not being addressed directly." Sally looked stunned with the repetition of her memory in the present. She recognized that in some ways Cliff was alone with his distress the same as she had been.

The following week, Sally told us, "I don't know how it happened, but I started to hear Cliff when he got into our bed in the middle of the night." Sally was able to discover from fragments of Cliff's description that he was being awakened by frightening dreams. Sally described, "I am now able to walk Cliff back to his own bed and to comfort him. We talk about his frightening dreams. I think Cliff feels deeply understood and comforted. That's what I wanted."

Within two weeks, Cliff was sleeping through the night in his own bed. Sally's insight that her childhood memory was being re-enacted with Cliff, combined with her wish to comfort Cliff, enabled her to hear him in the middle of the night. Now a mother, her revived memory of sleeping outside her parents' bedroom helped her to differentiate her own childhood wish to get into her parents' bed from her current wish to comfort Cliff. In addition, Sally now believed that her childhood memory was about what she thought her mother wanted: to not be awakened. She wondered whether her mother would have wanted to know about her nightmares and to comfort her. "I didn't want to bother or worry my mother. I'm not sure what she wanted." Sally's childhood memory had slightly, but meaningfully, changed.

4 Mother–Baby and Mother–Toddler Intersubjectivity

A Meeting of Minds

Intersubjectivity is an interaction between two people in which each is aware of the subjective experience of the other – a window into each other's minds that creates a profound sense of connection. Interactions that create moments of intersubjectivity are relationship building blocks. The emotional connection comes from feeling deeply understood by each other – a meeting of minds.

From birth to three years, intersubjectivity becomes more intense and recognizable. For a baby and toddler these moments build a foundation on which to discover one's own mind. Moments of intersubjectivity set in motion a life-long capacity for emotional intimacy and the satisfaction that comes with it.

For some mothers, friendships with other mothers provide a context for mother–baby intersubjective bonding. Nancy and Stephanie became best friends when their babies were 5 months. They had met in the playground and immediately clicked, although as Nancy described during a mothers' group, "We were very different. Stephanie was motherly, I was not. She quit her job and was enchanted by every moment with her baby. I continued my full-time work and never felt the thrill or connection that Stephanie enjoyed with her baby. I was just happy to see Micky reach each developmental milestone."

Nancy highlighted her mothering differences with Stephanie, the differences in their children who were now 3 years old, and her pride in her son's independence and emotional strength. Although she minimized their attachment to each other it was clear that she and Micky had a powerful, loving relationship, and Micky was thriving. Nancy's friendship with Stephanie was a part of it. The other mothers in the group talked about their first mommy-friends. Each one had a different story, but they shared important themes.

As the discussion continued, Nancy confided that she had had a prior pregnancy that needed to be terminated after seven months. Her baby had had a rare genetic defect: "The doctors told me it wasn't even a choice." Nancy and Stephanie's friendship, including all their differences in life experiences of loss and mothering style, and the children's developing differences, were crucial for Nancy as she was managing the ongoing impact of an earlier traumatic loss. In retrospect, Nancy was pleased with her mothering decisions, though they were different from

DOI: 10.4324/9781003352549-5

Stephanie's and she questioned them at the time. "I was afraid to get too close to Micky when he was a baby, but I guess we were close enough."

First smiles, pointing, learning to talk, communicating intentions – pointing to the future, and creating shared memory narratives – pointing to the past, are mother–child joint focus of attention interactions with heightened potential for moments of intersubjectivity. These everyday mother–baby interactions create feelings of meaningful connectedness: a sense of knowing what is in each other's mind.

First Smiles

A smile is an outward sign of an inner experience. Her baby's first smiles invite a mother to imagine the inner experience of her baby. Early smiles can activate a mother's awareness of her baby's dawning consciousness: her baby's awareness of interpersonal pleasure. Babies' smiles quickly become communications. During mother–baby mutual smiling, the internal subjective experience of each is sensed by the other. The smile of each influences the smile of the other. We can imagine in our words what this reciprocal interaction with a joint focus of attention to a shared inner experience contributes to a baby's developing sense of self and self with other. '*We are both smiling. Smiling with each other feels good to both of us. We delight each other. I am loveable.*'

Pointing

Joint focus of attention interactions initiated by a baby pointing are powerful mother–baby interactions that are endlessly repeated. For example: the baby points to a ceiling light. Mommy, excited by the invitation to know what her baby sees, looks at the light and says some version of "Yes, I see the light." Both mother and baby have a deep sense of knowing that they are both looking at the same thing. They have the same thing in mind. Their certainty is unquestioned. The interaction is compelling because of the inner experience of minds in synch: a joint focus of attention to sharing a perception. This self with other early experience of a meeting of minds will continue throughout life and may include the certainty of feeling understood. So much is happening emotionally, mentally, and interpersonally in this brief interaction triggered by a baby pointing.

Communicating Intentions – Pointing to the Future

When babies crawl towards an object that is not to be touched, for example an electric socket, stop to get Mommy's attention, smile, and then accelerate towards it, they are signaling their intention to touch the socket. This complex interaction pointing to the future without the finger gesture creates a joint focus of attention on the baby's intention and invites a response. This multi-faceted mother–baby interaction includes: the baby's memory of Mommy's limit – no touching the socket, the non-verbal signal to Mommy of an intention, a smile to make the interaction playful, and the expectation of being stopped. The interaction reflects the baby's internal conflict and creative compromise between the wish to please Mommy – an aspect of attachment, and other wishes that assert autonomy. The interaction provides the mother an opportunity to reinforce the limit; "You remember, the socket is not for touching. I will help you stop."

Creating Shared Memory Narratives – Pointing to the Past

Memory narratives are stories about things that have happened and the words to identify the feelings that accompany those events. Mothers co-create memory narratives with their babies and toddlers. The memory narratives they co-construct help babies and toddlers adapt to disturbing experiences, and to repeat pleasurable ones. While remembering together – a pointing to the past, babies and toddlers can feel safe, understood, and in control. Adaptive expectations of frightening experiences can be strengthened. Shared memory narratives of experiences that were difficult to understand can help babies and toddlers make sense of them.

Mothers, babies, and toddlers create memories together, but their contributions to the narratives are different. Memory narratives that include details from the child's point of view help babies and toddlers to mentally organize elements of an event and their reactions to it.

One-year-old Tod had gone to a petting zoo and got scared when a goat bleated. When Tod's mother was telling Tod's father about what happened, Tod's mother asked, "Tod, do you remember when you pet the goat and he bleated so loud? You got scared and cried. How loud did the goat bleat?" Turning passive into active and scared into safe, Tod imitated the goat's loud bleat, "Baa."

Sometimes mothers wish that their children will not remember an event. They may be convinced by well-meaning others that babies and toddlers will not remember. In some ways wishing or believing that a baby will not remember substitutes for wishing the event had never happened. However, when an event is not remembered explicitly with a narrative, it may be remembered implicitly as a feeling. Remembering with words how something felt is less disturbing than feeling it again.

Cody was almost 3 years old. While jumping on the living room sofa, she fell and cut her forehead on the corner of the coffee table. Cody's mother Joanna described the scene: "Cody cried in a way I had never heard before, a loud mixture of fear and pain. Her face was covered with blood but I could not see where it was coming from. I was overwhelmed and terrified. I shrieked, helplessly frozen for several moments until I gained control and called an ambulance. I think I really frightened Cody."

"Cody's father met us at the hospital. He was shocked silent. I cried hysterically while trying to comfort Cody who was screaming as the nurses immobilized her for the sutures. I was so scared. The doctor told us that she expected the cut to heal well. Cody was given a lollipop." This was the story Joanna told me on the phone. Medical healing had begun; emotional healing would take more time.

The next week Joanna and Cody returned to the mother-toddler group. Cody, with a small Band-Aid on her forehead, eagerly entered and began to play with the dollhouse. She vigorously and repeatedly jumped the little girl doll on the small dollhouse sofa. Abruptly her play stopped. After a brief pause the jumping was repeated, and then repeated again, and again. She was unable to develop her play, or to play with anything else. It seemed as though Cody had begun to use play to process the accident but was unable to elaborate her play into a useful scenario.

Joanna entered and almost threw herself onto a bench with a sigh of despair. She told the other mothers the story of Cody's accident as she had told it to me on the phone and added, "Since the accident last week, every time Cody hears an ambulance siren, which happens often, she begins to scream uncontrollably. It lasts about 20 minutes. The only thing that stops her crying is a lollipop." The stunned mothers mirrored Joanna's horror and feelings of helplessness as they listened silently.

The repetition and abrupt ending of Cody's play jumping the doll on the sofa, the crying when she heard ambulance sirens, and the lollipop to soothe her seemed to be Cody's incomplete fragmented memory of the accident. The jumping had preceded the accident and the lollipop was how it ended. The entire middle, including her mother's terror and crying, her father's silence, the blood, the ambulance ride, being restrained, her pain, and fear were activated each time Cody heard ambulance sirens.

Cody's parents had felt too overwhelmed to talk with Cody about the accident, and Cody needed help to construct a useful memory narrative. In Joanna's words, "It was so frightening and we felt so guilty. I just hoped Cody would forget about it. I guess we need to talk about it." The following week Joanna brought the memory narrative book that she, Cody's father, and Cody had created about the accident, the treatment, and the recovery.

Cody began to act out in her pretend play the shared memory narrative. At the beginning, Cody and her parents read the book frequently and played accident and going to the hospital. In a few days, Cody's crying when she heard an ambulance siren diminished and then stopped. Sirens now triggered the memory narrative, not the feelings of terror. She was able to remember many details of the accident: Mommy crying, the ambulance ride to the hospital, Daddy's silence, the treatment, and all the frightening feelings that could be talked about rather than relived. For a while they continued to read the accident book, talk about the accident, and to play going to the hospital. Within a month, the accident play had stopped, and the book remained mostly on the shelf.

It is possible that Cody no longer cried when she heard ambulance sirens because she had forgotten, but an alternative explanation is that Cody stopped screaming when she heard ambulance sirens because she had developed a shared memory narrative to help her to think about, talk about, and pretend in play many elements of the accident. She was no longer alone with her memories without words to describe what happened and how she felt. In addition, she now had Mommy and Daddy's comfort.

Learning to Talk

Babies are surrounded by language, repeat the sounds they hear, and words begin to emerge. When a mother is uncertain about the meaning of her baby's sounds, she may rely on the context to attribute meaning to them. The baby's approximation of a word, in combination with the mother's enunciation of the word and attribution of meaning to it, create a new word for the baby. For example, when the mother attributes meaning to the babbling sounds her baby makes or imagines that her baby said Ma and responds as if her baby said Mama, they have created a word together.

Often mothers are the only ones who understand their toddlers' emerging language. We can imagine what it might feel like to a toddler when Mommy is the only one in the whole world who understands. In these ways, the language acquisition process is about attachment, meaning making, and feeling understood.

Separateness of Minds

A baby's discovery of, and the interactions that highlight the separateness of, minds are a developmental process related to intersubjectivity and the meeting of minds. For example, it is story-time and the baby points to the bookcase and indicates a book choice. Mommy gets the book, but the baby rejects it and points again. Mommy gets the book she believes her baby is pointing to now, and the baby also rejects this book. This interaction is repeated several times until the baby accepts a book. This frequent mother–baby interaction is often experienced by a mother as her baby's deliberate attempt to annoy her or her own inability to understand her baby. Another explanation is that the baby is practicing having something in mind that Mommy cannot know until the baby lets her know. The baby has created an interaction that substantiates the separateness of minds. Experiencing both the meeting of minds and the separateness of minds is valuable.

During the first three years, mother–child interactions that highlight the separateness of minds often become increasingly angry. For example, the family was gathered for dinner. Charlie was 30 months and did not want the bread that was on the table. He had something else in mind and asked his mother for some toast. His mother was happy to toast some bread and provided the additional choice of cutting the crust off or keeping it on. Making a choice requires having two things in mind. Charlie made a choice, "No crust."

When the toast was the light brown color Charlie liked, his mother presented his crustless toast to him. Charlie rejected it, "I want toast with crust. I don't like this toast." Frustrated, Charlie's mother reasserted her intention to please him, "You asked me for no crust." Charlie made it clear, "That's not what I want now." This is a typical 2- to 3-year-old version of exercising a separateness of minds. Toast without crust was not what was in Charlie's mind now. He changed his mind; minds are flexible. A child's needs to feel understood and simultaneous needs to establish and maintain the separateness and complexity of minds may create challenges. Charlie was also learning about the limits of his ability to control his mother. She told him, "You have two kinds of bread, toast without crust and bread with crust. You can choose."

Learning Codes of Behavior

Codes of behavior, the dos and don'ts of everyday life, include needed information to live in the world of people: the family, the sandbox, school, and eventually the wider world. Moments of mother–child intersubjectivity are possible during limit-setting interactions related to learning codes of behavior. In fact, moments of intersubjectivity can make it easier to learn the hardest lessons. When a young child feels understood, when a baby's and toddler's thoughts and feelings are recognized and accepted as understandable, it is easier to learn Mommy's codes of behavior – Mommy's thoughts and feelings.

Mateo was 18 months and desperately wanted to tie his own shoes all by himself. He was unable to do it, but he persisted. In a rush to meet friends at the park, his mother gently tried to offer some assistance. Angry and asserting his autonomy, Mateo smacked her in the face. Startled and angry, his mother yelled at him, "No hitting." Mateo did not want to hurt his mother, he loved her. Her disapproval and the threat of losing her love were terrifying. Mateo started to cling to her and cry; his attachment needs felt threatened. Perhaps he also felt some remorse. Mateo's mother was moved by his distress. Gazing lovingly into each other's eyes she said, "I know you want to tie your shoes all by yourself. You were very angry when I tried to help you, but there is no hitting even when you are very angry. I got startled and yelled at you. You got scared." Moments of deeply knowing each other's subjective experience and one's own are part of everyday life for mothers, babies, and toddlers.

5   Child Development Information and Self-Reflective Questions

The child development information and self-reflective questions in this book were used during mother-baby-toddler groups at the Sackler Lefcourt Center for Child Development. The information focuses on mother–child interaction and the developing mind. The questions have no right or wrong answers. Their value is in the thoughts and feelings they stimulate. Some of the questions and answers may be surprising or even startling. These may be among the most useful. Some of the questions may not have answers. Their value may be in thinking about the question.

Mothering Style

Each mother has her own mothering style. It may be similar to others', but the specifics are unique. Authenticity can be an inherently valuable attribute. In one mother's words, "At first I did not think I was a very good mother. In many ways I was ridiculous. But at the same time, our mothers' group helped me believe that some of my feelings were universal and my idiosyncrasies were more than okay. They were me."

Some of the self-reflective questions address mothers' fluctuating feelings of authenticity. Some questions are about a child's sensitivity to mothers' authentic feelings in moments when she is exhausted, bored, or in a rush to leave and tries to conceal it. One mother's words capture this experience, "They are little mind-readers." Some answers will reaffirm convictions about aspects of child development theory with which you agree. Some answers will be consistent with the kind of mother you want to be. Moments when you have doubts about your mothering, and moments when you follow advice that does not quite fit with your own ideas or style, may come to mind.

Research and Theory

Ideas about child development are based on research, theory, and personal experience. The developmental information and self-reflective questions focus on the underlying meanings of behavior, and thoughts and feelings that motivate behavior. The information includes ideas about babies' and toddlers' underlying autonomy strivings and attachment to their mothers that are sometimes aligned and sometimes

DOI: 10.4324/9781003352549-6

clash. When the underlying meanings of behavior cannot be known, what is imagined by the mother is important because it influences mother–child interactions. The child development information and questions can add to your imaginings in ways that can help to resolve difficulties, and achieve mothering goals.

Mothers' personal reactions to expert opinion are important. Childhood memories may be central to reactions – those parts you want to embrace and those you want to reject. For example, the following information and questions about parental nudity in front of children were presented in a mother-toddler group; "Each child and children in general at various ages react differently to seeing their parents naked. You may remember seeing your parents naked and liking it, not liking it, or being indifferent. How does your toddler react to seeing you naked?"

Each mother in the group talked about her own childhood memories and current nudity with her toddler. Tania insisted that she thought family nudity was important, "I do not want my children raised in a sexually uptight home like I was raised. I want my children to be more uninhibited." In response to Tania's clearly stated goal and her own childhood memories related to a "sexually uptight home," I asked further questions about their children's reactions to seeing both parents naked. The details of each child's reaction provided important information for each mother.

Mirabella had been bathing with 18-month-old Scott since he was a baby. Scott had seemed indifferent to her being naked, but lately there had been a change. Mirabella described that Scott had begun to repeatedly touch her nipples, "I don't know why all of a sudden he started to touch me. Seeing me naked must have a different meaning to him now. I like bathing with Scott, but I definitely do not want him to touch my breasts in any way, and I don't want to keep saying no to him. It sounds so rejecting."

Mirabella re-evaluated her decision to bathe with Scott because it was triggering his strong repeated impulse to touch her breasts, was providing him the opportunity, and was motivating Mirabella to repeatedly say no. Charli added to the discussion: "I noticed lately that Shira is touching herself more; she's actually masturbating. Maybe all the family nudity is overstimulating. We all shower together every day and walk around naked." Cynthia remembered, "I didn't like seeing my mother naked. It didn't happen often. I like being naked, but not in front of Michelle. I just realized when I'm naked and Michelle walks in I rush to cover myself. I wonder what that's like for her." Juliette said, "In general I don't feel comfortable naked, I feel self-conscious about all my flabby skin, but when I'm naked in front of my son Asher I know he doesn't care about my cellulite; he doesn't even notice. I feel good being naked in front of him. I'm not sure how he feels." Lucia added, "It seems like mothers and children have reactions to same-sex nudity and opposite-sex nudity." Tania concluded, "I guess being naked can have different meanings. Right now, the amount of family nudity in my home seems just right for me, Liam, and his dad. In time, I know it will need to change."

New findings and changing cultural attitudes influence science: what gets studied and how findings are interpreted. For example, recently gender identity has been getting more political, legal, and scientific attention. The impact of father-child, and sibling relationships, on development has been less studied and less written about than the mother–child relationship; this leaves a gap.

The specific ways in which ideas about child development apply to each mother and child are determined by many things. Understanding a memory that is triggered by scientific information or expert opinion may be useful in assessing the personal value of the information. A memory triggered by a self-reflective question may help to specify the things you want to do the same as your own parents, the things you want to do differently, and why.

The comment, "I turned out okay," is often discussed in mothers' groups. Turning out okay in spite of childhood experiences is different from turning out okay because of childhood experiences. The way in which we get to where we end up may be important. Children are resilient and learn to adapt to their experiences. The child development information and self-reflective questions can help to sort out decisions about the kind of developmental process you want for your baby and toddler. Outcomes are more difficult to predict.

6   Describing Your Baby and Toddler

While mothers watch their babies and toddlers, in some moments they imagine what their child's experience is, and in others they focus on their own thoughts, feelings, and memories that are triggered by what they see. In some moments they may think about completely unrelated things. There is a moment-to-moment shifting of attention. A mother's description of her child is a mingling of what she sees and her thoughts and feelings about what she sees. As you watch your baby or toddler, a specific moment may jump out as most salient.

Jemma described Marco: "He's a very happy baby. He's especially happy playing with his dad. I was watching them yesterday; all of a sudden Marco's face lit up with a big smile and I remembered one time when my father was giving my twin brother a piggy-back ride and my stomach hurt so badly. They always had so much fun together. I just realized that when my husband is playing with Marco, I often ask him to walk the dog. It's as if I want them to stop playing. What I wanted was my father to stop playing with my brother. I want Marco to have fun with his dad."

Jemma's description of Marco as a happy baby triggered her memory of her painful jealousy and led to her insight about the meaning of asking her husband to walk the dog.

A baby's name in some ways is a description of the baby. The choice of names is influenced by personal, family, and cultural meanings of names and traditions. The traits of a wished-for child may contribute to the names chosen. Nicknames have additional meaning. When Gina was describing her many pet-names for Anita, she realized they were all foods: cupcake, muffin, honeybun, etc. With a gasp, suddenly she remembered her mother always saying, "I'm going to eat you up!" and her mixed feelings. She believed her mother was being affectionate, but she also remembered worrying about being eaten. Her worries were intensified when her mother read *Hansel and Gretel* to her, "Hansel and Gretel were clever enough to escape the witch who was planning to eat them, but I was worried."

Descriptive Traits

Babies and toddlers have distinctive physical, personality, and behavioral traits. Some traits are age related and others are enduring. Some are innate and others are learned or reactive to experience. Certain traits may be more appealing than others.

DOI: 10.4324/9781003352549-7

Some mother and child traits fit together and others clash. Some traits may create challenges for both a child and a mother.

Veronica described Marnie: "In many ways she's like me. She needs time to get used to new things. I have great memories of my mother pushing me on the swing, but it took a while. I was eager for Marnie to have the same fun and waited to introduce the baby swing until she was 14 months. I thought she would be comfortable by then, but as soon as I tried to put her in the swing she began to kick and scream. I was just like Marnie; slow to warm up. My Mom helped me learn to love the swing. I helped Marnie to push her special Bunny in the swing. She liked pushing Bunny and then she wanted me to push her. She now loves the swing. It still takes me a long time to get used to new things." Veronica was describing her own and Marnie's temperament.

Babies who scream loudly, and are difficult to soothe, may in time adjust to all the new internal and external stimulation they experience and be able to be comforted more easily. When babies and toddlers are given the time and support needed to adjust to new people or activities, even if they have a sensitive temperament and are slow to warm up, they can feel increasingly secure that things that at first may be frightening or disagreeable can become enjoyable.

Temperament

There are several innate traits that are called temperament. They are relatively predictable ways of behaving; however, they can be influenced by how they are responded to. They can be intensified or diminished. Temperament traits include activity level, novelty seeking or avoidant (sometimes called shy or slow to warm up), persistence or distractibility, reactivity to sensory stimulation, and predominant mood. A description of a baby or toddler often includes some temperament traits.

A stage of development or life experience can trigger the same behavior as temperament. For example, when Lucy was 17 months her activity level and novelty seeking were medium; her reactivity to sensory stimulation was low; her predominant mood was happy. When Lucy was 19 months she tripped in the playground, fell, and cracked a tooth, which then needed to be filed down. After the accident and the dental procedure, which were painful, frightening, and included the loud sound of a drill, Lucy's behavior changed dramatically for several weeks. Her activity level became generally low, she became clingy to her mother in new situations, and hypersensitive to noises that had never bothered her before. Lucy began to startle easily, wake during the middle of the night crying, and was difficult to comfort.

Lucy's mother did not think that her temperament had changed. She believed that Lucy was reacting to the events that often raise body anxieties for children her age: cracking a tooth and having it filed down almost to the gum-line. Lucy's mother used play and a shared memory narrative to help Lucy. "You had a scary accident. You tripped and fell and broke your tooth. It hurt! The dentist needed to file your tooth. The filing made a loud noise. Your tooth looks very little now, you can barely see it. The dentist said a big new tooth will grow. It will take a long time, but in a few years, you will see your new tooth." Lucy and her mother's pretend play included taking her teddy bear to the dentist and filing the teddy bear's tooth. Lucy particularly enjoyed making the loud drilling noise, which seemed to represent her fear.

Children Lucy's age, whatever their innate temperament, external behavior, or life experience, have thoughts and feelings that may trigger anxiety about parts of their body breaking. When an accident occurs or surgery is required, body anxieties may intensify and a sense of body damage may persist. A toddler's feelings (in our words) might be, '*There is something wrong with my body, there is something wrong with me.*' Creating shared memory narratives and pretend play can promote emotional healing.

Development and New Meanings

In addition to temperament and life experiences, new physical abilities and new cognitive meanings influence behavior. For example, when babies start to roll over, sit, and then to crawl, the motivation to keep moving can be strong. Changing diapers can become a challenge. A seemingly cooperative smiling baby, who had appeared to luxuriate in the pleasure of being tenderly cleaned while holding a toy and gazing at Mommy, now twists and squirms to be free of constraint while Mommy wrestles to contain the overflowing poop.

Reactions to separation during the first three years can have different underlying meanings at each phase. An 8-month-old can fear, '*Mommy does not exist when I do not see her.*' An 18-month-old can fear, '*Mommy does not love me.*' When a 30-month-old does something that makes Mommy angry, a separation can trigger intense fear that, '*Mommy does not love me anymore because of what I did and will never come back.*' These descriptions of the underlying meanings of separation provide ways to understand a baby's and toddler's strong reactions.

The underlying meaning of protests to separation, and at times clinging, may be an indication of a toddler's internal struggle with conflicting wishes: on the one hand, the wish to cling and on the other, the wish to run away with excited curiosity to explore. A toddler expects from experience to be swooped up in Mommy's arms when heading for danger or too far away, and relies on Mommy's availability as a secure base when needed. Toddlers are developing the ability to keep these feelings inside during separations. Your baby will gradually learn that you exist even when out of sight, separations are followed by reunions, and angry feelings resolve. You leave for a while because you have other things you want to do, and that's okay; your baby and toddler will be well cared for by someone else until you return. It is a great deal to learn and can take a long time.

Along with feelings of security, with development there are new feelings of vulnerability. '*I need my blood. If I start to bleed, will I lose all my blood? If my smooth skin gets a bruise, and looks so different, am I still okay? If I get a haircut, am I losing a part of my body I need to be me?*' The way in which a baby or toddler behaves can be influenced by temperament, life experience, and new thoughts and feelings during a specific phase of development.

Descriptions

Bianca described Marty who was 18 months: "When Marty was a baby he looked just like my brother. I was not able to breastfeed because it was too weird. He still looks like my brother." Bianca's description of Marty was accompanied by a memory: "I saw my best friend having a drink with my brother at a neighborhood hotel, maybe they were having an affair." Bianca's memories that were triggered while describing Marty included sexual fantasies about her brother of which she was unaware. The sexual meaning had influenced her decision not to breastfeed, and other decisions that kept her at a distance from Marty. As Bianca became more aware of her sexual feelings about her brother, she was able to interact more with Marty and became a secure base for him. When Marty was 2 years, Bianca's description of him changed, "Marty no longer looks like my brother, he really looks just like my husband."

A mother's prediction, sometimes an aspect of her description of her child, can lead to insight. Janice described 3-year-old Jonah: "I think Jonah will be gay. There is something wrong with his play. He only performs roles and wants me to be his audience. Since the moment he was born, I have thought he was gay. Why do I always think he will be gay?" For the first time, Janice was questioning her thinking. Her self-questioning led to a change. The following week Janice noticed, "Jonah has stopped playing roles and stopped wanting me to be his audience."

Janice's beginning to question why she thought Jonah was gay changed something between them. It was not clear what had changed; maybe Jonah no longer needed to play a role because he felt seen by his mother in a new way, or the meaning of Jonah's play had changed for Janice. The interesting part of this story is not whether Jonah was or would be gay, but for the first time since Jonah was born, Janice questioned her belief. Her belief that was part of her description of Jonah changed from a prediction to a fantasy that she wanted to understand.

Description of Your Child

The following questions and your answers may remind you of traits that also describe you, your partner, a sibling, or your parents. People you know who have the same traits as your child may influence how you feel about the trait.

- How would you describe your baby/toddler?
- When did you first observe these traits?
- How do the traits you describe influence your interactions with each other?

You may have different reactions to a trait you have described if you think it is innate, acquired, phase specific, or reactive to an experience either recent or long ago.

- Which of the traits that describe your baby/toddler do you think are innate? Acquired? Phase specific? Lifelong?
- In what ways does your belief that a trait is innate, acquired, phase specific, or lifelong influence your reactions to the trait?

As you describe your child, you might be wondering about what the traits you describe are like for your baby/toddler.

- Which traits that describe your baby/toddler are challenging for you? Challenging for your baby/toddler?
- How do you help your baby/toddler adapt to challenging traits?

You may credit yourself for some of your baby's/toddler's traits and blame yourself or someone else for others. The similarities and differences between you and your child may have an impact on your reactions to a trait. Your baby/toddler may be different from you, or how you had wished or imagined. You may wonder how you can influence your baby's/toddler's developing awareness of and attitudes towards the traits that you describe.

7 Child Development Themes and Subthemes

The developmental information and self-reflective questions in Chapters 8 through 13 are organized by age and categorized by six interconnected themes: Mother–Child Interaction; Body and Mind Awareness; Emotion Regulation; Play; Learning; and Mothers' Childhood Memories. Mother-child interaction is the overarching theme that encompasses the others. Following are brief descriptions with some examples.

Mother–Child Interaction

Mother–baby and mother–toddler interactions have underlying thoughts, feelings, and intentions; they have conscious and unconscious meanings. Developmental theories provide useful paradigms for understanding many interactions.

In some ways, mothers interact with their babies and toddlers not only as the children they are, but also as the ones they are developmentally becoming. For example, 16-month-old Winslow stood up in the bathtub with a cup of water. Poised to spill the water on the floor, he stopped and smiled at his mother. Winslow's mother said, "I can see you are trying to stop yourself. You know the water stays in the tub. I will help you to stop." In this way, Winslow's developing impulse control that was revealed when he paused and smiled at his mother was supported by her and the floor stayed dry. Recognizing emergent developmental steps can be useful.

Expectations

Mother–baby and mother–toddler interactions lead to expectations. That is, babies and toddlers make mental predictions based on their experience. Even a very young baby begins to expect a repetition of what has already been experienced. A baby who is fed when hungry will begin to expect the breast or bottle when feeling hungry. This expectation helps the baby's expression of hunger – crying – to become a communication and gradually helps the baby learn to wait.

A 10-month-old baby after a good sleep may awaken, play alone for a while, and then signal Mommy with a cry. Hearing Mommy's voice, "I'm coming," the baby stops crying. The reinforced expectation to see Mommy further helps the baby to shift attention from feelings of hunger to the expectation of seeing Mommy, feeling

DOI: 10.4324/9781003352549-8

the nipple, and the flow of milk. The expectation calms the baby. The satisfied expectation of Mommy's arrival intensifies the pleasure of their reunion and is reflected in their joyful greeting.

Expecting safety, shared pleasure, and the gratification of needs promotes mother–baby attachment, secure base interactions, and an ongoing secure sense of well-being. There will be many questions in the following chapters about expectations at different ages. There will be questions about what you would like your baby and toddler to expect.

Older babies and toddlers learn to expect Mommy's approval and disapproval for specific behaviors. They want and need their mothers' approval and are highly motivated to behave in ways to get approval and maintain feelings of self-worth. This may be difficult to believe because they so often behave in ways that get disapproval. There will be examples of this paradox and the child development theories that explain it.

Mothers teach their children codes of behavior. The ways in which a mother's expectations of her toddler's behavior become her toddler's own codes of behavior and self-expectations will be outlined. Some of the questions in the following chapters will be about identifying emerging internal conflicts that reflect the process by which your codes of behavior are becoming those of your baby and toddler.

Developing Sense of Self

Mother–baby and mother–toddler interactions influence a child's developing sense of self, and sense of self with other. How you understand your baby and toddler will influence your child's own self-understanding. Your child's sense of self will in some ways reflect what you like and what you do not like about your child. In many ways, mothers are their babies' and toddlers' mirror. This may sound like a huge responsibility; but it can also be an enormous advantage. Just as all people have parts of themselves they like and do not like, all mothers have things they like and things they do not like about their children. The challenge for both mothers and children is adapting to both.

Affectionate Interactions and Angry Interactions

Every mother–baby and mother–toddler relationship, in addition to pleasurable affectionate interactions, includes angry interactions. A baby may cry angrily when Mommy takes a dangerous item away, but then quickly shift attention to an offered substitute. A 2-year-old may reject a substitute, and kick and scream for 20 minutes when Mommy puts the vacuum cleaner away interrupting a favorite play activity. A mother's anger may escalate when this happens in front of company.

Mothers, babies, and toddlers learn to adapt to angry outbursts, their own as well as each other's. They develop ways to repair the ruptures in their loving feelings and return to loving interactions. They learn to expect repairs. Angry interactions intensify as children develop. During a mothers' group, one woman confessed, "I now understand why some mothers spank. I would never do it, but I never could understand it before; now I understand it. I never imagined how angry, helpless, and frightened I could feel." The other mothers agreed.

The child development information and self-reflective questions by age will address the rupture and repair process of affectionate mother–child interactions at each developmental phase. Some of the questions will address your memories of this process with your own mother, which may or may not be the process you want with your child.

Developing Self-assertiveness

Babies and toddlers assert themselves. They grab things they want and reject those they do not want. Interactions that support assertiveness contribute to a developing positive sense of self and can help a toddler to cooperate. During a mother-toddler group, 22-month-old Jessie took her shoes and socks off. Her mother looked delighted and praised Jessie for being able to take them off, even though she had wanted Jessie to keep them on. "Wow! You know how to take your shoes and socks off all by yourself, but here you need to wear shoes and socks." Jessie smiled with pride. This recognition helped Jessie easily accept her mother putting her shoes and socks back on because she felt proud of her achievement. Jessie also knew that her mother was proud of her. Many of the self-reflective questions will address mother–child interactions that are triggered when babies and toddlers assert their autonomy.

Separation and Reunion

Separation and reunion sequences are a unit. Babies gradually learn to expect that separations will be followed by reunions. Babies' reactions to separation from Mommy can begin as young as 6 weeks, reach a peak of anxiety at around 8 months, and escalate to include intense angry and fearful protests.

Saying goodbye, an important part of separation, helps babies and toddlers to prepare for an imminent separation. It also enables them to know that they can expect to be told before separations. This expectation helps prevent unnecessary anticipatory anxiety and hypervigilance. A baby or toddler may protest an expected separation vigorously, but a protest is different from being overwhelmed. It may be difficult to differentiate a protest from being overwhelmed, but it is a useful distinction; angry protests can be acknowledged.

Mothers' decisions about when and for how long they separate from their babies and toddlers and with whom they entrust their care, are determined by many factors, and will be addressed in the following chapters by age.

Body and Mind Awareness

Two exciting areas of discovery during their first three years are bodies and minds: both their own and Mommy's. Babies aged 2 to 3 months repeatedly move their hands in front of their eyes. Why do babies typically do this? It feels good; they are gradually learning about having an intention and the power to achieve it. They are also learning that their hand is part of themselves. We can imagine in our words a baby's experience of all they can do with their hands, '*My hand is part of me, I can move it. I can see it when I want to, most of the time. I can even put it in my mouth and suck it. I then feel my hand being sucked and my mouth sucking my hand.*' At about 4 months, '*I can put my two hands together and get a big feeling touching and being touched at the same time.*' These are compelling body–mind experiences. Body and mind awareness develop in concert.

Babies and toddlers experience body pleasure and body pain. They actively explore all their bodies can do and feel. They are curious about their bodies. Their body experiences can trigger mothers' strong reactions, vivid childhood memories, and mothering goals.

Rebecca, 33 months old, touched her labia and asked her mother, "What is this?" Kaitlyn had been referring to her daughter's genitals as "private parts" and "down there." Those were the only words her own mother would use. Kaitlyn was determined to learn the words for the parts of her own genitals that she had never wanted to know and had avoided learning. She did not want her daughter to have the same sexual inhibitions that she had had and believed that knowing the words and talking together would help.

Babies and toddlers also learn about their mind: their inner world of thoughts, feelings, wishes, and fears, and the conflicts among them. They learn about the complexity of minds: making choices and changing one's mind. They become proud and possessive of their ideas, '*I said it first. Don't copy me.*' They also learn about their mother's mind: when both of their minds are in synch – a meeting of minds, and when they disagree with each other – the separateness of minds.

Family Diversity

Emerging body and mind awareness are influenced by similarities and differences within families – including sex, race, religion, language, physical traits, disabilities, and family composition. Parents make decisions about which get talked about, when, and how. Some reactions to differences and similarities may be more neutral and others linked to intense feelings, and mothers' childhood memories. Details will be discussed in chapters by age.

Internal Conflict

As babies and toddlers develop, internal conflicts gradually emerge. Attachment needs and needs for autonomy begin to clash. Babies and toddlers need to feel loved, approved of, and protected, and at the same time they strive to feel autonomous and self-reliant. In one moment, they push their mothers away and in the next seemingly cannot get close enough.

When Martine was 23 months, and her mother began to talk to another mother during a group, Martine stopped her play, climbed onto her mother's lap, held her mother's cheeks lovingly in her hands, and rotated her mother's face seeking her gaze. This familiar interaction communicating, '*Mommy, I want all your attention, all the time,*' alternated with asserting autonomy. As soon as Martine captured her mother's gaze, she slid off her lap and said, "Go away Mommy."

During the first three years, wishes to please Mommy conflict with wishes for autonomy and to please oneself. Interpersonal conflicts sometimes reflect internal conflict – the mother's, the child's, or both. Whining is sometimes a toddler's compromise between two opposing wishes: the wish to please Mommy by renouncing a wish and the wish to demand something to please oneself. In other words, sometimes toddlers are of two minds; they have an internal conflict.

Sybil said to her 26-month-old daughter, "Gretchen, I've told you no more cookies, don't ask me again." Gretchen whined for more cookies. Gretchen's wish to please herself by continuing to want and demand another cookie was conflicted with her wish to please her mother by not asking for or even wanting another cookie. Her internal conflict was revealed in her whining – not her regular assertive voice.

Sybil preferred that Gretchen not want another cookie. She wanted to please her daughter, "I don't like to say no to her, but she had enough." Sybil's internal conflict about saying no was embedded in her statement, "Don't ask me again." Both Sybil's and Gretchen's internal conflicts were being negotiated interpersonally. Sybil became aware of her own conflict and acknowledged Gretchen's, "I know you really want another cookie. You are asking in your squeaky voice instead of your strong voice because I said, don't ask me again. I should not have said that. I always want to know what you want and what you think. You can always tell me. Tomorrow, you can have another cookie."

These may seem like subtle and complex distinctions for a 2-year-old but having them in the mother's mind was useful to resolve the conflict between them about more cookies, to acknowledge and validate the toddler wanting more cookies, to address the whining, and to reaffirm the limit. Throughout *When Mothers Talk* the importance of children knowing their own minds is highlighted: what they think, want, like, do not like, and do not want.

Emotion Regulation

Identifying feelings with words helps to promote emotion regulation. The developmental information and questions organized by age identify some of the specific ways babies and toddlers behave when they feel anger, frustration, fear, sadness, and shame.

Overwhelming Feelings

Babies and toddlers need help to process overwhelming feelings. Tammy was 17 months and frequently pinched and hit herself, creating red blotches on her arms and legs. When this happened during a mother-toddler group, her mother Linda froze in an angry stare. Tammy had no way to process her feelings or to regulate her emotional state without her mother's help. Linda became aware that her own anxiety was triggered by Tammy's behavior, which seemed "inexplicable and crazy," and it was easier to feel angry than to feel scared and helpless herself as she had felt as a child when her sister pinched and hit her. This insight helped Linda to temper her own fear and anger that further frightened Tammy.

After identifying both Linda's and Tammy's fear of each other, it became clear that the immediate trigger for Tammy hitting and pinching herself was the approach of another child. Tammy seemed afraid that she would be hit, that a toy would be taken from her, or that she would grab a toy from or hit the approaching child. In response to her fears of other children, and to control her own impulses which also frightened her, Tammy hit and pinched herself.

With these new meanings of Tammy's behavior, Linda was less angry. She began to protect Tammy from her fear of other children and fear of her own aggressive impulses towards other children. For example, Linda said, "I am not going to let Sammy take the truck, I'm going to help you to keep it." Linda also helped Tammy to wait her turn for a toy she wanted, or to trade toys. "I know you want the puzzle Josie is playing with, I will help you to wait. We can play with the shape-box while you wait." Feeling safer protected Tammy from her own aggressive impulses, which also frightened her. Pinching and hitting herself abated and then stopped.

Play

Babies and toddlers play for pleasure, to learn, for social interaction, to master trauma, and to adapt to everyday stresses. Early play contributes to their developing sense of self. Pretend play, sometimes called imaginative play, develops gradually and provides a glimpse into their inner world: their wishes, fears, conflicts, and trial solutions. Babies and toddlers can "say" things in play that they cannot say in words.

Play and Everyday Stresses

Mother–baby and mother–toddler play are opportunities to master everyday stressful events. Peek-a-boo, a game about separation and reunion, is one of the earliest games introduced by mothers. The separation is brief, and the reunion is joyful. Toddlers create their own elaborations of hiding and finding games. For example, after mastering peek-a-boo, 10-month-old Harper created a new game. She repeatedly threw a small ball across the room and crawled to retrieve it. In addition to the pleasure of mastering the physical feat, Harper's play had meaning. Her game reinforced her learning that the ball existed even when it rolled under the sofa and she could not see it. It also gave control of separation and reunion to Harper, unlike when separated from her mother, which she could not control. Harper was playing peek-a-boo with the ball. Pretend play created by a baby or toddler has particular learning power.

Doctor visits, haircuts, and having a shampoo are often stressful; pretend play can modulate the stress. The pleasures and tensions during mealtime inspire frequent pretend play. The details of a toddler feeding a doll or toy animal can provide useful information about the meaning of meals to the toddler. Renee was 2½ years old. Her mother Chandler was horrified as she watched Renee play: "I could not believe what

I saw. Renee was feeding pretend oatmeal to her doll, spoon after spoon, jamming it into her face and saying, you need to eat more! One more bite! You are a bad girl! I always thought that I was encouraging Renee to eat. I never called her a bad girl. Maybe she feels forced and like a bad girl when she doesn't eat more."

Play and Life Lessons

Play with manipulative toys, in addition to practicing manual dexterity and cognitive abilities, provides important information about basic principles. A jack-in-the-box or activity-box with cranks, levers, and buttons to open doors and make things pop up and be seen, can help babies and toddlers to learn that objects exist even when they are not seen – object permanence. They also learn that thinking the door to open or wishing the door to open is not enough, they need to physically open it. The power of minds is limited.

With another popular toy, a toddler bangs the ball, it drops into a hole, and comes out the bottom. It takes a strong whack and makes a loud noise. This play, in addition to being a pleasurable, aggressive game of peek-a-boo with the ball, is reminiscent of the body – food goes in and poop comes out. This meaning of the play to toddlers can be compelling as their ideas about pooping evolve. Adults may also find this play engaging. Everybody eats and poops.

Play with construction toys, block building, and stringing beads provides repeated experiences demonstrating that the world is made up of objects that have component parts that can be assembled, disassembled, and re-assembled in the same form or differently. As in language, the same words can be strung together differently to create sentences with different meanings. In contrast, puzzles have one way in which they can be put together and completed. It is a different life lesson. Both construction toys and puzzles provide the repeated pleasure and reassurance that when things fall apart, they can be put back together. Often scattering the pieces of a completed puzzle or knocking down a tower is as much fun as putting them back together. All play has underlying meanings.

Play and Body Integrity

The adaptive creativity of toddlers' play is captured in the following examples. Savannah was 24 months. While ice-skating with her family, her mother accidentally stepped on Savannah's finger in a way that ripped off her nail. Savannah and her mother were both devastated. After a dash to the emergency room, several painful injections to numb her fingers and an x-ray, the doctor bandaged her entire hand. They were told that her nail might not grow back.

A week later, after the bandage was removed, her finger was healing, and the nail was growing back, Savannah's main play activity for several weeks was shredding pieces of paper, crumpling the pieces together into a ball the same size that her bandaged hand had been, and binding the clumps together with scotch tape. This activity was repeated many times a day. The corners of the living room floor were piled high with these put-together body repair constructions. Savannah's play represented the accident, the medical treatment, and most importantly the healing. Savannah created the play to cope with the feelings damage to her body evoked. When her feelings of body integrity were restored, the play was no longer needed.

Brody, 22 months, created a new game. Each evening after his bath, he sat naked on the edge of his bed and opened and closed his legs, slowly exposing and hiding his penis between his thighs. Brody's mother was curious about the meaning of his play until she remembered his bath with his cousin Autumn who was visiting for the weekend. She believed that Brody had created this game in response to his reaction to the boy–girl genital difference. In addition, she thought that his play was a reaction to Autumn trying to touch his penis and both mothers shouting, "No!" Brody's play repeatedly confirmed his penis was always there. Brody played this peek-a-boo game with his penis every night for about a week.

The child development information and self-reflective questions by age explore the feelings with which babies and toddlers wrestle, and the ways in which they use play to adapt.

Picture Books

Reading picture books to toddlers creates a joint focus of attention to the pictures and the story, to their meaning, and the feelings evoked. Picture books are frequently read and re-read because their themes are not only important during early development but are relevant throughout life. The shared parent–toddler attention to these themes can be enriching for both mother and child.

Rose and 20-month-old Melanie provide a dramatic example. They were struggling to find each other: in other words, to connect emotionally. Though unaware, Rose kept her distance from Melanie both physically and emotionally. Melanie's development was significantly delayed.

Rose had the lightest skin in her family and among her friends as a teenager, and because of it escaped much of the racist discrimination they experienced. Melanie's darker skin activated Rose's long-held feelings of fear, shame, and guilt about the color of her own light skin. Although she was not aware of it, Rose felt safer being distant from Melanie, but was missing the kind of relationship with Melanie that she wanted, and Melanie was suffering.

With the help of developmental consultations and Rose's insight, Melanie and Rose began to connect emotionally. Reading *Mommy, Where Are You?* became captivating to them both. Sitting on separate chairs, they read the book many times a day. The reading routine brought them together physically and emotionally. The story resonated with their struggle and reflected their gradual success emotionally connecting with each other. While reading the book, Melanie could always find the Mommy by lifting the flap that hid the Mommy, and Rose could always enjoy the pleasure of the Mommy being found.

Once Rose and Melanie were able to play together, talk to each other, and be physically affectionate with each other, Melanie listened to *Mommy, Where Are You?* cuddled on her mother's lap. Reading *Mommy, Where Are You?* had acquired new meaning. In Rose's words, "When Melanie found me, she found herself." I think Rose's words also meant: when I found part of myself that I had rejected, I found Melanie.

Play with Peers

Babies are interested in other babies: looking and smiling at each other, and touching – sometimes gently, sometimes not. Babies vocalize with each other in turn-taking rhythms as if they are having a conversation. They imitate the sounds of each other. They may pass a toy back and forth. Toddlers with adult help can build a tower together or create a marching band. Items that other toddlers wear may capture their attention, for example eyeglasses and barrettes. Toddlers may be more interested in a toy when another child is playing with it. It seems that their interest is beyond the intrinsic properties of the toy, but rather is connected to their social interest with each other. Some toddlers are motivated to be part of a group activity, others are slower to warm up to close interaction and may prefer more distance; however, watching and being watched are also interactions.

Motivation for social interaction is pre-wired, highly adaptive, and captures mothers' attention. Most mothers are interested in their children making friends. When 13-month-old Kevin crawled next to Bella, his mother said, "It may look like Kevin is interested in the truck Bella is holding, but I know he wants to be close to her. He really likes Bella. I think he says her name."

Learning

All learning has emotional underpinnings and meanings. In addition to learning a task from trial and error, a baby or toddler in our words learns some version of, '*I can do it myself; it was hard and took a long time, but I did it.*' With instructional learning, the task is learned, and '*I can learn from others*' is also learned. Learning from observing and imitating Mommy, in addition to learning the behavior, for example please and thank you, a child also learns '*I can be like Mommy in many wonderful ways.*'

Mother–baby and mother–toddler teaching–learning interactions by imitation are occurring all the time. For example, 32-month-old Troy, with a serious expression began to repeatedly bend his arm at the elbow, fold it across his body, and look at his wrist. His mother was curious and somewhat concerned because Troy did it so often it started to look as though he had developed a tic. She asked, "Troy, what are you doing?" Troy said, "I don't know, but you do it all the time." Troy's mother realized that he had been carefully observing her look at her watch and was doing what he had seen her do. Toddlers are highly motivated to imitate Mommy.

Teaching-learning interactions include imitation, instruction, and physical help. Each teaching-learning approach may be more suitable for certain tasks, specific children, at particular ages, and for each parent.

Learning Codes of Behavior – The Dos and Don'ts of Everyday Life

Learning acceptable codes of behavior often clashes with babies' and toddlers' own wishes and impulses. When teaching and learning the dos and don'ts of everyday life, emotions can run high. The overarching goal of most early learning about ways to behave is emotional development. Emotional development includes mental capacities to regulate emotions, wishes to please Mommy – an aspect of attachment, the ability to inhibit behavior that Mommy disapproves of, to achieve adequate resolutions of ambivalence, to tolerate frustration, to wait, and to find satisfaction in substitute gratifications when needed. These mental abilities importantly include the development of a conscience – a personal sense of right and wrong. These mental capacities are the pillars of behavior.

Sensitive and attuned mother–baby and mother–toddler interactions can promote the development of these mental abilities. A mother's attention to both the external behavior she wants her child to learn and her child's inner world of thoughts and feelings can result in behavioral learning and emotional development that complement each other.

Because babies and toddlers want and need Mommy's approval, they become more self-observant. Internal conflict emerges about satisfying their own wishes and impulses that are unacceptable to Mommy, for example throwing food on the floor. In this way, interpersonal mother–baby and mother–toddler conflicts about behavior increasingly become a child's internal conflicts. Mothers' expectations of their baby's and toddler's behavior gradually become the child's own standards. As your baby learns your behavioral expectations, gradually your codes of behavior mostly will become your child's own aims and self-prohibitions.

Consistency and Inconsistency

Most learning requires multiple teaching-learning interactions, and while consistency is often emphasized, inconsistency is also important. Inconsistencies help children to adapt to change and to be responsive to variations and nuance. It is as though they are learning this is the rule all the time except when Mommy is on the phone. Some things are okay in private, but not in public. Some things I only do with Daddy, some things I only do with Mommy. I can eat French fries with my hands, but not spaghetti. We usually take a bus, today we are taking a taxi. These are some examples of inconsistencies that are of value. In addition, there are few non-negotiable, non-flexible behavioral limits or ways of being. It takes many slightly different repetitions, changes in routine, and contexts to learn all the variations and respond accordingly.

The dos and don'ts of everyday life need to be learned in a way that they can be appropriately applied, and when there is uncertainty a baby or toddler can check back with Mommy as a secure base. A startle in response to a mother's prohibition may indicate a degree of hyperarousal that may interfere with processing the limit and its flexible parameters. An example of this occurred with 18-month-old Jeremy who frequently startled when reprimanded by his mother. Unable to check back with her, he entered the playroom, froze, pointed at the toys, and said, "No touch, no touch."

Part of the long-range goal when teaching babies and toddlers the dos and don'ts of their everyday lives is allowing some space for conflict, mistakes, and the inconsistencies, complexities, and nuances of the things they are being taught. This complexity starts in the mother's mind and will be evidenced in her child's growing adaptation to the changing demands of the environment.

Learning with and without Help

When a baby or toddler is struggling to achieve a task, for example to roll over, walk, do a puzzle, or self-feed, how do you decide when to help and when not to help? Many things may influence your decision, including how much mess will occur and how much more work for you, your assessment of your child's ability to tolerate the frustration, your ability to tolerate your child's frustration, and your ideas about the value of learning from success, mistakes, and failure. Sometimes memories of being too pushed, not pushed enough, painful failures, and embarrassing mistakes influence mothers' decisions.

Self-assertion, Aggression, and Passivity

Mothers may be reactive to interactions between children when they view their child as too aggressive or too passive. Ginny weighed two pounds at birth and had many related medical complications. Her mother Miriam was convinced Ginny would be small her entire life and would need to be assertive, confident, and strong. When Ginny was 20 months, according to her mother she had become "too aggressive" with other children. "Nobody wants playdates with her anymore." As Miriam described Ginny's hitting and grabbing behavior in the sandbox, she noted, "I just realized, since she was very young I have always done everything I can to promote her assertiveness. She is so tiny. I see her as so vulnerable. I don't want her to be bullied. Maybe I am promoting her hitting and grabbing."

In response to a series of group questions including, when would you like your child to be more assertive? Bethany explained, "Otis is a very sweet boy. He shares his toys all the time. He's generous and nice. I think he takes after me. But when Otis is playing with something and another child approaches him, he just hands over the toy. I used to think that was good and other children would like him. He's now 2½; I don't know how to help him stand up for himself." As Bethany spoke, she included vivid childhood memories of her father spanking her brother, and her brother hitting and teasing her. She recognized that her inhibition of Otis's assertiveness was related to her fear of male aggression. Her childhood memories had been activated by having a son.

After the mothers' group discussion, Bethany and Otis began to play a fencing game with toy swords, and Bethany helped Otis to assert himself with other children; for example, to hold on to toys he was playing with. Otis began to stand up for himself and to build friendships. Bethany became more comfortable with healthy aggression. Dangerous male aggression became a memory, not a universal male trait to be feared. Bethany reflected, "I had wanted Otis to be a nice boy, not a bully like I remember my brother and father. I was afraid of them. I was afraid to

help Otis stand up for himself. Even that seemed too aggressive. We are both having fun with the swords."

Apologies

Opportunities for apologizing and accepting apologies arise when toddlers interact
with each other; hugs may turn into tackles and kisses into bites. Mothers have
different approaches to helping toddlers and sometimes disagree with each other.

Recognizing distinctions between apologies as social convention or as expressions of remorse and forgiveness can be important. Promoting the development of a
toddler's capacity for remorse is a goal and may require processing the complexity
of feelings underlying the interactions rather than a precipitous apology. For example, when 34-month-old Sara hit Patti, "You were very angry when Patti grabbed
your car. You hit her so hard, she cried. You got scared. I think you felt sorry that you
hit her, you did not want to hurt her."

Mothers' Childhood Memories

Childhood memories can add an important personal perspective to the anecdotes,
theories, and research findings presented in this book. The best approach to many
challenges during the first three years may be embedded in each mother's own
memories.

Repetition of Childhood Memories

Some mother–baby and mother–toddler interactions are repetitions of a mother's
childhood memory; however, what is being repeated may be disguised or hidden.
When mother–child interactions are perplexing or stressful they may be linked to
an unrecognized childhood memory.

Deidra frequently said things that she thought were mean to her 16-month-old
daughter Mandie and she did not know why she kept doing it. "The mean words
just spill out of my mouth. My mother says very mean things to me, she always
has. I hate it. I don't know why I keep doing it to Mandie." Identifying specific
childhood memories of pushing her mother away and linking them to her current
interactions with Mandie helped Deidra to recognize that talking mean was a way
to feel close to her own mother. "Lately, I've been pushing my mother away. I want
to feel close to her even though I am so angry at her. Maybe talking mean to Mandie is a way to feel close to my mother while I push her away." This insight helped
Deidra to be the kind of mother she wanted to be, not mean.

Body Sensation Memories

Mothers have intimate contact with their baby's or toddler's bodies. Their own
early fantasies and body experiences can be aroused and may be repeated. For
example, Beatrix told a mothers' group about a nighttime ritual of gently fingertip
tickling her daughter's arm, back, and tummy before sleep as she had been tickled

when she was a little girl. One night, pointing to her genitals, her 2-year-old daughter said, "Mommy, tickle me there." Beatrix was startled. She had not remembered or realized that the tickling was arousing, "In that way." During the present moment tickling her daughter, reliving the past replaced remembering.

Sibling Rivalry Memories

Sometimes a mother's rivalry with her own sibling is reactivated and repeated with her toddler. Joyce characterized herself as shy and reserved. She described her 2-year-old daughter Jill: "She's such a showoff. Jill's always trying to be the center of attention. I don't like it. I'm not like that." Joyce's reserved demeanor was different from her exuberant outgoing daughter's. In addition, her revived memories of her older sister whom she believed, "did everything better, she was always in the spotlight" had triggered a ferocious rivalry with her daughter that she felt she was losing. As Joyce began to recognize that she had displaced feelings that she had toward her sister onto Jill, she became able to differentiate her painful childhood memories and continued rivalry with her sister from the normal needs of a 2-year-old to be admired.

In Summary

The child development information, self-reflective questions, and examples in the following chapters are organized by age and categorized by the themes discussed above. What occurs during each stage of development influences the next. Developmental steps taken in early phases continue into the next phase and lay a foundation for later phases. Emergent steps in development can be identified and supported.

Mommy-friends

Each chapter by age begins with a mother's story about a friend or group of friends during her early years of motherhood. Some mothers are eager to meet other mothers, some not so interested. Some women are motivated, but life circumstances make it difficult or impossible. Four themes emerge in mothers' stories about their friendships when their children are babies and toddlers: 1. Feelings of loneliness and anxiety, 2. Activated childhood memories, 3. Self-criticism, and 4. Mother–baby and mother–toddler loving interactions vicariously enjoyed.

8 Birth to 6 Months

Mommy-friends

Marjorie and Polly lived in the same apartment building and met in the mailroom when they were both seven months pregnant. Marjorie explained, "I had gotten a Mother's Day card that amused us both and we became fast friends. Charles was a difficult baby from the moment he was born. He screamed all the time. It was so stressful. I was sleep deprived and had gained over 40 pounds. I was miserable. Polly had an easy, smiley baby who slept through the night at 3 months. I was very envious, and I was sure it was my fault that my baby was so difficult. My friendships with Polly and her easy baby were important to me. When we were all together, I was okay. They made everything feel better.

"When Charles was 2 years old, Polly moved to Florida; I was so sad. I met Francine, whose son Peter was also 2 years. We became good friends. Charles had become an easy toddler. Peter was wild and difficult. I could not see anything Francine did that was causing Peter's very challenging and sometimes frightening behavior. Every day he ran out of the playground and Francine chased after him. She was always calm and patient. I was afraid that Peter might be kidnapped or run over by a car. I now had the easy child, and my friend had the difficult one.

"This reminds me; my older sister frightened me all the time. She told me I better sleep with one foot out of the bed so I can run away fast when the tickle monster comes to get me in the middle of the night. I was terrified. Nobody helped or protected me. Francine was amazing, the opposite of my mother. Francine always ran after Peter to protect him. When I was with Francine and Peter, I always felt safe and everything would be okay."

When navigating the emotional rollercoaster of early motherhood and the activation of childhood memories, friendships are important for many mothers. The acceptance and support mommy-friends give to each other, with all their similarities and differences, can help mothers be less self-critical and more self-forgiving. Mothers can get vicarious feelings of safety and comfort from being included in a loving mother–baby relationship.

First Mommy-friends

When a baby is born, an entanglement of the mother's feelings is aroused. While there are many pleasures, the ongoing demands of infant care and a crying baby

DOI: 10.4324/9781003352549-9

can be worrying and wearing. Stresses for mothers during this phase may include a multitude of new tasks with feelings of being a competent woman dissolving into feelings of uncertainty and the enormous responsibility of a baby's survival. For many mothers, sharing the pleasures with a friend can be enriching and sharing the challenges can be important.

An interest in friendships with women who also have babies may begin to emerge. Work schedules may interfere. Lifestyle or other relationships may make it more difficult or less needed. During middle-of-the-night feedings, isolated windows lit across the street or across the city or town may capture a mother's attention and imagination "I am not alone; other mothers with their babies are near." An affinity with mothers and their babies passing in the park or standing close on a supermarket line may rush to the front of your mind. Babies' photographs shown at work that evoke shared joy with other mothers and personal longings may trigger wishes for a mommy-friend.

- How has your life changed since your baby was born? How has what you think about changed?
- What impact has your baby's birth had on your relationships with other people?
- What impact has pregnancy, childbirth, breastfeeding, and caring for your baby had on your body?

The above questions may have awakened many feelings, both comforting and disturbing. You may be aware of how your answers influence your interactions with your baby. The following questions are organized according to theme headings: Mother–Child Interaction; Body and Mind Awareness; Emotion Regulation; Play; Learning; and Mothers' Childhood Memories.

Mother–Child Interaction

The developmental changes during the first six months of a baby's life are monumental. The pleasures of mother–baby interactions gradually increase. First smiles emerge and augment the mother–baby attachment process. Mother–baby interactions, including mutual gaze, synchronized "conversations," and tender touching promote capacities that lay a foundation for your baby's future interactions and deepen your relationship with each other.

As you get to know your baby, as maturation unfolds, and your relationship evolves, you are discovering more and more about your baby and about yourself as a mother. Your baby may have strong likes and dislikes. Some may be aligned with yours and some not.

For the first five months of Jinni's life, she settled into nursing easily. She focused on sucking vigorously; nothing distracted her. When Jinni was about 5½ months, it seemed to her mother Billie that everything had changed. Jinni periodically stopped sucking and turned her attention to gaze and smile at her mother. At times

Jinni twisted her entire body around to scan the room, yanked Billie's nipple, and then resumed nursing. Jinni's developing social interests changed the way she liked to nurse. Feedings took much longer. Billie enjoyed the playful interactions and her baby's growing interest in the world, but she sometimes felt more in a rush, and did not like the nipple pain from Jinni's yanking.

Billie realized that this was Jinni's way of socializing during a meal and when Jinni smiled and reached up to touch her mother's face, Billie smiled. However, in addition to the time it took, there was something else about nursing and socializing that Billie did not like, especially when her husband was watching.

Over time, Billie and Jinni established a rhythm that included some long playful feedings, some quick snacks, and some long, drowsy, wake–sleep feasts. Billie learned to break the suction created by nursing before Jinni twisted completely around, and Jinni learned not to yank Billie's nipples when she wanted to look around. Though the specifics are not known, both Billie and Jinni contributed to this mutually regulated, pleasurable pattern. Billie described, "Sometimes I end a feeding and sometimes Jinni does. Sometimes they are long and sometimes short." We can imagine that in some ways Jinni was beginning to learn about her own intentions and the reciprocity in relationships.

Likes and Dislikes

Your baby's likes and dislikes will influence your interactions with each other. Likes and dislikes may be related to age, temperament, or life experiences. One baby may not like being swaddled. Another may like a bath but not a shampoo. There may be important caretaking activities that a baby dislikes intensely. Understanding the specifics of what a baby is reacting to may be useful in finding ways to help the baby to adapt or to adapt to the baby.

> - What are some of the things your baby likes that you do not like?
> - What are some of the things your baby does not like that you are trying to help your baby adapt to?
> - When your likes and dislikes, and your baby's likes and dislikes, clash, how do you decide what to do?

Babies have an innate sucking reflex. The ability to suck and a baby's need to suck are both independent of and aligned with needs for nourishment. There is individual variation in the amount of sucking each baby needs. For some babies, sucking needs can be satisfied by sucking a bottle or breast nipple during feedings. For others, a pacifier or thumb may be needed for additional sucking. A baby's sucking likes and dislikes combined with mothers' preferences will influence their interactions with each other.

Plans to care for a baby and the actuality are different. Your decision to breast or bottle feed may have been made many years ago, or more recently. You may have made decisions about pacifiers and sleep. Your decisions may be firm or may be changing as you get to know your baby. Understanding the reasons for your decisions including developmental theory, personal meanings, your baby's likes and dislikes, and how your decisions relate to childhood memories can deepen your self-understanding and inform your decisions.

- What interactions are you having with your baby that you did not anticipate having?
- What interactions are you not having with your baby that you had thought you would have?
- What decisions are you re-evaluating?

These questions and your answers may have brought to the front of your mind some feelings that you had not anticipated. You may have talked about them or kept them private.

Babies' Developing Expectations

During the first six months of life, mother–baby interactions create a foundation for developing expectations. Although a baby does not yet have these explicit thoughts or words, a baby does have these experiences and gradually develops these expectations. '*When I am hungry, Mommy feeds me. When I am distressed and cry, Mommy picks me up and I am comforted. When I am scared, if I am close to Mommy, I feel safe. Sometimes Mommy goes away, then she comes back.*' We can imagine with our words what a baby's developing sense of self is with these expectations, '*I am safe, I am loveable.*'

Your baby may be showing beginning indications of expectations. For example, when your baby wakes for a feeding and cries, your baby's expectation to be fed may get triggered when you pick your baby up, begin to prepare a bottle, or sit in your favorite nursing chair. Your baby's expectation may not get triggered until the nipple touches your baby's lips. Expecting to be satisfied will get triggered at some point and your baby will calm, be able to grasp the nipple, start sucking, and continue to suck until the milk begins to flow.

- What expectations do you imagine your baby has?
- What routines have you established with your baby that will or have created expectations?

A mother may wonder about her baby acquiring certain expectations. In the following example, the mother's worries about "spoiling" her 6-month-old and her conflicts about responding to her baby's cries were activated. Zina wondered, "When I'm in a different room and Callie cries, I always feel she is calling me a bad mother. I am not sure I should go to her. I don't want to spoil her." In other words, Zina was not sure she wanted Callie to expect her to come when she cried. Zina continued, through tears, "My mother always called me a bad little girl. I never knew what to expect. I think Callie needs me; she should be able to expect me when she is distressed."

• How does your baby recover when distressed?

Expectations of gratification and comfort, and developing mother–baby attachment, build resilience and the ability to cope with and recover from the ubiquitous inevitable frustrations, discomforts, and pains of everyday life that a baby experiences.

Attachment

There has been a great deal of research about mother–baby attachment, many scientific papers, on-line information, and published books. Attachment is one way to describe the mother–baby relationship. A baby's growing attachment is the result of the expectations the baby has developed that promote feelings of safety including protection when frightened and comfort when distressed. A baby's signals of distress and a mother's sensitive and empathic responsiveness are at the core of a baby's attachment security.

Mother–baby attachment is ubiquitous, but the specifics of each mother–baby attachment relationship are unique. Attachment evolves and looks different at each phase of development. Your baby's attachment to you and your attachment to your baby motivate many of your interactions with each other. The following questions focus on your baby's developing attachment relationship with you, what it feels like to you, what you imagine it feels like to your baby, and how it influences your interactions with each other.

A mother's sense that her baby knows her may be visceral, but unarticulated. She may know it because it is obvious, because she feels it, or presumes it. She may be unsure.

• When does your baby cry for you?
• When and how is your baby comforted by you?
• What distresses for your baby are eased by being held by you?

The impact of physically painful or emotionally disturbing experiences for a baby is mitigated when being held by the mother. In part, this is an innate physiological phenomenon that becomes more psychological with development. In other words, your baby's growing attachment to you increases your baby's ability to be comforted by you and for your proximity to insulate your baby from disturbing impingements including loud noises, a looming stranger, hunger, or pain.

Your baby's pain from an injection and recovery are eased when being held by you. Mother–baby attachment also promotes distress reactions to separation, fear of strangers, and increased demands to be held by you.

• How does your and your baby's growing attachment relationship influence decisions about separations?

As your baby's unique attachment to you is developing, your feelings about separations may change. Many aspects of attachment may be exceptionally pleasurable, others may feel like endless demands, and some may trigger frightening thoughts.

Mothers' Typical Fears

During the first six months of their baby's life, mothers may have nightmares about their babies, or daytime fears of bad things happening to them. Lorraine, the mother of a 3-month-old, announced during a mothers' group that every time she walked past a door while holding her baby, she thought about the possibility of his head banging against the door frame. Nickie then reported that every time she closed the car door, she imagined that she had slammed it on her baby's hand. These kinds of thoughts are frightening and typical for mothers with babies this age. In some ways they increase mothers' vigilance to protect their babies. Frightening thoughts about hurting your baby may be triggered by your own childhood memories. Your own accident may not be remembered in the moment, but the feelings may have been awakened.

• What frightening thoughts about your baby have you had?

In addition to powerful feelings of love and attachment, and fierce motivation to protect their babies, mothers' feelings during the first six months may also include boredom, loneliness, guilt, anxiety, and anger. Mothers' frightening thoughts about their babies getting hurt or lost, the adaptive function of the thoughts, the memories that might trigger them, and the related feelings that intensify them are typical. The angry feelings that mothers have towards their babies can increase their fears, and feelings of horror about their fears. As mothers discover how common the frightening thoughts are, and as their babies develop, these images and frightening thoughts usually diminish.

Body and Mind Awareness

Body and mind awareness develop together. Body experiences affect the mind, and mental states, thoughts, and feelings affect the body. Each ability a baby acquires that we see from the outside, for example putting hands to mouth and sucking fingers, is accompanied by the baby's mental experience of it. We can imagine in our words a baby's dawning awareness, '*It feels good to suck my fingers. It is like sucking a nipple in some ways, and different in some ways.*'

> - Which body parts does your baby touch, look at, or move purposely?
> - What body games do you play with your baby?

Body pleasure, body pain, being touched, and self-touching are part of body awareness and contribute to a baby's developing sense of self. Babies react to their body sensations: they smile and grimace. They cry when they feel pain. Babies kick their feet with exuberance and acquire a robust laugh. They touch their feet, genitals, tummies, ears, and hair. Some babies, having discovered their voice and how loud they can squeal, practice it frequently.

> - What body explorations does your baby enjoy?
> - What body pain has your baby had?
> - Which parts of the body does your baby like touched or kissed by you? Which parts of the body does your baby not like to be touched?

When babies feel the urge, they poop, pee, sneeze, hiccup, burp, and spit-up. They shiver and startle. Acknowledging a baby's reactions to body sensations contributes to the sensations becoming known by the baby and shared with mommy – a joint focus of attention. Babies have different sleep, feeding, and bowel rhythms; some are regular, others more irregular. Some may be influenced by routines; others are more internally determined. Babies' bodies, their insides and outsides, and all their body sensations become part of their emerging sense of self. We can imagine in our words a baby's response to Mommy's attention and care of her baby's body, '*Mommy looks at me; she touches me lovingly. Mommy takes care of me. Mommy knows when I sneeze or cough. Mommy knows all the parts of me.*' During mother–baby body-play, a baby's experience may be something like, '*Mommy and I have fun together when she kisses my feet. Mommy knows these sensations feel good to me. When I feel pain, Mommy knows how I feel and comforts me. Mommy knows when I poop.*'

Joint Attention

When mothers and babies watch together as the mother slowly moves a toy, they are sharing a joint focus of attention on the toy. At some point the baby may look at Mommy and realize they are looking at the same toy.

> - When do you and your baby share a focus of attention on a toy?

Joint attention to a toy, mutual smiles, and mother–baby shared emotional states gradually contribute to your baby's growing awareness of your minds in synch.

Your spontaneous empathic response to your baby's discomfort when you pull a tight shirt over your baby's head is registered in the subtle changes of your facial expression and resonates with your baby's experience – a brief moment of joint attention to your baby's feelings.

> • When do you and your baby have a joint focus of attention to your baby's feelings?

Empathy

Mother–baby joint attention to the baby's feelings is an empathic interaction. For example, Jessica was 6 months and struggled to swat a bell to make it jingle. Jessica's mother was uncertain about when to help her: "I feel so frustrated watching her, but I know when she finally rings the bell herself she is thrilled. Sometimes I tell her that I know it's so hard and then she does it. I think she feels my empathy for both her frustration and her pleasurable success."

> • What are the moments when your baby might be aware of your empathy?

As your baby experiences your empathy, your baby's self-understanding develops. For example, your baby grimaces at the taste of new vitamins. The spontaneous empathic change in your facial expression and your words reflect and validate your baby's experience. *'These new vitamins taste different. I am not sure I like them. Mommy knows how I feel and I know that Mommy thinks they are good.'* In other words, your empathy promotes your baby's self-understanding and understanding of you.

Gender

Cultural ideas about gender, that is what it means to be male or female, continue to evolve. Laws and customs related to being male or female change. Attitudes about gender may be different today from when you were a little girl. You may remember your reactions when you discovered the sex of your baby. You may have observed the reactions of others.

A mother's wishes to have a boy or a girl may have emerged years before her baby was conceived and may be related to specific life experiences. During pregnancy, ideas and hopes about having a boy or a girl may intensify, fade, or vary. Musings that play with both possibilities may surface. A mother's wishes and fantasies about the sex of her baby may be overshadowed by the baby felt moving inside her body, seen on a sonagram, or by her baby at birth.

> • What information does your baby get from you and from others about being a boy or a girl?

The sex of a baby is identified either before or at birth; gender identity gradually unfolds. Information and questions in the following chapters will track the development of the awareness of sex differences, gender, and gender identity during the first three years. Your baby's developing gender-related behavior may influence your ideas about gender.

Emotion Regulation

Babies express what they are feeling. As mothers respond to their expressions, the feelings expressed become communications. For example, when a baby feels cold and cries, and Mommy comes and warms her baby, over time the cry becomes a communication, '*Mommy, I am cold, warm me.*' Your baby's expectations to be responded to will gradually enable your baby to calm and to wait when needed. Expectations contribute to emotion regulation.

> • What expectations does your baby have that are beginning to contribute to emotion regulation?

Babies have different thresholds for over arousal and under arousal that influence emotion regulation. Some babies can fall asleep or nurse in a noisy room, others need quiet. Some startle easily and may take a while to re-regulate. Some require greater stimulation than others to become alert.

Being Soothed and Self-soothing

Soothing mother–baby interactions contribute to a baby's developing ability to self-soothe. All human beings, including babies, children, and adults, at times benefit from emotion regulating interactions with others. When distressed, empathy from a friend, a hug from a spouse, or kind words from a stranger can be soothing.

Crying and being comforted are frequent mother–baby interactions. A baby's crying is stressful for the mother, and triggers empathy for her baby and a strong motivation to soothe her baby. This is a valuable system because it can promote sensitive caretaking; but it is a fragile system. When her baby continues to cry, a mother's feelings of helplessness and anxiety can become intense. Her feelings of frustration and inadequacy can become overwhelming. Since mothers' well-being is essential, also built into the system is a mother's increasing ability to understand her baby's distress and find ways to comfort her baby.

During a first mother-baby group, 3-month-old Candi began to cry. Regina, Candi's mother, explained, "See, this is what happens. She just cries. She's very difficult." After a few minutes of loud crying, Regina stood up and began walking back and forth gently rocking Candi in her arms. After a few more moments of crying, Regina said, "Maybe I should leave."

The other mothers urged Regina to stay and commiserated with her distress. I added, "You are welcome to stay. During our group, the babies are going to do all the things they do – cry, poop, eat, spit-up, sleep, smile, coo, and more. Babies of 3 months are learning how to transition from awake to sleep and sleep to awake. They are learning about what it feels like to poop and to burp. They may have strong reactions to these internal experiences and may for a while. They are also learning about what it feels like to be in a mother-baby group for the first time."

This allusion to the mothers' feelings and implicitly to mother–baby mutual arousal, triggered the mothers' recognition of some discomfort and a shared laugh. Everyone relaxed. I continued, "These may be some of the meanings of Candi's crying. We are going to talk a great deal about the meanings beneath the surface of the babies' behavior: what we imagine and what research has found."

In a few minutes, but what seemed to Regina like forever, Candi calmed, and then fell asleep in her mother's arms. Regina was in a sweat as she criticized herself, "I guess I'm just not a natural mother. I need to teach her to behave better." Regina's negative attributions to Candi then spewed out. "She looks like a crazy baby. Her stringy blond hair is so wild." Regina minimized her own painful feelings about herself as "not a natural mother" and bolstered positive self-feelings by negative attributions to Candi.

The mothers' group discussion shifted to childhood memories. Regina recalled, "My mother only cared about how I behaved, never about how I felt. When I was in a school play, as I was walking on stage, I told my mother I was very nervous. She told me that there is nothing to be nervous about, I have a nothing part. I was so hurt and angry." Regina realized that her current feelings of inadequacy as a mother and her anger towards Candi when she cried were rooted in childhood memories.

Gradually Regina shifted her focus from an evaluation of Candi's behavior to empathy for how Candi felt. Over time Regina became more empathic to Candie's distress because her reactivated anger towards her own mother was identified and her long-held feelings of inadequacy were not activated by Candi's crying. Her reactions to Candi became increasingly disentangled from childhood memories; she became more empathic to Candi and better able to soothe her.

- What does your baby find soothing when distressed?
- When is it difficult to soothe your baby?
- What feelings are aroused and memories awakened when it is difficult to comfort your baby?

Laughing

At around 4 months, babies begin to laugh. Mother–baby interactions that evoke repeated laughter can be thought of as emotion regulation play. The mother initiates and repeats a comical action and her baby's laughter repeatedly erupts in response to the simultaneously expected and unexpected, surprising and frustrating, yet predominately pleasurable elements. For example, while maintaining a mutual gaze, a mother put her 5-month-old baby's pacifier in her own mouth and as her baby reached for it the mother spit it out beyond his reach with a playful popping sound. The baby laughed uproariously. This playful interaction was repeated several times.

The baby's laughing response included familiarity with pacifier sucking; surprise mixed with some displeasure to see his pacifier in his mother's mouth; further surprise mixed with displeasure as he attempted to grab it and Mommy spit it out with a playful noise that gently startled him and the pacifier flew out of Mommy's mouth beyond the baby's reach – an unexpected and frustrating event in a playful context. The rising and falling intensity and shifting of emotions during the interaction, the intuitively well-synchronized timing and rhythm of their turn taking, and their loving playfulness were essential elements of the interaction: a mother–baby game of emotion regulation traversing the threshold between pleasure and unpleasure that evokes laughter. When displeasure, including a startle, frustration, or hyperarousal, is too intense or predominates an interaction that evokes laughter, the baby's laughing sounds more like crying.

> • What are the interaction details with your baby that trigger your baby's laughter?

Words to Identify Emotions

A baby's emotions include happy, sad, angry, surprise, fear, uncertainty, frustration, and affection. Gradually, learning feeling words contributes to the development of emotion regulation. Having words to identify feelings makes them more manageable and more shareable. Identifying your own emotions with words will gradually contribute to your baby understanding you. Your baby is learning that everyone has feelings.

> • What emotions does your baby have? When are they evoked?
> • Which emotions, yours and your baby's, do you identify for your baby with words?

Your baby's changing and recurring emotions will gradually become recognized and contribute to your baby's developing sense of self. Babies also become aware of Mommy's empathy when feelings arise. We can imagine in our words a baby's emerging experience of this process: '*Sometimes I feel happy, affectionate, sad, angry, or afraid. They are all part of me. Mommy knows all my feeling parts.*'

Play

During moments of face-to-face mother–baby play, which include mutual gaze, shared smiles, gentle touching, and melodic sounds and phrases, a baby experiences the shared pleasures of intimate, reciprocal interaction. These kinds of early play interactions are unique for each mother and baby. These original mother–baby interactions may provide a foundation for intimacy throughout life: the quiet pleasures of affectionate, subtly synchronized being together.

At times your baby may "ask" you to play. Teri was almost 6 months and awakened from a long nap. After several minutes of looking at the mobile over her crib, she cried for her mother. Believing that she was hungry, her mother Zora lifted Teri out of the crib, placed her in the nursing position, and raised her shirt. Teri did not want to nurse, she wanted to play. She lay in her mother's arms, gazed up into her mother's eyes, smiled, and touched her mother's lips. Zora thought that this was Teri's way of asking her to sing their special song. After several verses, Teri nursed.

> • What face-to-face games do you and your baby play?

Play with Toys

Beginning play with toys provides the opportunity for babies to learn about how things work and promotes a sense of self that can make things happen; shake a rattle and make it jingle.

> • What kind of play with toys does your baby like? Not like?
> • What happens when your baby is struggling to achieve a task with a toy?

Caitlin realized that her uncertainty about helping James to push the button on the activity box, or letting him struggle to do it himself, was related to her memories of her own struggles about what it meant to her and to her mother to do homework by herself or with her mother's help. Caitlin recalled, "If I got my mother's help, I felt completely inadequate. If I did my homework by myself, I feared it would be unacceptable." Understanding the link between her childhood memory and her conflict about helping James enabled Caitlin to make decisions about helping James based on her interactions with him and his responses, rather than in response to her reactivated childhood memories.

For some babies, being on their tummies is not comfortable and therefore play with toys is difficult during tummy-time. They may sleep on their backs and be unfamiliar with the tummy-time position.

Play with Mommy's Things

Babies may want to touch and fondle objects that their mothers wear, like the silky edge of a nightgown or a glittering necklace. The intrinsic properties of the object may be appealing, but a baby's interest may come from both growing mother–baby attachment and the baby's beginning ability to mentally connect the object with Mommy. The object is mentally linked to Mommy, but it is also separate from Mommy and can be possessed by the baby. Your baby's developing ability to mentally connect an object with you, and to use that mental connection to feel emotionally close to you while touching the object, is an emergent developmental step that may be practiced frequently.

- What items of yours does your baby want to touch or hold?
- Is there a special soft toy you give to your baby frequently?
- Do you imagine your baby has formed, or will form, a special attachment to it?

Mother–Baby Play

Some play with your baby may be pleasurable for you, and other kinds may be frustrating or boring. Your various feelings about play with your baby may be related to specific details and indicate what kinds of play will be most rewarding for you both. Robyn described the most pleasurable play she had with 4-month-old Remy: "I lay on the sofa with a pillow behind my head and my knees bent. Remy is seated on my lap, leaning back against my thighs. It is a perfect position for a conversation and a song. We hold hands. Our eye contact is intense and intimate. Actually, I think it's the first time in my life I have had such an experience of connectedness. At this age, other kinds of play can be boring for me."

- What kinds of play with your baby are most pleasurable for you?
- What childhood memories are related to the kinds of play you like with your baby and the play you do not like?

At this early phase, face-to-face mother–baby play has special significance. It includes nuanced, synchronized, interpersonal relatedness.

Mothers' Childhood Memories

Pleasurable Memories

Mothers' pleasurable childhood memories, with and without awareness, influence many interactions with their babies. Responsiveness to the enormous demands of motherhood may be traced to pleasurable memories. Pleasurable memories are sometimes re-enacted with a baby to substitute for or to ward off painful feelings, thoughts, and memories. For example, Blair's mother died three years before her baby Kyra was born. Since Kyra's birth, Blair had missed her mother in a way she had not before. When Kyra was 2 months, Blair joined a mother-baby group. During every group until she was 5 months, tenderly embraced in her mother's arms, Kyra slept while the other babies were physically active and socially interactive.

When Kyra was approaching 5 months, Blair was ready to describe what she liked about Kyra sleeping throughout every group: "I like the way her body feels. I like the feeling of her weight on me, warm and still. I can feel the rhythm of her breathing, gentle bursts of her breath on my neck, and her heartbeat." Blair had captured the specifics of an experience from long ago: fragments of an implicit body sensation memory. Blair painted a vivid picture of the meaning of these interactions with her baby, "My mother had a stroke when I was 3 years old and became completely paralyzed. My grandmother took care of me. I remember every day holding my grandmother's cold hand as we walked into my mother's bedroom, my heart pounding with excitement to be close to my mother. My grandmother lifted me and lay me down on my mother's body. She felt warm and still. I don't remember how long I lay there or when we stopped having these wonderful visits. I miss my mother more since Kyra's birth; my mother will never know Kyra. It's so sad." The mothers listened to every detail. Blair was moved by their empathic responses.

In addition to missing her mother more since Kyra was born, and thoughts about what her mother was missing, Blair's feelings of childhood loss had been reactivated and specific memories emerged: "My mother was not able to come to my grade-school, high-school, or college graduations." With the support of the mothers' group and the shared pleasures of motherhood, Blair realized, "Kyra sleeping on me during mother-baby groups is a way to remember the good parts of being with my mother without remembering all that was lost. But so much is being lost while she sleeps."

Blair's insight about the connections between her childhood memories of body closeness with her own mother, her feelings of loss as a child, and Kyra sleeping on her during the mothers' group, and what was being lost while she slept, led to Kyra staying awake. Rather than sleeping on Blair, Kyra began to manipulate toys, kick with delight, and interact with the other babies. Of course, Kyra was now older but something else also seemed to have happened. Though the specifics are not known, with the support of the mothers' group, Blair's insight about what she was reliving with Kyra led to a change that contributed to Kyra staying awake.

- What childhood memories have influenced you as a mother?
- What childhood memories, both pleasurable and painful, do you think are being relived with your baby?

Painful Memories

Cora and Lizzie are another example of the impact of a mother's childhood memories on mother–baby interactions. Though unaware, Cora's childhood memories about her mother's absence were being repeated with 5-month-old Lizzie. Cora explained, "My Mom worked all the time. Other people took care of me. When I woke in the morning my Mom was still asleep and when I came home from school, she wasn't there." Cora's feelings about her mother's absence were not remembered.

Cora also described, "I work all the time, just like my mom. I feel so close to my mother even though she has lived on the other side of the country since I was very young and I rarely see her. Sometimes I don't see Lizzie for four or five days. I leave for work before she wakes up and often don't get home until she is asleep. When I do see her, she won't look at me no matter what I do. She's angry at me because I work all the time. I don't know why I stay at work too late to see Lizzie." Cora's life-long yearnings for closeness with her own mother were interfering with mother–baby attachment with Lizzie.

Cora felt close to her mother who lived far away, and she felt rejected by Lizzie from whom she distanced herself. Cora's emerging insight that being like her mother by "working all the time" was a way to feel close to her mother, but contributed to her avoidance of Lizzie triggered their first mother–baby shared smile and mutual gaze. Cora began to spend more time with Lizzie and mother–baby attachment began to emerge. In Cora's words, "We are beginning to bond."

Highlights: Birth to 6 Months

The first six months of motherhood are filled with moments of deep pleasure and enormous stress. When a mother's pleasurable interaction with her baby can be linked to a pleasurable childhood memory, a positive aspect of her relationship with her own mother may be remembered.

Dahlia had a fond memory of her mother that came to mind when Jed was 4 months old. "At night, before I put Jed in his crib, I sit in the rocking chair and cradle him in my arms. It's a wonderful time. I always hold his foot in my hand as he drifts off to sleep. It reminds me, when I was a little girl, every night my Mom told me to call her when I was ready for a goodnight kiss. Every night, I hid under the covers and called her. She entered my room singing, where's Dahlia? My feet would feel all tingly tickly and I would giggle. I only had that tickly feeling in my feet when she sang my name. My mom was not the best Mom, she often wasn't there; but every night her good night kiss was the best."

---

9   6 to 12 Months

Mommy-friends

Doreen recalled a lonely time in her life. "I was 10 years old, my father had left, my parents got divorced, my mother and I moved to New York City, my mother was depressed, and I had no friends. I felt so alone. I lived across the street from a small playground filled with mothers, babies, and little children. It looked like a happy place that I frequently walked past on my way home from school. Sometimes I went in and sat for a while. It always helped me feel better.

"Lara was born in early October. She was great, and I was so happy to have a baby. But it was a long, lonely winter. I wanted to meet other mothers and babies. On sunny days, even when it was freezing cold, we went to the playground. But week after week, even when the sun was shining bright, the playground remained cold and empty. I was with my baby but felt so alone. In April, the playground became the warm, gathering place I was waiting for. I met my first mommy-friend; we formed a mothers' group. Everything felt better."

Doreen's childhood loneliness was reactivated when her baby was born. The winter playground bleakness she describes not only reflects the stresses of new motherhood but also her deep feelings of childhood loneliness that were reactivated. Doreen created a family of mommy-friends.

Mother–Child Interaction

The developmental steps from 6 to 12 months build on those of the first 6 months, lay a foundation for the future, and continue into the future. Mothers may wonder, "what is my baby thinking?" but they also attribute meaning to their babies' facial expressions and vocalizations. Mothers put into words their babies' subjective experience, including thoughts, feelings, and intentions. They empathically understand: "You are trying so hard to stand up." "You spit out the spinach. You said no!" "You are so happy to see Granny."

Babies' physical abilities rapidly develop during this phase. They begin to sit, crawl, stand, and then to walk. They are highly motivated to practice their newly acquired skills. Their autonomy increases, their access to the world around them broadens,

DOI: 10.4324/9781003352549-10

and their curious explorations intensify. Anything they experience as constraint may be protested. At the same time as they crawl, walk, and then run away, mother–baby attachment intensifies. For mothers, new pleasures and new challenges emerge.

Your baby has a new alertness; a personhood that is more definable, an individuality that is describable, and likes and dislikes that are identifiable. Your relationship with each other has its own unique features. Your baby's feelings of safety and vitality are tied to your interactions with each other. You have a history together and shared memories. Your bond with each other is deepening.

The child development information and questions that follow will highlight the developing complexity of a baby's mind and the ways in which babies feel understood and try to understand their mothers.

Understanding Each Other

A mother and her baby are discovering what can be known about each other's inner world of thoughts and feelings. If your baby tries to grab the cookie you are eating and you give some to your baby, we can imagine that your baby feels understood by you. But, what happens when you understand what your baby wants but you are not going to give it to your baby?

Being understood when a wish is not gratified can make it easier for a baby to manage the frustration and angry feelings that are evoked. Identifying feelings with words can promote feeling understood and self-understanding. Increasingly with development, feeling understood can help a baby to wait or shift attention to a substitute. For example, 10-month-old Serena, while sitting on her mother's lap, tried to grab her mother's coffee cup. Her mother moved the cup out of reach and said, "No!" Serena screamed. Her mother said, "I know you want my cup. You sound angry. Here is your cup." While Serena may not have understood all her mother's words, she felt her mother's empathy for her frustration and anger. Serena accepted the substitute her mother offered.

- When does communicating that you understand how your baby feels increase your baby's ability to manage feelings of frustration or anger?
- When does understanding your baby not help?

Empathy

Empathy for babies promotes their self-understanding. For example, Glenda was 7 months and startled and cried when the jack-in-the-box clown popped out. Her mother communicated that she understood what Glenda's startle and distress felt like. With a popping and startle tempo in synch with the jack-in-the-box and sounding like an accelerated heartbeat, her words to describe what happened, "The clown popped out, so fast," also communicated that she understood how Glenda felt. Glenda tried to push the clown back into the box to see it pop out again; her mother helped. The second time the clown popped out Glenda startled again, but this time she looked at her mother; she did not cry. Her mother repeated, "Yes, the clown popped out." The third time, Glenda did not startle. She knew that her mother understood, and she knew what to expect. She looked at her mother and smiled.

Sharing Thoughts and Feelings

There is much said about the inability of babies to share. The following questions will highlight the ways in which babies do share thoughts and feelings.

Mothers and babies share the pleasure of mutual smiles, surprise at something unexpected, and some fears. Mother–baby feeding each other may be one of the earliest sharing interactions with an object. A familiar sharing game often initiated by a baby handing an object to Mommy has been called: "I give it to you; you give it to me." An object being passed back and forth to each other is a repeated, brief sharing. The turn-taking is reminiscent of having a conversation – a sharing of thoughts and feelings.

Babies 6 to 12 months become increasingly motivated to communicate or share their subjective experiences: their pleasures, interests, fears, pains, and uncertainties. They want to know that Mommy understands them; and they want to understand Mommy. They sometimes participate when mothers talk; they join the conversation. For example, Patricia was describing to a group of mothers how angry and embarrassed she was when 12-month-old Lulu had her first temper tantrum in the supermarket. "Lulu was having fun loading the shopping cart with me. As she sat on the shopping cart seat, pointing to items on the shelf, I handed each item to her, and she threw it into the cart. But it was enough, and it was time to leave. I had already collected many items we didn't need because Lulu was having so much fun. When I told her no more and refused to give another item to her, she began to kick and scream."

As Patricia was describing this scene, Lulu crawled past the other mothers and babies to get next to her mother, looked at her intensely, lay on the floor, kicked her feet, and let out a long, loud shriek. Lulu wanted to join our conversation. She wanted her mother to know that she understood and remembered the angry feelings.

Babies are beginning to learn that angry feelings can be talked about together and memory narratives can be co-constructed, "Lulu, it looks like you want to join our conversation and show us what happened. You remember, you and Mommy were both angry."

- When does your baby look at you to communicate thoughts and feelings?
- When your baby is uncertain, when does your baby look at you to know what you think or feel?

Your baby may sense your feelings even when you try to conceal them or do not explicitly communicate them. For example, Erika realized that when she is going out for the evening and wants to leave after 11-month-old Julianna falls asleep, it always takes longer for Julianna to fall asleep. Erika wondered, "Julianna seems to know that I am going out after she falls asleep so it takes longer. I'm tense and I'm rushing her to sleep. It's so hard for me to say goodbye. I feel like I'm sneaking out. Maybe saying goodbye while she is awake would be easier for us both." Adrianne, another mother in the group said, "Whenever I am angry at my husband, Jesse wants to be held. I think she feels scared. I always felt frightened when my parents fought. Maybe I should say something to her."

- When does it seem that your baby is reactive to feelings you are not acknowledging or are trying to conceal?

The mother–baby relationship is unique. A mother's ability to see the world through her baby's eyes can be remarkable. Her impulses to protect her baby can be fierce. A baby's reactivity to Mommy's emotions is also highly attuned.

Pointing

Babies begin to point during this phase of development. This common, frequent gesture is full of meaning. A baby pointing initiates a mother–baby joint focus of attention. Often the objects that a baby first points to are at a distance, for example a ceiling light or wall clock. Pointing may expand to include airplanes and birds. Pointing to objects at a distance highlights that the primary aim of early pointing is to achieve a joint focus of attention.

While pointing, in order to confirm that a joint focus of attention has been achieved, a baby's gaze may shift between the object being pointed at and Mommy's line of vision. Even without a gaze confirmation, both mother and baby have a strong conviction that they are both looking at the same object. How do they know this? What are the micro-communications that convey this? This sense of certainty may be related to the certainty of being and feeling understood.

A baby's pointing is insistent and calls for a response. When your baby points at a ceiling light, some version of, "Yes, I see the light" and the implicit communication of, "I know what you are looking at, and you know that I am looking at the same thing" is satisfying to you both. You both know that you have the same thing in mind. Your minds are in synch. A baby's discovery that each object has a word is often highlighted in discussions about pointing. I am highlighting the emotional significance of pointing that includes the mother–baby shared experience of a meeting of minds.

- When does your baby point to have a joint focus of attention with you?
- What do you imagine it is about your response that motivates your baby to repeat pointing?

Your baby's repeated aim of pointing is to have what is in mind understood by you – the essence of a verbal conversation. This connection between the finger pointing gesture and language is supported by the observation that among the first words many babies say is the word "this" or "that" – verbal abstract designators.

Communicating Intentions – Pointing to the Future

Intentions can be shared. A baby signaling an intention is a pointing to the future without the finger gesture. For example, at around 10 months, with a glance and a smile across the room that gets Mommy's attention, a baby's intention to play with the dog's food can be clearly and quickly communicated.

While babies seek their mothers' approval, and are highly motivated by their approval, in some moments babies may signal an intention that is known will get disapproval. A baby's signal of an intention to do something Mommy disapproves of may be an assertion of autonomy, a confirmation that the baby remembers the prohibition, and an effort to get help to stop. The details of this complex interaction are of interest and can contribute to teaching the dos and don'ts of everyday life. For example, "I see you remember there is no touching Fluffy's food. I will help you to stop."

- When does your baby signal an intention that is known to be disapproved of?
- When does your baby signal an intention to see if you think it is safe?

Your baby wants to please you, but not always. Sometimes your baby's explorations, curiosity, and gravity experiments are more compelling and conflict with wishes to please you. Your baby trusts you and wants to know what you think is dangerous, but sometimes protests. During the first three years, while your baby is gradually learning all the dos and don'ts, communicating intentions that you disapprove of may increase.

Separateness of Minds

A baby gesturing "No," and then saying the word "No," are significant developmental achievements. The word "No" indicates a baby's emerging self-assertiveness and highlights the separateness of minds. Daisy, 9 months, did not like her morning vitamins. When her mother tried to give the liquid vitamins to her on a spoon, Daisy sealed her lips and turned her head. When Daisy's mother put the vitamins into an eye dropper and handed the eye dropper to Daisy, she eagerly took it and sucked in her vitamins all by herself. Daisy now felt in control: doing, rather than being done to. Feeling in control can promote awareness of one's own mind and autonomy. The gesture and word "No" express and communicate autonomy, separateness, individual wishes, and assertiveness. I am highlighting the exciting developmental meanings of "No," not the mother–baby conflicts that come with it.

> • When does your baby gesture or say "No"?
> • When do you accept your baby's "No"?

When mothers say "No" to their babies, communicating that they understand what their babies want and offering a substitute can help the baby accept Mommy's "No" and shift attention. For example, 11-month-old Charlotte pulled the lid off her sippy-cup and delighted in spilling and splashing puddles of milk on the table. Her mother Christina explained: "At breakfast, when Charlotte spilled her milk and was making a mess, I grabbed the cup out of her hand and yelled at her. She got very frightened and cried hysterically. It reminded me of the times my mother yelled and terrified me. I was older, but still it frightened me. When Charlotte did it again at lunch, I decided to respond differently. I gently took the cup away from her and said, 'I see you want to spill and splash. I think that means you are all finished with lunch. There is no spilling milk. I'm going to clean this mess and get a basin of water and some cups for spilling.' It was amazing. She watched while I cleared away her plate and cleaned the milk. That was three days ago, she's not spilled the milk again."

While an 11-month-old may not understand all the words, the complex meaning of the words that included disapproval, the prohibition of spilling milk, validating the fun of spilling and splashing, and the choice of playing with water were clearly communicated. Charlotte was able to shift her attention and have fun playing with the water.

> • When is your baby able to shift attention?
> • When does your baby persist and reject a substitute?

Shifting Attention

There is a potentially useful distinction between the idea of a baby shifting attention and the goal of distracting a baby. A baby who is being distracted is passive, has no agency, or control. Distracted, is being done to the baby. Shifting attention includes a sense of a baby's agency and either implicitly or explicitly includes the recognition and validation of what the baby wants; the baby does the shifting. The baby is not tricked; the limit is explicit. For example, "I know you want to play with my eyeglasses. My glasses are not for playing; I am stopping you. You can play with these toy glasses."

> • When does acknowledging your baby's wishes and feelings help your baby shift attention to a substitute? When does it not help?

As babies develop, feeling understood and clearly knowing the limit can help them to shift attention and discover their own minds. While feeling understood will not always help a baby to shift attention and accept a substitute or to wait, and communicating understanding may not always be practical, when it does happen it can provide a valuable experience for a baby that in our words can come to include, *'Mommy understands me. I understand myself. Mommy knows what I want, but Mommy's "No" is clear. I have choices. I can shift my attention.'*

Angry Interactions

All relationships, including mother–baby love relationships, have angry inter-actions. In other words, there are ruptures and repairs of loving interactions. Often the ruptures are triggered by the baby's "No" or the Mommy's "No." For example, it was time for 12-month-old Denver to be in his car seat. His mother Sandy had used all her ingenuity to avoid a struggle. However, as she lowered Denver into the seat, he arched his back and stiffened his legs. Neither coaxing nor physical strength could settle Denver into the car seat. Denver screamed and Sandy yelled. Both Sandy's and Denver's "No" were strong. They were both angry. It is often surprising how frustrated and angry mothers and babies can feel.

- When does your baby get angry at you?
- When do you get angry at your baby?

The distress for both mothers and babies caused by the eruption of angry feelings and the rupture of affectionate interactions is attenuated by the developing expecta-tion that ruptures of loving feelings get repaired; angry feelings dissolve and loving interactions return.

Attachment

Mother–baby interactions during the first year lead to mother–baby attachment; an emotional bonding. Mothers' attention and sensitive responsiveness to their babies promote the security of attachment. It is the meaning to a baby of Mommy's kiss that soothes the pain; the meaning grows out of attachment. Part of the meaning is, *'Mommy is close, I am safe. Mommy understands.'* Another part of the meaning is the expectation from experience that, *'It will feel better.'*

You may wonder when to protect your baby and prevent emotional or physical pain, and in what situations to help your baby cope with painful feelings. Babies need both protection and learning to manage many kinds of distress. A few drops of water splashing on a baby's face during a bath may communicate it is okay when your face gets wet; more water may be overwhelming; preventing a baby's face from getting wet at all or quickly drying it, may intensify discomfort or anxiety about getting wet when it is not warranted.

- When do you protect your baby from physical or emotional pain?
- When do you help your baby to cope with physical or emotional distress?

Ellie described the following situation: "Joe was playing with a helium balloon tied to his stroller. He repeatedly pulled it close and then let it fly up. All of a sudden the balloon came untied. He cried, bereft, as he watched it fly far away. I needed to decide whether to buy him another balloon or help him to cope with the loss. I decided to help him cope with his feelings. I said, 'The balloon came untied and flew away. You are so sad.'" Decisions about when to protect your baby from difficult feelings and when to help your baby cope with them may be related to your own childhood memories.

- When does a kiss or other emotional comfort soothe your baby's distress or pain? When does it not?

Identifying a baby's distress with words can begin to convey empathy. For example, "Your cookie broke into little pieces; I know you are disappointed. You want the big cookie, but it crumbled! You can eat all the little pieces and they will taste yummy." While these words may be complicated, the sound of your soothing voice and communicating your feelings of empathy may comfort your baby.

Babies' Interest in Objects Connected to Mommy

Your baby's ability to mentally connect objects to you is developing further. If you regularly wear a necklace or other item, your baby may reach to touch it. It is physically separate from you, but mentally connected to you by your baby. The television remote does amazing things, but its appeal may come from your baby mentally connecting it with you. As your baby's attachment to you develops, your baby's interest in items that have been mentally connected to you intensifies.

- What items of yours does your baby want to play with?
- Which are okay with you, which not? What happens?

Adults have similar experiences of linking the meaning of objects to people. The scent of the shampoo used by a boyfriend long ago can continue to evoke powerful feelings years or even decades later. Sexual arousal might describe the experience that is awakened. These feelings have more to do with memories than the intrinsic properties of the scent.

Mother–Baby Attachment Disruptions

Mother–baby attachment is a powerful and resilient dynamic. When the emotional bonds of attachment are disrupted or strained, they can be repaired. When Mackenzie was 7 months old, her mother Doris discovered the affair her husband had been having for two years and became depressed when he asked for a divorce. She stopped playing with Mackenzie and delegated her care. Mother–baby attachment was disrupted. Doris joined a mother-baby group. During the group, while Doris ignored Mackenzie's distress and rejected her efforts to get close, I identified any indication of Mackenzie's attachment to her mother: for example, a subtle glance at or slight movement towards her mother. The other mothers commiserated with Doris's anger at her husband and her sadness. However, Doris was not able to feel loved or needed by Mackenzie, or loving towards her. She continued to ignore Mackenzie and to appear detached from the other mothers.

After six weeks, something changed. For the first time, sitting close to the other mothers, smiling, and holding Mackenzie tenderly on her lap the way some of the other mothers were holding their babies, Doris had a new idea, "Mackenzie has discovered her bellybutton. Maybe she remembers being attached to me." Doris's image of prenatal umbilical attachment with Mackenzie was the beginning of the repair of their ruptured emotional attachment relationship.

Separations and Reunions

Families have different patterns of separating from each other and reuniting. You may have returned to work, be planning to return to work, decided not to, or be uncertain. Childcare arrangements and feelings about this separation from your baby may be complex.

In some families, three generations live together; others live in different cities or countries. In some families, people announce when they intend to leave a room, even if briefly, and where they are going. Some parents travel without their babies and little children, others do not. Reunions in some families always include a kiss. In others, reunions are more casual. Understanding the ways in which patterns of separation and reunion have evolved in your family and what they mean may be useful to make decisions for you and your baby.

- When are you and your baby separated?
- How does your baby react?

Mothers' childhood memories can influence mother–baby separations and reunions. Diana recalled, "My mother and sister were never home after school. Every day I was always alone in my room, but at 4 p.m. every day my dad opened the front door and whistled the same tune. It was a special hello just for me. I always answered him with a long, singsong 'Hi.' When Zev was 6 months I returned to work. He's now 1 year old and it is still very hard for me not to see him all day, but every day when I come home I whistle the same tune my father whistled. Every day, Zev comes to the door as fast as he can. We have the best hug."

Diana's childhood memories of loneliness, the distant but loving reunions with her father, and the "best" reunion hugs with her son capture the sadness of separation, the pleasure of reunion, the reactivation of childhood memories, and the changes that can occur with the next generation. Diana was able to have reunions as a mother, that she was unable to have as a child.

During this phase of development, your baby may get more distressed by separation. You may have established separation and reunion routines that include goodbyes and greetings. If you have introduced peek-a-boo, your baby may begin to initiate variations. For example, peek out at you from behind a chair.

Each mother and baby plays their own version of peek-a-boo, and while the specific differences may have meaning, they all share the main elements of the game: brief separations, followed by joyful reunions.

- How do you and your baby play peek-a-boo?
- What other games of separation and reunion do you play?

Saying goodbye to each other before mother–baby separation helps the baby to be active rather than passive, to expect the separation, and to be prepared for the feelings that will be evoked. Having some of the distress before you leave can make it easier to cope with the feelings when you have left. Being cared for in your absence by someone your baby knows can make it easier to adapt to separation.

- How does your baby react to saying, waving, or kissing, goodbye?
- How does your baby react to reunions?

Sleep

Sleep is a kind of separation, and a baby's reactions to separation may influence sleep–wake patterns. Bedtime routines can help babies to develop expectations about sleep including separation from Mommy, no more play, etc. Routines can include dimmed lights, a feeding, and a song or story with a cuddle. Sleep routines can promote a readiness to sleep: a lowering of excitation, coziness, and a sense of security. The sense of security comes from your baby's expectation of your availability when needed, and your continuing care and protection. Mothers can create sleep routines that can promote a readiness for sleep; falling asleep is something the baby does.

- What sleep routines are beginning to be established with your baby?
- If sleep is difficult, in what ways might your baby's daytime experiences contribute to the difficulty?

Babies gradually establish sleep patterns that fit with adult sleep schedules and family lifestyle. The process is different for each mother and baby. There are maturational, behavioral, physiological, and psychological components to sleep. The meaning of sleep to a mother can play a role in her baby's sleep patterns.

Ester was 9 months and was waking every three hours. Her mother Adrianna was unaware that her "checking" on Ester, tiptoeing into her room throughout the night, was waking her. She was also unaware that her "checking" was related to childhood memories. When Adrianna was 5 years old her mother had had a stillbirth. Adrianna realized that her memories of what she was told throughout her life, and her mother's ongoing depression and anxiety, were triggering her own night waking and "checking" on Ester. With this insight, Adrianna resolved the "sleep problem."

- What experiences of separation or loss, yours or your baby's, have influenced your baby's sleep?
- What difficulties related to sleep does your baby have that are inexplicable?

Mothers who have experienced the death of a parent or sibling, or other significant loss or separation, may have interactions with their babies that affect sleep patterns. Mothers' memories of nightmares can also have an impact. Both everyday experiences and more significant life events influence babies' sleep patterns. Innate traits may also play a role.

Reunions

A baby's reaction after some mother–baby separations may be surprising. Shari described 12-month-old Axl: "I went away for the weekend. When I came home, Axl looked totally confused, he didn't recognize me." Two other mothers in the group had similar experiences. Kristen added, "Kiara was angry at me, not confused. She wouldn't even look at me."

Another explanation is that during mother–baby separations, babies are beginning to imagine Mommy, envision her. This is a way to feel close to Mommy when separated. The image or sense of Mommy that a baby imagines is a composite that is based on many different ways Mommy has looked: happy, angry, busy, and playful; Mommy with wet hair, dry hair, etc. When babies are reunited with their mothers after separations, they may be trying to reconcile their mental image of Mommy during her absence with the actual, specific way Mommy looks when they are reunited. Your baby and young toddler's facial expression and reaction to you after a separation may reflect this adaptive mental process.

Likes and Dislikes

Babies this age are highly motivated to pursue their likes and reject their dislikes. They like, in fact they are propelled to practice, their newly acquired motor skills: to sit themselves upright, to crawl, to stand, and then to walk. Their motivation is strong and their attempts to overcome any obstacles that arise are vigorous. This may present challenges to changing diapers, airplane travel, car seats, etc.

Sometimes what appears to be a baby's dislike is a response to something new or unexpected. Greg was 7 months. He had eaten several vegetables and fruits and had enjoyed them. When his mother introduced avocado, an expression of what looked like disgust crept over his face. His mother assumed his expression meant the taste and texture were new to him; they were unexpected. Next time, instead of putting the avocado into Greg's mouth, she put the spoon close to his lips so he could take the avocado off the spoon with his lips himself. After a few tentative explorations with his tongue and lips, Greg opened his mouth wide.

- When is having more control to explore a new experience useful to your baby?
- When does your having more control help?
- How do your food preferences influence your baby's food likes and dislikes?

At 10 months, Katia began to protest being dressed and undressed. Her mother Jill decided to help Katia to be more active in the process rather than passive. Jill described this during a mothers' group: "Dressing and undressing Katia had become impossible. Now I put the shirt armhole next to Katia's hand and say, 'Katia, push your arm into the sleeve.' When getting undressed I say, 'Katia pull your socks off.' Dressing and undressing have become much easier. It may take a few minutes longer, but it's worth it." Sylvie, another mother in the group, had a strong reaction: "It sounds like that may have worked once, but I don't think you can rely on it. Also, she needs to know who's in charge." Jill snapped back, "I'm in charge of when I give control to her. Maybe I can't rely on it, but I think it's good for Katia to have more control when she can." Mothers also want to feel in control; but often do not.

As children develop, their needs to be active and to feel in control become increasingly important as an expression of self. In other words, they want to feel, '*I am doing this or I choose this.*' In other moments, the pleasures of total passivity or being out of control or excited may predominate. The pleasures of both being active and being passive, in different moments, continue throughout life.

Expectations

Babies are creating memories: not with words yet, but as expectations and body memories. For example, '*When I smile at Mommy, she smiles at me, it feels good. When I am scared, Mommy holds me and comforts me. When I go to the doctor's office and get a shot, it hurts.*' A baby's expectations during this phase, both pleasurable and painful, may be visible. For example, every day at around 6:00, when she hears the jingle of Daddy's keys as he steps into the apartment, 11-month-old Jessa scurries to the front door. Her expectation of seeing Daddy intensifies the pleasure of their reunion. On the other hand, as soon as Jessa enters the doctor's office she begins to cry. Her mother says, "You remember, the doctor gave you a shot last time. It hurt. No shot today. Just a checkup." With development, remembering with words can replace a triggered fearful response. If Jessa is going to get another shot her mother says, "Yes, you remember the shot you got last time. It hurt. You are going to get another shot today. I will hold you and then you will feel better."

- What expectations does your baby have?
- When is shifting an expectation to a shared memory useful?

Maturational Milestones

Mothers monitor their babies' maturation and nurture their development. For example: Libby was eager for 10-month-old Johnny to crawl, and believed he could. She placed him in the middle of the room and walked away as she said, "I know he can crawl; he even can pull himself up to stand. Maybe he's lazy." Johnny remained still and looked down at the floor as his mother walked away. It seemed as though, for Johnny to crawl, he needed to feel that he could lean on his mother, feel her strength, and borrow some of it for himself. Libby wanted Johnny to crawl, but it was unclear whether she wanted him to follow her as she walked away. For Johnny to crawl towards his mother, he needed to expect that she would satisfy his needs for closeness. To crawl away from his mother, he needed to feel emotionally close to her, and to know that he could return to her as a secure base.

Recognizing that Johnny felt sad as she walked away, Libby returned and sat next to him on the floor. He leaned against her, and she caressed him. After a few moments, Johnny placed his hands on his mother's thigh, straightened his arms, and propped himself up in a crawling position. He then turned away from his mother, crawled to the other side of the room, and then back to her. Intuitively something happened between Johnny and his mother. Maybe when Johnny's mother returned and sat next to him, in addition to feeling empowered by her strength, the expectation of being able to return to his mother when he crawled away was activated; he could feel her wishes to be close to him. Both physical and emotional readiness may be needed for some maturational achievements.

• What does your baby seem physically capable to do, but is not ready emotionally to do?

Some babies seem capable of walking but are not ready to let go of Mommy's finger to walk completely on their own. Others may hold an object in each hand as they take their first steps. In a way, they may be staying symbolically connected to Mommy as they walk away.

Body and Mind Awareness

Body and mind awareness develop together, each influencing the other. Learning body parts, experiencing body pleasures and body pains, the achievement of motor abilities to sit, crawl, stand, and to walk all have mental components. A baby's exhilaration in response to the achievement of walking highlights the mind–body connection. Asking your baby, "Where is your nose? Where are your fingers? etc. is an early mother–baby body game. In addition to learning the names of body parts, your baby is learning, '*All these are part of me.*' These mother–baby interactions promote a baby's body sense of self.

• What body games do you and your baby play?

Identifying Body Parts

In a lively discussion about the words for genitals that mothers choose, Marina said, "Arial is only 11 months. I know many mothers from the beginning teach their daughters the word vagina even though they are not really talking about the vagina. I don't know what words to teach Arial, but I think it's important. What she is touching is her vulva. It's a part of her body that she has noticed, but I don't feel comfortable saying that word. Vulva seems too sexy. Labia feels too medical. Vagina is incorrect. No word feels right. I want Arial to feel comfortable with all parts of her body. I don't talk about her anus, but that's different. I'm amazed I am talking about this at all."

Jenna had different reactions to interactions with Stefan about his body. She told the mothers' group that her milk let-down reflex during breastfeeding was strong and pleasurable. She was happy to see Stefan touching his penis during diaper changes and baths and was teaching him the word penis. She had resumed sex with her husband after the recommended six-week abstinence following delivery and was delighted that her milk-spraying let-down reflex was triggered when she had an orgasm. Jenna's boastful declarations during the mothers' group triggered some envy, some embarrassment, some ridicule, and some inspiration. Marina said, "I think I will start to say vagina like most moms."

Mirror Image and Developing Sense of Self

A new perspective of self was emerging for 11-month-old Dakota as she explored her mirror image. When Dakota had been younger and her mother held her in front of the mirror, she seemed to focus on her mother's reflection. This time was different. With determination, Dakota crawled very close to the mirror. Anticipating a moment of discovery, her mother videotaped what happened next.

Dakota, with her forehead almost touching the mirror, looked carefully at her own reflection. She stuck her tongue slowly in and out several times. Her concentration intensified. She moved her head gently towards the mirror until her forehead and nose touched it softly. Her mother said, "Yes, you see your nose." Dakota wiggled her nose. She repeated ever so slowly sticking her tongue in and out and gently kissed her reflection. Her mother joyfully commented, "You are giving yourself a kiss." Dakota turned away from the mirror and looked at her mother with a big smile.

Dakota's new mirror play demonstrated an emerging sense of self: herself seen from the outside while experienced on the inside. Her mother watched with delight.

- How does your baby react to the mirror?
- What does your baby's reaction mean?
- If you hold a toy over your baby's head in front of the mirror, will your baby reach for the toy's reflection in the mirror, or reach for the toy?

Sense of Self

A baby's developing sense of self includes: a body sense of self and all the body can do and feel; a mind sense of self that has thoughts and emotions, likes and dislikes, intentions and agency; and an emerging sense of self in interaction with others. Our words to describe a baby's emerging sense of self might include: '*Mommy loves me, I am lovable. Mommy protects me, I am safe. I am learning new things, I am capable. Mommy is proud of me. Mommy is my mommy.*'

Gender

Designating the sex of a baby either boy or girl occurs before or at birth. Gender identity, what it means, and how it feels to be a boy or a girl, develop later. Gender identity has mind, body, social, and cultural components. In recent years, there has been increased attention to and controversy about gender in medicine, law, and politics. Picture books for young children and the marketing of toys have been influenced by shifting cultural attitudes about gender. The first box-cover of the game Battleship had a father and son playing the game and a mother and daughter washing dishes in the background. This would not occur today. The clothes babies wear today are sometimes less gender-linked than in the past. Some of the societal changes and controversies among experts have raised questions for parents.

- What is important to you about gender? What is not important to you about gender?
- What gender-linked toys or clothes does your baby have? Which do you avoid? How do you decide?

Identifying Mommy as a woman, Daddy as a man, and your baby as a boy or a girl may be everyday occurrences. Pronouns may be used as a reference to sex or to gender. Gender is in our consciousness. Allusions to what it means to be male or female begin to surface.

Many things influence the ways in which gender is expressed and communicated in mother–baby interactions. For example, Willow's mother Piper was distressed that people frequently thought 10-month-old Willow was a boy. Piper dressed Willow in what she considered "gender neutral" clothes, but clothes that the world around her seemed to view as boy's clothes. Piper resented "gender stereotyping" and did not want to conform to it until she realized that her nickname for Willow since she was 2 months was Will, "I just realized I am calling Willow a boy's name! I want her to be recognized as a girl. I want her to know she's a girl."

- Now that you have a baby boy or girl, what gender-related thoughts pop into your mind?
- What gender-linked interactions do you have with your baby?
- What gender-related goals do you have for your baby?

Some mothers may avoid gender-linked references, others may highlight gender. Understanding the influence of childhood memories on your views about gender can be informative. Your baby's growing awareness of and reactions to gender will provide important information to you about developing gender identity.

Emotion Regulation

Self-soothing and Being Soothed

Babies have an inborn system to maintain a state of equilibrium. When a baby's emotional equilibrium is disturbed, the system is activated to return to a state of equilibrium. A baby's system is immature, but active. When their equilibrium is disrupted, babies cry.

Both being soothed and self-soothing are part of the system. Experiences of each promote the development of the other. Some aspects of being soothed are internal. In other words, there is a self-regulating part to being soothed. When you are comforting your baby, and your baby is comforted, you cannot see the internal self-regulating processes within your baby in response to you.

Your baby may also have developed some observable self-soothing behaviors, for example thumb, finger, or pacifier sucking, rubbing a piece of soft fabric, or an attachment to a treasured toy.

- When is your baby comforted by you?
- If your baby uses a pacifier, how do you decide when to offer it?
- When is breastfeeding or a bottle used for comfort?

When close to their mothers, babies are better able to ward off distress and to calm when they are distressed. Both temperament and life experience contribute to the development of emotion regulation. Innate characteristics, including sensitivity to sensory stimulation or to emotional arousal, may make emotion regulation more difficult.

Expectations

As described earlier, babies' expectations can promote emotion regulation. A crying baby who expects Mommy to respond may stop crying when Mommy's voice is heard. Hearing Mommy's voice can intensify the security of expected gratification and prevent the baby from becoming overwhelmed or giving up. *'Mommy is close, all is okay.'*

- When do you see evidence of your baby's internal emotion regulation?

Increasingly as your baby develops, you will see evidence of your baby's response to your empathy. It will become apparent that, even when the frustration, fear, or pain continues, your baby will feel better when you are close and communicate that you understand. This is part of the mother–baby attachment relationship.

Treasured Toys

Your baby may have begun to develop an attachment to a cuddly toy. Treasured toys, or what were first described as transitional objects, include soft huggable teddy-bears, dolls, and fluffy bunnies. While these toys have appealing features, it is the meaning that a baby is able to attribute to the toy and the baby's capacity for attachment to the toy, that make it treasured and promote emotion regulation.

Babies' attachments to their treasured toys reveal important aspects of their developing minds including their growing abilities to tolerate feelings of frustration, anxiety, and ambivalence; the grief of separation and loss; intense anger and terrifying fear. Because of these developing mental capacities, and the baby's attributions to the toy, the baby is better able to manage these emotions when close to the toy.

The toy may have accompanied feedings since infancy or may have been among many toys huddled on a shelf and claimed by the baby. Either way, the attachment and the emotion regulation it enables are created by the baby and increase during the first three years.

Lyla had conflicted feelings about 12-month-old Marcie's growing attachment to a soft bunny and was preventing her access to the bunny. "I know an attachment to a toy is considered an important part of development, but Marcie wants it with her all the time. I'm afraid she is becoming too attached; it would be unbearable if it got lost." As Lyla spoke these words, she remembered her own lonely grief when her teddy-bear was repeatedly lost. "My older sister teased me all the time. She also tricked me. When I couldn't find my teddy-bear, she would tell me she found it; I would get very excited and then she would say, 'just kidding.' I think she hid it all the time. I know it's great to have a special toy but I've been trying to protect Marcie from the pain of losing it. Actually, I think I've been frightening Marcie by repeatedly warning her that her bunny will get lost. I've changed my mind. I will stop threatening her and do what I can to prevent her bunny from getting lost, but if it does I will help her cope with her feelings. Maybe there's no such thing as too attached."

- In what ways do your childhood memories of a treasured toy influence your interactions with your baby?

Words to Identify Feelings

As your baby develops, identifying feelings with words can contribute to emotion regulation. Using words to describe your baby's emotions can help your baby to begin to recognize and think about feelings – one's own and those of others.

- What emotions that your baby has do you identify with a word?
- What emotions of yours do you identify with a word for your baby?

While a group of mothers were talking about identifying their baby's emotions with words, Darlene had an insight: "I just realized that I often tell Kitty she's sad when really I know she's angry. Maybe I want her to feel sad rather than angry. Being angry is okay; she's entitled." Denni had a different thought: "When Freya cries, it feels like she is yelling at me. I always tell her she's angry. It was my mother who was always angry! Maybe Freya is feeling something else when she cries." Camila added, "I don't feel comfortable telling Beau that I'm sad or angry, but I'm sure he can tell when I am not my usual self. He always wants me to hold him. Maybe saying it would feel better to him."

Internal Conflict

Babies begin to have contradictory feelings and opposing wishes; in other words, ambivalence. For example, a baby may be frightened by the noise of the blender but may also be curious. The conflict may intensify the distress and make emotion regulation more difficult. Recognizing a conflict, or a potential conflict, can lead to emotion regulation. Cynthia was 10 months and cried every time her mother used the blender. Cynthia was delighted by the power she had to turn the ceiling lights on and off with the quiet flick of a switch. Stimulating Cynthia's curiosity about the blender, her mother taught her to turn the blender on and off. While being held in her mother's arms, Cynthia was helped to master her fear of the blender's noise by controlling it.

Recognizing your baby's internal conflicts related to attachment and autonomy, affection and anger, curiosity and fear, can help to resolve some difficulties. Recognizing the impact of your own internal conflicts on interactions with your baby may be more challenging. For example, Jillian believed that it was best for babies to sleep in their own beds. She did not think that co-sleeping was good for children or parents. By 4 months, Samantha was sleeping through the night in her own crib. After her last nursing for the day, Jillian changed Samantha's diaper and lay her down in her crib awake. As Jillian left the room, Samantha quickly drifted off to sleep.

This well-established routine changed when Samantha was around 8 months, when typically there is a rise in reactions to separation. As soon as her head touched the mattress, she sat herself up and began to scream. Jillian returned to Samantha, comforted her, lay her back down, and began to leave the room again. After many repetitions, Samantha fell asleep. When this pattern was repeated during the middle of the night, Jillian was frustrated and exhausted. Her conflict, of which she had been unaware, materialized. Determined to not take Samantha into her and her husband's bed, she moved a recliner into Samantha's room and fell asleep on it with her. "I'm not sleeping with Samantha in my bed, but I am sleeping with her on the recliner. It's really the same thing. I don't know what I want to do. I was never allowed in my parents' bed. I didn't think I would ever want to sleep with Samantha. Maybe I did and didn't know it."

- What conflicts do you have with your baby?
- What conflicts with your baby may be related to your own internal conflicts?

Following Advice and Mothers' Conflict

Advice to mothers is forthcoming about the importance of both meeting the developmental needs of babies and satisfying mothers' own needs and priorities. While the advice might make sense, mothers' worries, beliefs, and not enough time for everything may create conflict. Childhood memories may fuel mothers' conflicted feelings.

Milena was conflicted about letting 12-month-old Shep climb the stairs. He started walking at 9 months and loved to climb. Milena described the problem: "Shep wants to climb the steps all day long. He's very good at it, but he can't do it completely alone. I need to help him. My mother never let me climb to the top of the monkey-bars. I knew I could do it, but she would not let me do it alone and she wouldn't help me. I'm happy to help Shep on the stairs and it's good for him to learn to climb, but I cannot do it all day. It's too dangerous for him to do it alone and I don't want to put up gates."

Shep was determined to master the stairs and Milena did not want to repeatedly negotiate the stairs with him. After blurting out, "Maybe if he falls down the stairs then he will learn," Milena realized, "It's almost as if my anger would motivate me to let him do something dangerous – both anger at Shep and at my mother. I'm going to put up gates, even though I don't like how they look and I feel guilty about not helping him."

- When are you in conflict about letting your baby do something dangerous?

Preventing Accidents

There are two general approaches to preventing babies from having access to items and activities that are dangerous or fragile. One is preventing access to the object, or what has been called "babyproofing," and the other is mother–baby teaching–learning interactions. Both approaches are needed. For example, beginning to learn with Mommy about the pleasure of a flower's fragrance and enjoying its delicate beauty without touching it may be preferable to flowers being completely unavailable. Babies can learn to enjoy flowers. On the other hand, cleaning fluids that are poisonous are best stored in a locked cabinet out of reach.

- Which items have you decided to make inaccessible to your baby?
- Which items that your baby wants to touch, but that are not allowed, do you have teaching–learning interactions about?

Phyllis had a music box that she wanted to keep on the living room coffee table but she did not want Luella to touch it by herself. "My mother gave the music box to me when I got pregnant. It plays the lullaby she used to sing to me. I am teaching Luella that the music box is something we do together. She is now 12 months and walking around the coffee table holding on. When she wants to hear the music, she points to the box and says 'muba.' I think she is learning."

Mother–baby teaching–learning interactions about the everyday dos and don'ts and some of the special pleasures require many repetitions. Gradually your codes of behavior will become mostly your baby's and many of your delights that have been shared will be enjoyed by your child.

Play

Play during this phase of development is rapidly expanding. Exploration and discovery of how objects feel and look from every angle capture babies' attention. The wonder of bubbles floating in the air and items falling to the floor are captivating. Cups have insides and outsides, buckets can be filled and emptied.

Babies enjoy toys that enable them to experience their sense of agency – the self-satisfaction of '*I did it!*'; for example, to press a button and make a sound, or to open a door and see a clown pop out. The repetition of these activities has the additional pleasure of knowing what to expect.

> • When does your baby seem to feel the pleasure of, '*I did it*'?

Pretend Play

Pretend play to think about, practice, and control everyday life experiences begins to emerge. Your baby's imitations of you clapping or waving, and imitations of a dog barking or a cow mooing, may be linked to the development of pretend play. Babbling on your cell phone or trying on your watch may be precursors to role-play. Your baby may have seen you pretend to feed a baby-doll or toy animal and imitate you. When you push a toy car along the floor, you may imitate a car sound. You and your baby are building a repertoire of everyday pretend play scenarios.

> • What kinds of beginning pretend play do you and your baby do?

Reading Picture Books

The value of reading to babies is often emphasized. However, many babies are too busy to read; they are practicing to crawl, stand, and walk. Their motivation to master mobility and to actively explore the world around them is primary. However, the same baby who wriggles off Mommy's lap when she tries to read an age-appropriate, picture-book classic, may take a book off the shelf and pretend to read it.

Play Alone in the Presence of Mommy

Babies play with Mommy and play alone. Both kinds of play are pleasurable and promote development. A third category is: play alone in the presence of Mommy. That is, mother and baby are together but each focused on something else. For example, while you are reading the newspaper, your baby is emptying and filling a basket full of blocks, as you have done together. Occasionally you may look at each other, or you say something, or your baby gives a block to you. There is a simultaneous feeling of connectedness with each other and solitary pleasure – alone but not alone. Alone in the presence of Mommy has been described as contributing to the developing capacity to be alone.

- When does your baby have each of these experiences: play with you, play alone, play alone in your presence?

You may wonder how much of each play category is optimal for you and your baby. Of course, the exact amount that is right for each mother and baby, at each phase of development, is not known.

There are two complementary patterns of mothers' play with babies: following the baby's lead; and expanding or scaffolding the baby's play. A combination of both kinds of play promotes babies' play, learning, and pleasure, and simultaneously contributes to mothers' genuine interest in the play.

Learning

During this phase of development, babies learn a great deal. Babies learn by themselves through trial and error, and mothers teach their babies. There are different kinds of teaching–learning interactions, including verbal instruction, physical maneuvering, and imitation. For example, when saying "bye-bye" to Daddy, JoEllen waves Michael's hand with her hand and says, "Michael, say bye-bye." When JoEllen and Michael hand things to each other, she says, "thank you" without an instruction. JoEllen expects that in time Michael will imitate her thank you, learn the words "bye-bye," and wave. Learning is highly motivated by attachment.

Different teaching–learning approaches may be more suitable for different tasks, at different ages, for different children. Mothers may favor one approach. Some things you are teaching your baby may be with a combination of imitation, instruction, and physical help.

- What are you teaching your baby by imitation? Instruction? Physical help?

Learning Foundations

Many mother–baby teaching–learning interactions during this phase create a foundation for future learning. Expecting a baby to learn them now would be premature. For example, Caroline described an interaction with 11-month-old Jimmy: "I don't expect him to clean his room, but while I am throwing Jimmy's dirty clothes into the hamper, I say, 'dirty clothes go in the hamper. Here is your sock, you can throw it into the hamper.' He is thrilled to do it."

Learning About Poop

In some ways, when your baby poops and you identify what is happening, your baby is learning that you are interested in pooping and poop, and it is something you can communicate about with each other. A foundation for future learning to use the potty is being created. Children are interested in the things their mothers are interested in. Defecating is a pleasurable body experience that triggers interaction with Mommy – a joint focus of attention, a word, and body care-taking mother–baby interactions. Your baby is experiencing, '*Pooping feels good. Mommy knows when I poop. It must be important.*'

- What is your baby learning about poop and pooping?

Codes of Behavior

As babies begin to explore the world around them, and practice all their new abilities, telling your baby "No" will be more frequent. The list of dos and don'ts is long, and the help babies need to learn them is ongoing for a long time. At the same time, there are many opportunities for "Yes." Approval is highly motivating. Eventually your codes of behavior mostly will become your toddler's own dos and don'ts, and the ability to stop, even when impulses are strong, will develop.

Babies this age are beginning to expect disapproval of certain behaviors. Babies are learning what it means and what happens when Mommy says "No." In our words, a baby's developing expectation might be, '*When Mommy says "No," she helps me to stop myself, she understands what I want, and why it is important to me.*'

Cathy was trying to teach 9-month-old Paul not to play with her hair. He fondled it gently but sometimes it got tangled in his fingers and he pulled it. Cathy wanted him to stop. "It started about a month ago when he was nursing, but now he wants to do it whenever I'm holding him. It feels too sexy when he does it gently and it hurts when he pulls it. I stop him, say 'No,' and offer him a soft toy lion with a long mane, but nothing helps. I think playing with my hair is linked to his pleasure nursing, but I want him to stop. Even when he is not nursing, he wants to do it. I think he gets angry when I stop him. Luckily, he recovers quickly. I don't act angry, but I feel angry."

- What dos and don'ts are you beginning to teach your baby?
- What is your baby learning about loving and angry interactions?

Gradually, with many repetitions of being told "No," being gently prevented from playing with Mommy's hair, and being offered a substitute, Paul's impulse to play with his mother's hair seemed to have vanished. Another explanation is that not fondling Mommy's hair became Paul's own way of being with Mommy. Paul accepted the toy lion as a substitute and started to sleep with it. He also learned that his and his mother's angry feelings do not last; loving feelings return.

Regi was approaching 1 year and began to dip his hands into the bowl of food his mother was spoon-feeding him and rub it into his hair. Maxine explained, "I don't know why he does it, but I say 'No' and stop him. He freezes for a few moments and then does it again. Nothing helps." Alexa said, "I know what you mean. I was trying to teach Buck not to throw food on the floor, but I was able to give a ball to him instead. There's no substitute for putting food in Regi's hair. Finally, Buck started to look at me with a special look before throwing the food so I could give him the ball to throw." Alarmed, Maxine said, "I just realized that every time Regi rubs the food in his hair and I say "No," he startles. Maybe I am frightening him. I used to jump out of my skin when my mother yelled at me. I think his startle and then freezing may prevent him from learning and developing the ability to stop himself or signal me before he does it. Also I realize, I've been avoiding letting him feed himself because I don't want the mess. Maybe he needs more finger foods and his own spoon."

Gradually, repeated mother–baby teaching–learning interactions that prevent excessive amounts of fear or anger and incorporate new abilities help babies and toddlers to adopt for themselves the codes of behavior that surround them. The long-range goal of repeated limit-setting is that the baby develops self-disapproval of the behavior.

Yes and No

During the first months of life, babies begin to imitate the sounds of words they hear. Babies understand language before they are able to talk. You may have strong convictions about what your baby understands, or you may be uncertain. Zelda, Blossom's mother, often prefaced communications to her daughter with the word "Yes." It was her manner of speaking, "Yes, you did it, yes I understand. No jumping on the sofa, yes jumping on the floor." Blossom acquired a "No" gesture when she was about 7 months; she turned her head and closed her lips when she did not want another bite to eat. One of her first spoken words was "Yes." The word "Yes" was linked to good feelings. When babies hear yes, they learn to say yes.

> - When do you say "Yes" and when do you say "No" to your baby?

Gestures and Early Words

Gestures, precursors to words, typically begin to emerge during the first year. Gestures and their meanings include: pointing, '*Look at that*'; arms raised, '*Pick me up*'; waving, '*Bye-bye*'; and many gestures for the word "No," including head shaking or turning away, clenched lips, and hand pushing. "No" gestures are important acts of autonomy. Successful non-verbal communications lead to words.

The words, "Mama" and "Dada," are among those acquired early. They may be early words because of the ways parents respond to baby sounds that are approximations of the words. This highlights that language develops in an inter-personal context and the meaning and emotional significance of words matter.

- What sounds and babbling does your baby do that are approxima-tions of words?
- What response do you get when you talk to your baby?

There is a large body of literature about language acquisition, and much research and advice to parents. "Talk to your baby," is repeated, everyday wisdom.

Your baby cannot have a verbal conversation with you yet, but non-verbal re-sponses while you are talking may be seen. In many ways, you have been having non-verbal conversations with your baby since birth. While you are talking, you may notice changes in your baby's facial expressions and body movements. Your baby's eyes may scan your face, focus on your mouth, or you both may be riveted in mutual gaze. You may see the emerging, surging, peaking, and receding of a smile. Your baby may reach out to touch you. Your baby's lips may move in synch with yours. As you talk, your baby may attempt to imitate your words. These are parts of a non-verbal conversation.

Social Learning with Other Babies

Babies are interested in other babies: looking at them and interacting with them. When babies begin to crawl, they may approach each other and touch: sometimes gently, sometimes rough. They may pass a toy to each other. They may imitate each other. Babies are reactive to the emotions of other babies. A baby's cry may trigger a cry. Babies are innately social.

Mothers often recognize their babies' attention to each other and support their interactions. Chester was in a weekly mother-baby group. Myra, his mother, de-scribed his interactions with Abby. "I know this sounds unbelievable, he's only 9 months, but he always looks happy to see Abby. He watches her and is interested in the toys she plays with because he is interested in her."

Helping Babies Interact

Mothers may disagree about when babies need social help. When Chester grabbed a book away from Abby and she cried, Myra intervened to describe what happened and to help him give the book back: "You like to play with Abby. There is no grab-bing, you need to give the book back to Abby." Abby's mother thought adult help was unnecessary: "Abby can defend herself. I want her to grab it back."

- When do you intervene, and when do you think the babies can resolve a conflict themselves?

There are different opinions about when adult intervention is useful to resolve baby and toddler conflicts with each other. Some mothers and professionals believe that as long as they are not hurting each other, let them work it out; they will learn from the interaction. Others believe that adult help can teach standards of behavior and model ways to resolve conflict. In some ways, both ideas apply. The challenge is deciding which is more useful in which specific situation, with each child, and for each mother. Childhood memories may influence decisions.

Johanna had vivid, painful memories of being bullied as a child and was angry that her mother, counselors at camp, and teachers at school allowed it to happen. Maren had many guilty memories about aggressively teasing her younger sister, bunkmates, and classmates. For both mothers, understanding their own childhood memories that were reactivating intense feelings of guilt and anger, and impulses to retaliate or withdraw, helped them each decide when and what kind of adult intervention would be most helpful to their babies.

Siblings

Babies who have siblings may have a range of everyday loving and angry interactions with each other. They are rivals for Mommy's affection and attention. A baby's adoring gaze at an older sibling is frequent. A baby can be perplexed by, curious about, affectionate with, or disturbed by, an infant. Twin babies have a unique social experience.

Babies bring their experience with siblings to their interactions with other babies. Jazmine was 10 months and had a 3-year-old brother who frequently grabbed toys from her. Her mother Zoe thought it was, "No big deal," because Jazmine did not seem to care. She enjoyed her brother's attention and picked up another toy. When Zoe and Jazmine joined a mother-baby group, Zoe changed her mind. "Jazmine keeps grabbing toys from the other babies. It's as though she has learned grabbing is what you do with a baby. It looks as if she doesn't care when her brother grabs from her, but maybe she does. Or maybe she thinks it's okay because I act as if it is okay, but it's not. I want her to know it's not okay with me when her brother grabs from her or when she grabs."

Mothers' Childhood Memories

Emerging Fears

A mother's emerging fear about her baby may be a reactivated memory. Kari joined a mother-baby group with her twins Carson and Cassandra, who were 10 months. As they approached 1 year old, Kari developed a fear that they would be kidnapped, "When I see a car drive slowly past our house, I feel convinced of the danger and even though I know it probably isn't true, I get panicky."

Kari had been adopted when she was a newborn and grew up being frequently told that her adoption did not become final until she was 1 year old; the same age her twins would soon be. Kari's fear about her babies included the memory of her mother's anxiety that Kari might be taken away and reunited with her biological mother. Embedded in Kari's memory was also the idea that her mother had taken another woman's baby.

Kari believed, "Being adopted was never an issue for me. I have the best parents." When asked to tell us more about the car driving past her house, she said, "A woman is driving." When I asked who she thinks the woman might be, she blurted out, "Maybe it's my biological mother." Kari's awareness of her rivalry with both her biological mother and her adoptive mother suddenly emerged: "I had biological children, my mother could not. I am able to keep my biological babies, my biological mother could not keep me."

Kari's fears about her babies being kidnapped were rooted in her own guilty feelings of pride and pleasure in having given birth and keeping her babies; feelings she viewed as too aggressively competitive with both her biological and adoptive mothers. Kari's fantasy that her biological mother was driving the car and was threatening to kidnap her babies represented both Kari's fears of retaliation for her aggressive victories and a repair of disavowed feelings of loss by a reunion with her biological mother. Kari's kidnapping anxiety was resolved with these new meanings of her kidnapping fear. Her kidnapping fear faded away.

Reactivated Loss

Each week, Marlene entered the mother-baby room, placed 10-month-old George in front of the toy shelf, and walked to the other side of the room. George never looked at his mother or approached her. If a toy was handed to him, he briefly explored it in a low-key manner. Marlene longingly gazed at George from across the room.

During the third time the mother-baby group was meeting, Marlene confided, "I feel like I'm not George's mother. He thinks the nanny is his mother; I've turned his care almost completely over to her. She's with him more than I am. He laughs with her in a way that he never laughs with me." Marlene's next sentence provided a possible way to understand what was happening. "My mother died when I was 15 years old after a long, painful, and disfiguring illness."

Marlene was unaware that, to her, being a mother meant becoming sick, deformed, and then dying. Marlene loved George and wanted to be his mother, but as he developed, her childhood memories erupted and she became terrified. As Marlene talked with the other mothers about the sad, frightening details of her mother's illness and death, her happy pleasurable memories began to surface and were reflected in warm supportive interactions with the other mothers. Marlene was no longer alone with her feelings; she had a circle of mommy-friends. Becoming a mother became unlinked from dying. The pleasurable memories and developing friendships with mothers mitigated reactivated memories of horror.

Gradually, Marlene assumed more of George's care. She frequently bathed him; she ate breakfast with him every morning before going to work, and frequently dinner. Marlene and George resumed playing together. Marlene also began to tuck him into his crib at bedtime. She made up what became their special goodnight song. Psychologically, Marlene became George's mother. George thrived. The drooling that had drenched his face and shirt no longer flowed. Of course, George was now older, but something else that had changed between George and his mother may have influenced his weeping saliva. Mother–baby attachment is resilient and powerful.

Highlights: 6 to 12 Months – A Baby's First Birthday

A baby's first birthday is a major milestone. Mother–baby interactions are at the core of all that has been achieved. The excitement generated is a recognition of the extent of the baby's step-by-step development and an appreciation of the many pleasures and stresses during the first year of motherhood.

While some caretaking of your baby may have been shared or delegated, being a mother is full-time. Your baby's first birthday may evoke flashbacks of the past year: the pleasures and the stresses. You may be aware of changes in yourself having achieved the first year of motherhood. There is much to celebrate.

---

10 12 to 18 Months

Mommy-friends

Glena told the following story about her first year of motherhood. "I wanted to meet other mothers going through the same things I was. I felt very lonely. I didn't have any friends with babies. The playground seemed like the best place to meet other mothers. As I approached the benches surrounding the sandbox, I saw a woman sitting alone with a baby who looked about the same age as Gus. We quickly became friends. We did errands every morning together and had picnic lunches in the park. We often had dinner together. On rainy days we met at one of our homes. She was a lifeline.

"I had been working before I got pregnant, but none of my work-friends had babies. I needed a mommy-friend. It reminds me; when I was growing up I lived in a big apartment building. There were lots of children, but they were all much younger than I was. I always played alone. I wished I had a friend; but it was the best time with my mother. We cooked together every day."

Glena's story about her loneliness after her baby was born and her search for a mommy-friend is reminiscent of her childhood memories. Glena's mommy-friend satisfied both her wish for a friend and the reactivation of the pleasures of being with her own mother.

Mother–Child Interaction

The transition from baby to toddler is identified by walking and includes beginning to talk – new experiences of autonomy and new kinds of mother–baby interactions. The exhilaration of upright mobility and the multitude of exciting new discoveries are characteristic of this phase of development. Mother–toddler interactions provide the secure base from which toddlers explore the world and practice their rapidly emerging physical and cognitive abilities. They return to or signal their mothers when contact is needed. When a baby or toddler has a physical or cognitive disability, this stage may look different externally but internally, that is emotionally, it may have many of the same elements.

DOI: 10.4324/9781003352549-11

Attachment Needs, Autonomy Strivings, and Social Referencing

Toddlers are highly motivated to share their experiences with their mothers: their achievements, discoveries, and uncertainties. They want to know their mothers' thoughts and feelings. These non-verbal secure base interactions have been called social referencing. They are typical during this phase of development and are an outgrowth of mother–baby attachment. The interactions are filled with meaning. For example, 14-month-old Daniel crawled across the room away from his mother. He approached Felicia, used the toy shelf to pull himself up to standing, and tried to take the doll she was holding. With his hands remaining on the doll as Felicia held on tight, he looked back at his mother and non-verbally communicated, '*Mommy, I want this doll. Is it okay for me to grab it? I need help to get it or to stop myself.*' Or when a stranger gets close, Daniel looks at his mother quizzically wanting to know, '*Am I safe?*' Or when a child tries to grab a toy that Daniel is holding, he looks at his mother silently asking, '*Mommy, did you see what happened? What should I do?*'

- When does your toddler initiate secure base interactions with you?
- When does your toddler want to know what you are thinking?
- When and how does knowing what you think or feel influence your toddler's behavior? When do your thoughts and feelings seem to not influence your toddler?

While toddlers are motivated by both attachment needs and autonomy strivings and the tensions between them, mothers of toddlers are motivated to both support their toddlers' autonomous explorations and to keep them close. Sometimes these aims are in conflict. Sometimes a toddler's autonomy clashes with a mother's needs for closeness. Wendy described, "I keep saying I want Mia to play with the other children, but whenever she is on my lap touching base, I keep caressing her. Maybe I am keeping her too close."

- When are you aware of having conflicted feelings about your toddler's autonomy?

Implicit and Explicit Communications

There may be times when you intend to communicate safety, but you are uncertain and your toddler reacts to your underlying feelings. For example, Jennine had a life-long fear of birds that she did not want Denis to have. During their many walks in the park, whenever a pigeon approached them, Jennine said, "It's okay, hi pigeon." Each time, Denis cried and clung to his mother. After a mothers' group discussion of similar experiences, the next time a pigeon came close, Jennine tried a different approach. "I feel a little scared when a pigeon gets close to us; Daddy is not afraid of pigeons. We can clap our hands and the pigeons will fly away." Denis began to feel safer when pigeons approached. He no longer cried.

Because of the exquisitely attuned mother–toddler relationship and toddlers' emerging empathy, they are sensitive to their mothers' authentic feelings. In the above example, Jennine acknowledging feeling scared, that she and Daddy had different feelings, and being able to chase the pigeons away with a clap, helped Denis to feel less scared himself. After acknowledging her fear, Jennine felt less scared also.

- When does your toddler's behavior reflect your underlying feelings, not what you want to communicate?
- When do you want to conceal your feelings from your toddler?

Kaylee was 17 months and busy playing in the sandbox. Alyssa tried to take Kaylee's shovel as she had successfully done several times before. This time Kaylee said "No," held on to the shovel tight, hit Alyssa gently on the wrist, and ran to her mother.

Kaylee's mother Marietta believed that hitting was not the way to resolve disputes, and toddlers needed to be taught not to hit. But Marietta also strongly believed that children need to feel entitled to protect themselves and to stand up for themselves. "I always teach Kaylee there is no hitting, but I also try to teach her to feel entitled to protect herself. I think that's why she said 'No' very loud and hit Alyssa so gently. Kaylee wanted to know what I thought and I was confused about how I wanted to respond. I said, 'Alyssa is not allowed to grab your shovel. You told her No! You also hit her. You know hitting is not okay, so you hit her very softly. I think she heard you.'" Marietta believed that, in this situation, apologies and reprimands for hitting were secondary to the importance of feeling entitled to protect herself.

Collecting Treasures

When babies begin to walk, they may collect many treasures as they explore their surroundings. Your toddler may deposit many items on your lap; to a toddler, they are all precious – dirty sticks and stones, scraps of paper, toys, etc. As you hold your toddler's collection, while feeling held by you as if in your arms and in your mind, your toddler's explorations continue and expand. In this way toddlers fuel their internal mental sense of Mommy and create a bridge connecting the wider world with Mommy. This invisible bridge enables your toddler to feel emotionally close to you when at a slight distance learning about the world.

April and her mother Taylor were in a mother-toddler group for the first time. April was 15 months old and whimpered as she wandered aimlessly around the room. She was unable to play with the toys and unable to be close to her mother. April and her mother had no secure base or social referencing interactions. After a while, April approached her mother and dropped a doll next to her. Her mother did not respond; April walked away quietly crying. A few minutes later, April dropped the doll on her mother's lap. Her mother removed it and placed it on the floor. April walked away and continued to wander and softly cry.

Mothers' group discussion focused on the possible meanings of April dropping the doll next to her mother or on her lap. The idea that April wanted to watch her mother hold the doll to feel close and safe triggered Taylor's frightening memories of her father's alcoholic rages and her mother's fear and helplessness. "One night my father threw a lamp at the window. Shattered glass flew across the floor. My mother screamed. I'm not sure if the light bulb or the window broke, but I was terrified and felt so alone." April's frightened wandering aloneness and Taylor's ignoring the doll that April gave to her were enactments of her memory of fear and aloneness.

Taylor's response to the links between her childhood memory and her interactions with April, and mothers' group support, enabled her to respond to April intuitively and empathically. Taylor said, "I think April feels the same way here as I remember feeling when my father threw the lamp." The next time April dropped the doll on her mother's lap, Taylor held it. Her initial awkwardness holding the doll revealed remnants of her childhood terror. Gradually as Taylor felt safer in the group, she embraced the doll tenderly. April began to hand the doll to her mother frequently and then to sit on her mother's lap. Her mother cuddled and caressed her. Social referencing when April was at a distance began to include mutual glances and smiles. The mother–toddler "doll-play" had provided a symbolic bridge to mother–toddler secure base attachment interactions.

April was no longer distressed; she felt held by her mother and safe, as did Taylor with the support of the mothers' group. April's independent play became more organized and focused. She was able to both initiate physical contact with her mother when she needed it and to connect with her emotionally from a distance. They shared an intersubjective experience of: '*I see you, you see me, you are thinking about me, I am thinking about you, we are safe, we are emotionally connected.*' In time, the doll remained on the shelf. April's mother had become a secure base for April.

- When does your toddler give items to you to hold while exploring or playing at a slight distance?

Differentiating Needs and Wants

Rosie voiced a concern that many mothers have: "He needs to learn; he can't have everything he wants." Learning you cannot have everything you want is an important life lesson. Toddlers have frequent experiences of not getting what they want – there are many potential learning opportunities. Meeting developmental, physical, and emotional needs is essential. Gratifying all wishes is not possible, practical, or necessary. Many things toddlers want are not good for them. Sometimes mothers' worries about their children learning they cannot have everything they want are related to their own feelings of deprivation.

As Rosie and 16-month-old Wayne were entering the mother-toddler room, seeking a secure base, Wayne looked up at his mother and reached to hold her hand to feel safe while walking into the loud, crowded room. Rosie gently moved her hand away and said, "He needs to learn, he can't have everything he wants." Rosie's painful memories followed: "When I was a little girl, my older sister teased me all the time. When I told my mother that my sister was teasing me and I needed her help, she always told me, 'You can't have everything you want. Don't be a tattletale, handle it yourself.' I knew I couldn't have everything I wanted. There were a zillion opportunities to learn it, but I needed my mother's help to feel safe. I could not do it myself. What I really want is to help Wayne feel safe." After a moment's thought, Rosie added, "I could say to him, 'I know you want to hold my hand because it's so loud here and there are so many people. I am going to stay very close to you and help you walk in all by yourself.'" Differentiating between needs and wants was useful: Wayne needed a secure base, he wanted to hold hands. Rosie thought of another way to meet Wayne's need to feel safe.

Awareness of her memories enabled Rosie to recognize the variety of ways she was helping Wayne to manage feelings of frustration and anger when he did not get what he wanted, and ways to meet Wayne's needs for a secure base.

Angry Interactions

Toddlers are learning more about the pleasures of loving interactions with Mommy and the security Mommy provides. They are also learning more about the angry interactions that may begin to increase in frequency and intensity during this phase of development. Loving feelings predominate, angry feelings erupt, and loving feelings are restored; the anger dissipates.

The magnitude of mother–toddler anger may be surprising. A frustrating element may be that an intelligent toddler can seem completely irrational, but from a developmental perspective makes sense. Toby and 17-month-old Emily were ready to go on a picnic. Their picnic basket was packed with Emily's favorite snacks. As they approached the door to leave the building, it was raining. Toby said, "Look, it's raining. We cannot go to the park for our picnic. We can eat our picnic upstairs." Emily screamed for what seemed like a long time. "No, stop the rain. Stop it, stop it."

Toddlers view their mothers as omnipotent. From a toddler's point of view, Mommy is all powerful – she can kiss a booboo and it feels better, so certainly she could stop the rain. Toby on the other hand felt unjustly accused of not stopping the rain. Toby reminded herself that toddlers are not always rational from an adult perspective and reassured herself that Emily's anger would subside. She did not mount a defense, instead she said, "I know how disappointed you are." Emily calmed. She may not have known the meaning of the word disappointed, but she did know how she felt. She also knew that Mommy understood her feelings.

Internal Conflict

Toddlers' attachment and autonomy needs are both strong and increasingly create internal conflict that promotes interpersonal conflict. Avery had a good example: "We were at a birthday party last weekend and the children were crawling through a tunnel. Kris, after sitting on my lap and watching for a while, wanted to go through with the other children. He wiggled off my lap, approached the tunnel line, and waited for his turn. When it was his turn, he started to cry and ran back to me. He then tried again, and the same thing happened. The third time I walked with him to the tunnel holding his hand and said, 'I will go in with you.' Kris seemed pleased. But when I tried to go into the tunnel with him, he threw himself on the floor and screamed, 'No Mommy!' I said, 'I know you want to do it all by yourself, and you also want me to be close.'" This phase of development is filled with conflict; toddlers gradually learn to resolve internal conflict.

Expectations About Angry Feelings

For both mothers and toddlers, the expectation that loving feelings return after angry feelings subside contributes to confidence in the rupture–repair process. Toddlers come to expect that their mothers will keep them safe, teach them what they need to know, share their pleasure, and soothe their pain. Mother–child attachment dynamics are strong and resilient. But it is not so simple. Mother–toddler relationships become increasingly complex. We can imagine the complexity in a toddler's mind using our words: '*I am safe, but sometimes I get hurt. I am loved, but sometimes Mommy disapproves of my behavior. I have so much to learn from Mommy, but sometimes I protest learning. Mommy and I love each other, but sometimes we feel angry. After we get angry, we get un-angry.*'

> • How would you describe the rupture–repair process of loving and angry feelings with your toddler?

Rupture and Repair Model

The game with blocks, "build it up and knock it down," which is extraordinarily pleasurable to many toddlers, provides a model for the rupture and repair cycles in love relationships. A toddler's excitement and urgency to knock a block tower down again and again, and to see Mommy restore it each time, may capture the valued reassurance of the fundamental permanence of the structure: it can always be rebuilt. '*No matter how angry I make Mommy, she loves me.*'

Separation and Reunion

During this phase of development, separation protests may intensify. Waving and saying goodbye enable toddlers to expect the separation and how it will feel, to be active rather than passive when separating, and to ease the distress. Separation play including peek-a-boo, hide-and-seek, and imaginative scenarios increases.

Denise, 18 months, combined play and saying goodbye. It was time for Alyx, Denise's mother, to leave for work. Their usual routine had included Denise and her babysitter walking Mommy to the elevator and Denise pressing the elevator button. As usual, Alyx stood next to the front door and called for Denise: "It's time to say bye-bye, I'm going to work." Denise ran in the other direction and hid behind the curtains. In this way Denise achieved two things: she delayed Mommy leaving and she actively did the leaving rather than passively being left. Together, Alyx and Denise turned hiding behind the curtains into a game of hide-and-seek that created a joyful separation and reunion game of mastery before an actual separation. Denise hiding behind the curtains and the happy reunion with Mommy became part of their goodbye routine.

- What games and routines help your toddler with separations?

During Separations

The longer a separation during the first three years, the more stressful it becomes. However, toddlers have begun to develop strategies for coping with separations that can be supported during separations: the longer ones and the shorter ones. The toddler's knowledge that, '*We always say goodbye before Mommy leaves; Mommy exists even when not seen; I can think about Mommy and imagine her when I don't see her; and separations are followed by reunions*' helps toddlers to adapt and can be reinforced during separations. A secure relationship with the substitute care-taker, conversations about Mommy, reunion plans, and sometimes a phone call, can help toddlers to cope.

- What are some of the instructions for caretakers while you are away?

Following, are some of the things Sean's regular babysitter Sasha said to him when his mother was at work: "Mommy is at work. I think she is sitting at her desk with her computer. Remember we said bye-bye after breakfast. Mommy gave a kiss to you. Mommy will be home after we play, have lunch, go to the park, and have a bath. Let's draw a picture for Mommy. You can give it to her when she comes home. I will tell Mommy we talked about her when she was at work."

Sean's babysitter's comments that helped him cope with separation included: a specific way to envision Mommy at work, a shared memory of Mommy's goodbye kiss, the specific sequence of activities after which Mommy would come home, and some details and preparations for their reunion.

Alone in the Presence of Mommy

A toddler's experiences of being alone in the presence of Mommy may be relevant to the developing capacity to cope with separation. Every morning, when Devlin took a shower, Mario played with his blocks. Mario and his mother could not see or talk to each other; the shower noise was too loud, and the glass was opaque. Mario seemed to feel emotionally with Mommy, while alone in the presence of Mommy.

> • When are you and your toddler together while each of you is focused on something else – alone with each other?

Separation and Sleep

Typical toddler worries related to separation can influence sleep. Frightening dreams at night and experiences during the day can also affect sleep. Toddlers and parents need sleep, and sleep difficulties are stressful. When there are sleep problems, understanding the details including associated thoughts, feelings, and memories of both the child and the mother can be useful to resolve them.

Annie was in the NICU for ten days after birth. She was a strong, healthy newborn who needed to be treated for an infection. Her mother Florence was discharged from the hospital when Annie was 2 days old. Every day from 5:00 a.m. to midnight Florence took care of Annie in the NICU; she breastfed, played with her all day, and returned home to sleep each night while her husband stayed with Annie. But Florence was not able to sleep. She tossed and turned for a few hours, then returned to the hospital. This early stressful separation from Annie and the anxiety it triggered lingered.

Both Annie and Florence continued to wake throughout the night and have difficulty falling back to sleep until Annie was 17 months and Florence connected a childhood memory to both of their sleep difficulties. "I just remembered, when I was 8 years old, I had meningitis and was in the hospital for about a month. My Mom visited me during the day, but at night I was alone. All through the night the nurses woke me to take my temperature, listen to my heart, and check my IV. My Mom always said that I almost died. I think when Annie was in the NICU in some ways I was reliving my own childhood trauma. I didn't realize it."

After Florence's insight about the connections between her childhood memory, the NICU, and her and Annie's current sleep difficulties, gradually both Annie and Florence began to sleep with fewer disruptions. Separations during the day also became easier for them both.

> • When your toddler has difficulty falling asleep or staying asleep, what are the feelings and memories that contribute?

There are two complex developmental milestones that are popularly called "training." For decades, learning to use the toilet has been called "toilet-training." Up until more recently it was the only mother–toddler teaching–learning or mutually regulated interaction that was referred to as training. In recent years, another developmental achievement has been popularly described as training: "sleep-training." The designation "training" suggests that the process is something the mother does or demands and the child obeys. The term training further suggests that the internal world of babies and toddlers, temperament, or life experiences do not matter in these mutually regulated, teaching-learning interactions; but of course they do. While many child development theories, books, and parents include the emotional responses of toddlers to learning to use the toilet, the term "toilet-training" has persisted. The emotional meanings of sleep to parents, babies, and toddlers are getting more attention now.

Likes and Dislikes – Meals

During this phase of development, toddlers may begin to have strong food preferences. Self-feeding increases and the mess expands. Food can be extraordinarily pleasurable and delicious, or unpleasant and disgusting. Food is necessary for survival, is a symbol for love, and is negotiated for autonomy. Meals can become fertile ground for mother–toddler power struggles.

Your responses to your toddler's food likes, dislikes, and eating messiness may be influenced by your ideas about nutrition, table manners, your own food preferences, and childhood memories.

- How would you describe your toddler's eating?
- What do you control about food? What does your child control?

In the middle of a mothers' group discussion about food, Meri described family meals: "JoEllen is 15 months and a very picky eater. She hardly eats anything. My husband always eats food off my plate; it's disgusting. I tell him not to, but he can't keep his hands to himself. JoEllen always tries to feed me; I want to feed myself. She won't let me feed her and she won't eat herself. She eats so little; I'm worried." Family meals had become fraught with power struggles, disgust, worry, and anger.

After a momentary pause, Meri blurted out how her mother and father always eat off each other's plates and feed each other: "It's like they are having sex at the table in front of everybody. They actually lick each other's fingers; it's disgusting." Another mother in the group asked Meri how these thoughts about her parents that popped into her mind were connected to her husband eating off her plate, her reaction to JoEllen trying to feed her, and being a picky eater. Meri answered, "I just realized that my disgust reaction to my husband is really about how I have always felt watching my parents eat since I was a little girl. Maybe my reactions to my parents also influence how I react to JoEllen and food."

Meri's reflections led to a change. She began to share some foods at the table with her husband and to let JoEllen feed her. JoEllen began to taste the food she was feeding to her mother; her repertoire of liked foods expanded. Meal-time pleasure for all increased.

Body and Mind Awareness

Descriptions of toddlers' favorite activities often include music. Musical rhythms, melodies, and lyrics capture their attention. Responsiveness to music may be related to awareness of body rhythms including the heartbeat, breathing, and walking. Mother–toddler dancing to music may be a new shared pleasure that builds on other synchronies.

Pooping

From the beginning of a baby's life, whether naked or in a diaper, pooping gets the mother's attention: before, during, or after. Toddlers gradually learn that their mothers are interested in their poop, and it is something that can be talked about together. When naked, urinating also gets mothers' attention.

Mothers introduce words for body parts, body sounds, and body products. For example, when Warren was pooping, his mother Ruby said the same words she remembered her mother saying to her younger brother, "Poop coming." When Warren was about 2 years old, he began to say, "Poop coming!" He also learned the word "toot" for passing gas and learned to differentiate poop coming from toot coming.

- What interactions do you and your toddler have about pooping, tooting, and peeing?

Your toddler may look at you before or while pooping, and in this way signal you that poop is coming. If autonomy strivings predominate, your toddler may crawl or walk behind a sofa to focus on the pleasurable body experience and to enjoy it without interruption, competing stimulation, or signaling you directly. Going to a special place to poop indicates body sensation awareness, a beginning ability to inhibit the impulse to poop, and a signal to you that poop is coming. Other toddlers may continue their play while pooping as if nothing is happening.

- What happens before, during, and after your toddler poops?

Some toddlers may practice starting and stopping a urine stream and beam with amazement at this accomplishment. Early mother–toddler interactions related to pooping and peeing are the first steps towards a toddler announcing poop and pee are coming and learning to use the potty.

The question often raised by mothers, "When should I start toilet-training?" can be reframed into recognizing where you and your toddler are in a collaborative, ongoing, interactive process about learning to use the potty.

Gender

Gender identity develops gradually. Toddlers are surrounded by references to gender: some are explicit and others they infer. A toddler's developing thoughts and feelings about gender may be revealed in play and other behavior. Mothers may wonder about how they want to respond. Their own politics and ethics may clash with their ideas about child development. For example, when Keith was 18 months and was watching his mother put on lipstick, he puckered his lips and asked, "Mommy, me too?" When Jayne was 17 months, she stood in front of the toilet with her hands on her genitals and urine dripping down her legs and said, "Making pee-pee." Keith's mother responded, "Women wear lipstick, you are a boy and will be a man when you grow up like daddy." Jayne's mother said, "Girls make pee-pee sitting on the toilet, you are a girl like Mommy." While the world may be more complicated, each mother believed that her response, which highlighted a sex difference, acknowledged a gender difference, and designated her child either a boy or girl, was the best response in the moment.

> • What do you want to communicate to your child about gender at this phase of development?

Designating Who Is a Boy and Who Is a Girl

Based on their own observations and what they have been told, toddlers begin to identify who is a boy and who is a girl. They create categories based on culturally prevalent styles of clothes and hair, and designations they hear. Toddlers are interested in boy–girl differences. For example, '*Girls wear dresses and pants. Boys wear pants, they don't wear dresses. Girls have long hair; boys have short hair.*' Some toddler categories may seem rigid in that they do not include all possible variations, but they serve toddlers' needs and beginning ability to make sense of the world they perceive. Categories become more complex with development. For example, '*Most boys have short hair, but sometimes boys have long hair.*'

> • What is said by you and your toddler about being a boy or a girl?

Observations of role differences at home may begin to capture a toddler's attention, get linked to gender, and be generalized, '*Mommies cook dinner, daddies wash dishes.*' Gradually early stereotypes expand and include more variation, '*My Mommy cooks, Finn's Daddy cooks.*' Family composition can influence a toddler's awareness of and interest in gender: '*Girls grow up to be mommies, boys grow up to be daddies. I have two mommies.*' Parents' preferences to avoid gender themes, or to highlight gender differences or similarities, may also influence toddlers.

- What is your toddler's awareness of sex differences?
- In what ways do you contribute to your toddler's awareness of gender?

You may be reading or hearing contradictory ideas about the development of gender identity. There is much that is unknown. You will gain a wealth of information as you watch your toddler's interests, ideas, and feelings about gender evolve.

Mothers' Wishes for a Boy, Wishes for a Girl

A mother's reactions to learning the sex of her baby may include the fulfillment of a wish, a disappointment, or an entanglement of feelings that can neutralize a prior preference for the sex of her baby. In other words, in response to her actual baby, a mother's wished-for baby can fade, and her actual baby can be claimed as "my baby."

Sloane's yearnings for a daughter intensified when she gave birth to her third son. She brought a photo of her 17-month-old middle son wearing a dress and blond curls almost to his shoulders, to show to the mother-baby group. Her words conveyed both her wish and her grief, "He would make such a pretty girl." We were able to begin to talk about Sloane's grieving for the daughter that she would never have and her pleasure in the photo as a pretend realization of her long-time wish to have a daughter. Sloane became able to differentiate her wishes to have a daughter from her deep love and profound pleasures with her sons. In a dramatic gesture, communicating the complexity of her feelings and conflicting impulses, Sloane tore up the photo and demonstrated that her actual sons were more valued than her wished-for daughter. She decided, "It's time for his first haircut."

Parental Nudity in Front of Toddlers

Discovery of the male–female genital difference is thought to occur around 16 months and can influence reactions to seeing parents naked, as well as to seeing other children naked. For example, Davina had bathed with her mother since she was a baby and seemed to have had no reaction to seeing her mother naked. When she was about 17 months, she began to try to touch her mother's pubic hair.

Awareness of male–female genital differences and child–adult genital differences can also influence children's interest in their own genitals. Philip had always bathed with his older sister. It was convenient and they had fun. After he turned 16 months, Philip began to hold his penis whenever he and his sister were naked together. This change in his behavior may have been a reaction to a new awareness of the male–female genital difference and its meaning to him. His mother Arizona decided to bathe them separately. Trish, another group-mother confronted her: "Isn't it better for him to learn about boy–girl differences?" Arizona said, "Yes, it's important to learn about them in a way that's comfortable, not in a way that makes him so nervous." Claude added, "Ellie acts as if she doesn't notice; maybe that's her reaction to noticing."

- How does your toddler react to seeing you naked? Daddy naked? Other children naked?
- What are the possible meanings of your toddler's reactions?

Mothers have their own preferences about being naked in front of their children; recognizing the changing behavior of children that may be reactive to seeing parents and siblings naked can be useful to make decisions about family nudity at each stage of development.

Genital Curiosity, Sensations, and What Gets Talked About

Genital curiosity increases during the toddler years. There is enormous individual variation. Mothers talk about their toddlers' emerging interest, exploration, and touching for pleasure. Mothers' stories about their toddlers' genital touching may include mothers' own feelings aroused and childhood memories activated.

Toddlers are proud to show their naked bodies and to have them admired. They may enjoy total abandon being naked. There are innate and acquired individual differences in their body explorations, and how much and what kind of genital pleasure each toddler seeks. A toddler's body excitement can be contagious or barely noticed. Toddlers may be curious about each part of their genitals: how they look, smell, and feel.

During a mothers' group, Elianna described Louisa's discovery at 18 months: "Louisa's older brother was taking a bath and she was sitting on the floor naked with her legs spread, exploring with her fingers. I was so surprised when pointing to her clitoris she said, this is my little penis. I was happy about her discovery and told her that's her clitoris. I wanted her to know it's great to have a clitoris. She said, 'no Mommy, that's my little penis.' It seemed important to her in the moment to think about it that way, I don't know why, but I stopped myself from insisting it's her clitoris."

Mothers make different decisions about what gets talked about with their toddlers. Lenore thought that when Phoenix showed her his erection, he seemed worried. Lenore explained, "The other day Phoenix said, 'Look Mommy, my penis is hard.' I thought he needed some reassurance. I said you have an erection. I thought telling him that there is a word to describe his experience would lessen any worries he might have." Scarlett, another mother in the group, said, "I'm not sure I want to have those kinds of conversations with Felix."

- What genital exploration does your toddler do?
- When and how does your toddler seek genital pleasure?
- What aspects of your toddler's genital exploration and pleasure do you and your toddler talk about?

Boys are aware of their erections and may want to know what Mommy thinks. They may have discovered their scrotum and testicles. Girls are aware of their vulva, and may have discovered their clitoris, vagina, and the scent of their vaginal secretions. They may want to know what Mommy thinks. The genital pleasure toddler boys and girls experience may be apparent. Their pride may be palpable, inhibition may be absent. Individual variation is huge. While the aim of toddlers' pleasure in touching their genitals is not orgasm and the specifics of their fantasies may not be known, we can think about toddler genital pleasure as sexual because it involves the sex organs.

- What do you want to communicate to your toddler about genital pleasure?
- How do your childhood memories influence your interactions with your toddler about body pleasure?
- What is your toddler learning about body pleasure now that you believe will lay a foundation for the future?

We might say that each mother simultaneously celebrates her toddler's body and all it can feel and do, while she also teaches her toddler the norms of her culture and family codes of behavior. In other words, mothers communicate that genital pleasure feels good but is not something to do at the dinner table, while playing with friends, etc. It is good to be curious and explore your body in private, but not okay to explore Mommy's body. There are parts of genital pleasure that get talked about and parts that are private. In general, toddlers quickly learn both the approval of body pleasure and curiosity, and the limits to pursuing them.

Mothers' Reactions to Sexually Related Behavior

Many things influence mothers' reactions to their toddlers' sexually related behavior. As an adult, Kathleen knew that childhood genital exploration and touching for pleasure were considered normal; but her own childhood memories of shame and guilt were activated when 16-month-old Amber started to touch her genitals.

"Amber has started to rub herself. She likes it, but I'm afraid she is going to hurt herself. I think it's normal but I'm worried. I was not allowed to do that."

When Amber developed some genital irritation and the pediatrician wanted to catheterize her to make a diagnosis, Kathleen was unable to tell him that she thought the irritation was from her "rubbing," not from an infection, "I felt too embarrassed and guilty to tell the doctor." The terror and pain that Amber experienced being catheterized and the fact that she did not have a urinary tract infection, amplified Kathleen's guilt. "It's all my fault. If I had told the doctor, she would not have needed to be catheterized. I felt too ashamed and guilty to tell the doctor."

Genay had similar childhood memories of shame and guilt, but a different response to her daughter Charlene's genital explorations. Genay remembered, "I had my first orgasm when I was 10 years old. I discovered while lying in bed before sleep, if I rubbed my legs together in a special way I had this amazing feeling. I was so excited; I told my mother. She told me never to do it again. It was a bad thing to do, and I could hurt myself. I tried not to do it, but it felt too good to stop. I never told my mother again. When Charlene touches herself, I tell her that I know it feels good. I don't want her to feel the guilt, shame, and fear that I felt."

Mothers and Sex

Mothers are surrounded by their toddler's emerging body curiosities, discoveries, and pleasures. At the same time, in addition to the demands of toddler care, mothers may have experienced enormous body changes from pregnancy, childbirth, and breastfeeding, and the ways in which they influence a woman's sexual desire, arousal, and satisfaction. The process for each woman to re-establish or establish satisfying sex in a changing family with new roles, new identities, and new stresses is sometimes a challenge.

> * In what ways is your sex life the same as before your baby and in what ways is it different?

Emotion Regulation

Aggressive behavior may be triggered when toddlers feel angry, frightened, over stimulated, or frustrated. When toddlers want something, they may be assertive and grab it. When they are frightened, they may hit. When they are over stimulated, they may bite. Toddlers are learning to identify their feelings and to inhibit impulses. Gradually, words can take the place of action: '*I am so angry; I feel like hitting.*'

Fears

Young toddlers may begin to acquire a variety of typical fears including loud or unexpected noises, looming objects, animals and insects, and fears of body damage.

Haircuts and cutting nails may become terrifying. Mommy raising her voice can be frightening. It is the meaning a toddler attributes that makes some things frightening. In other words, a toddler's own thoughts and feelings can be scary. Early fears are a precursor to typical later fears of the dark, monsters, and witches. These common childhood fears become the fears that adults seek to re-experience in horror and suspense films and books.

The emergence of typical fears throughout early development is thought to have an evolutionary survival basis. For example, when babies' survival is completely dependent on their mothers, fear of separation from Mommy and fear of strangers protect them by keeping them close to their mothers. When babies begin to crawl, and then to walk, a fear of dogs may emerge with the new ability to avoid proximity to dogs. Fear is a signal of potential danger. With help from their mothers, toddlers learn to assess what and if action is needed when they feel scared.

- What fears does your toddler have that are related to this phase of development?
- How are your toddler's fears related to life experiences? Yours and your toddler's?

Fears and Pretend Play

Kimberly was 16 months and was terrified of dogs. Kimberly was so frightened in their presence that she kept her distance and demanded to be held by her mother while vigilantly keeping her eyes on the dogs. Her mother Tara did not understand Kimberly's "hysterical" reaction. "I don't know why she's so scared. Most of the dogs are small and quite calm; she's never been bitten, but I was. I guess I'm still scared." Tara decided to buy a toy dog. The handle of the leash had two buttons: one made the dog walk and the other made the dog flip over. Tara and Kimberly created a variety of start and stop games with the toy. Kimberly was able to control the dog's walking and flipping at first with her words and her mother pressing the buttons, and then by herself. Her fear of dogs diminished, but never went away. Some fears become intergenerational.

Typical Bumps and Bruises

Zeke was almost 19 months and was beginning to cry louder and longer after typical toddler bumps and bruises. His mother Marla believed it was important to reassure children when they got hurt, and not to over-react. Her response to Zeke was, "It's nothing, you're afraid not hurt. You don't need to cry." Marla's surface calm and attempts to reassure Zeke were not helping him; he frequently became overwhelmed and difficult to comfort. Marla's own childhood memories were activated. "My parents were holocaust survivors, everything that ever happened to me they thought was nothing. Even when I broke my leg, they said it was nothing. I guess it was nothing compared to what happened to them in

Auschwitz. I don't know what to say to Zeke when he gets hurt. I don't want to over-react."

Marla's memories of her parents' reactions to her pain and fear, what she was told and what she imagined about their suffering in a concentration camp, and their vivid tattoos that were a constant reminder, had interfered with Marla getting her parents' understanding and comfort and were influencing her interactions with Zeke. He, like Marla, was not feeling comforted or reassured. Unlike Marla who had learned not to cry, Zeke continued to cry.

After linking Marla's childhood memories of her own pain and fear that she suffered silently to her current interactions with Zeke, Marla changed her response to Zeke's pain. For example, when Zeke got a minor bump: "I saw you bumped your head on the table; it must have startled you. Do you want a kiss?" When he got a bad bump as she embraced him and gently kissed him: "That looked like a hard bump, does it still hurt? Let me know when it starts to feel better." With this approach, Zeke's crying in response to injuries became more modulated and specifically reactive.

- How does your toddler react to bumps and bruises?
- How do you react when your toddler gets hurt?
- What memories are triggered?

When a toddler gets hurt, the mother's anxiety is triggered and leads to an assessment of the injury. For some mothers, their reaction in the moment is to their feelings of anxiety, not to the current injury. Being able to connect the felt anxiety to an activated memory can lessen feelings of anxiety and promote assessment of the current injury, and responsive comfort to the toddler. A mother's comforting caresses can become part of her toddler's emotion regulation, self-soothing, and resilience.

Self-consciousness and Embarrassment

During this toddler phase, feelings of self-consciousness and embarrassment begin to emerge. These new feelings indicate the ability of toddlers to experience themselves as seen from the outside in addition to how they feel on the inside. They have a beginning sense of how others see them.

- When does your toddler seem to feel embarrassed or self-conscious?

Feeling embarrassed is linked to self-disapproval. This developmental step is important to lay a foundation for the development of a conscience – an internal guide of right and wrong. Feelings of embarrassment also make toddlers vulnerable to being shamed and becoming overwhelmed with self-criticism. The development of a conscience is important, but harsh disapproval of a toddler can become harsh self-disapproval. Excessive embarrassment, shame, or guilt can make a child feel they are damaged, or inadequate. Toddlers need to become self-critical of certain behaviors. Teaching codes of behavior without humiliating a toddler or creating excessive self-criticism is sometimes a challenge.

Treasured Toys

A toddler's increasing attachment to a treasured toy is both an indication of a developing capacity for emotion regulation and promotes further emotion self-regulation. The toy may have objective qualities that make it appealing, but the toddler creates its meaning. Whereas many of the words a toddler speaks have been learned, the name and exact pronunciation of a treasured toy is often created by or co-created with the toddler. In some ways this may be part of its special meaning to the toddler and the entire family.

A treasured toy may be a valued sleep partner and frequent play companion, but seem ignored in moments. For example, Clarissa was 16 months. She slept with her Blanky every night, dragged it around the apartment, and took it with her outside. Sitting on her bedroom floor while Clarissa played with her baby doll, her treasured Blanky remained cast aside among a bunch of scattered toys. However, the moment her mother picked it up to return it to Clarissa's crib, Clarissa shouted "No!"

Toddlers keep track of their treasured toys to the best of their ability. They may protest it being thrown into the washing machine or left at home. Even if access is prevented, a treasured toy itself remains available. It can always be reclaimed. A treasured toy is never angry, sad, or busy. The ability to feel soothed while holding a treasured toy is constant because the soothing is embodied in the toddler's mind.

Not all children have treasured toys. Those who do not form an attachment to one special toy create other ways to achieve the same emotion regulation capacities. Thumb sucking, pacifiers, and bottles are similar to treasured toys in some ways, but different because of the ongoing direct body pleasure since infancy that they provide.

- If your child has a treasured toy, how are you influenced by the meaning of the toy to your toddler?
- If your child does not have an attachment to one special toy, what other behaviors seem to promote the development of emotion regulation?

A young toddler's attachment to a treasured toy, including the ability to endow the toy with emotion regulation capacities, increases during the first three years. A toddler's abilities to mentally perform the emotion regulation functions autonomously also increase. In other words, the toddler behaves as if the blanket or soft cuddly toy is doing the soothing, but in fact it is the developing mental capacities within the toddler's mind. Words to describe this process might be, '*I am loveable, even when Mommy is angry at me. I am safe, even when I feel scared. I love Mommy and she loves me, even when we are angry. Holding my blanket helps me have these feelings.*'

A toddler's emerging capacity for empathy may be seen with a treasured toy. When Andrea's mother was chopping onions, and tears were rolling down her cheeks, Andrea handed her treasured pink bunny to her mother and said, "Give a kiss to Mommy."

Play

Screen-time

The importance of toddler play is widely agreed upon. Screen-time is not traditional play, but it does have some elements that other forms of play also have. The potential value and potential harm of screen-time for toddlers have been questioned: answers differ; advice is widespread.

During past generations when innovations captured current consciousness, their impact was also questioned. It might be surprising to know that there were concerns about the influence on memory of the printing press; if information was in books, it would not need to be remembered. Worries surfaced that the telephone, television, and comic books would undermine wholesome values, family life, and sturdy development. The irresistible appeal and the potential damage of "too much" were emphasized in the past as they are now about screen-time. Of course, an exact measurement of "too-much" is never known, though at the extremes it may be clear. Mothers reading to toddlers is a highly valued activity; never being read to would be a loss; being read to all day would interfere with other valuable activities. Gradually, new technologies and forms of entertainment get integrated into the culture with huge individual variation.

Mothers make personal decisions for themselves about their own screen-time. Their decisions are based on competing interests and responsibilities, and the impact of their own screen-time on their toddlers. Mothers make decisions about their toddler's screen-time balancing what is known about the value of competing activities, especially mother–toddler play. They worry about the use of screen-time as a babysitter or for emotion regulation. Babysitting may be needed, and emotion regulation may be useful. There is much to consider.

- How does your own screen-time influence your decisions about your toddler's screen-time?
- How do your memories influence the decisions you make about screen-time?

When you are texting, emailing, or otherwise engaged with a device, your toddler loses your attention, as is also true when you are doing many other things. You may feel the pull towards your devices strongly. Your toddler is interested in the things that interest you. In addition, devices have intrinsic properties that appeal to toddlers: press a button and things happen. While your toddler's interest in screen-time may be increasing and digital game competence expanding, of primary importance to your toddler is you and your interactions with each other.

Rough and Tumble Play

Rough and tumble vigorous physical play increases during the first three years. Throwing toddlers in the air and catching them, wrestling, and some tickling are typical. In the context of loving playfulness, physical strength is both freely exuberant and restrained. The warning, "This will end in tears" captures both the fragility of the pleasure and the threat of danger. Mothers' related childhood memories may be vivid and reveal elements of the ambivalence. A frequent name remembered is "tickle-torture."

High-arousal rough and tumble play may be universal but individual differences are huge. The optimal amount or intensity for one toddler may be overstimulating to another. A toddler's experiences of rising excitement and the return to a state of equilibrium can contribute to developing emotion regulation and the ability to enjoy a range of interactive stimulation from quiet contentment to breath-taking exhilaration. Rough and tumble play usually occurs in the context of the intimate and safe parent-child relationship.

> - What kind of rough and tumble play does your toddler like?
> - How do your childhood memories of being tickled or wrestling influence rough and tumble play with your toddler?

Each parent and toddler has their own exciting and attuned rough and tumble play routines. Aspects of the play that are overwhelming to a toddler and trigger biting, hitting, or tears can be identified and modified.

Bellybutton Play

In many families, bellybuttons get attention. Not incidental to an interest in bellybuttons is that they are close to the genitals, are often concealed, both males and females have them, and they are sensitive to the touch. An aspect of the attention may be the fun of designating a bellybutton, either an innie or an outie. While both males and females have bellybuttons, and both males and females have innies and outies, the designation innie or outie may be a slightly disguised reference to the genital male–female difference and part of the excitement of bellybutton play.

It is noteworthy that adults in many situations continue to use the word bellybutton rather than navel. This may be related to the power of childhood experiences, meanings, and memories of the bellybutton. In addition, the bellybutton is a remnant of the biological mother–baby attachment.

Pretend Play and Shared Expectations

Mother–toddler pretend play about anticipated events is a way to plan for the future together. Shared expectations can help to mitigate the impact of potentially disturbing or overwhelming experiences. Wesley was scheduled for an appendectomy. Wesley's mother Parker wanted to help him to know what to expect, and believed that in addition to telling Wesley what will happen, pretend play would be the best way to create shared expectations. Parker described her plan: "We will play with surgical masks, syringes, gauze, a blood pressure-cuff, band-aids, and a stethoscope. I will tell Wesley that his doctor said that to get all better he needs something called surgery. We will be going to a special place for the surgery called a hospital. Many people wear pajamas at the hospital. I will emphasize that Daddy and I will be with him."

Wesley was 15 months when he had the surgery; familiarity with the medical equipment, words related to hospitals and surgery, and pretend play with Mommy were worthwhile. Wesley may not have understood all the words, but Parker was convinced that he did get the feeling of being close to her, being taken care of, and being safe. While Parker remained anxious about the surgery, play with Wesley also helped her to calm.

Wesley recovered well from his surgery. Doctor-play evolved from hospital and surgery themes into the details of well-baby-care doctor visits. For a while, Wesley's teddy-bear had a small band-aid on its tummy. One day Wesley took the band-aid off, threw it in the garbage and said, "All better. No more surgery."

Shared Memory Narratives, Play, and Life Stories

Some mother–toddler play and shared memory narratives evolve into life-long autobiographical stories. Wesley's story about the scar from his appendectomy maintained elements of the play with his mother before the surgery, their shared memory narrative after, and some new elements. When he was 3 years old, Wesley told this memory: "When I was a baby I had surgery. Mommy and Daddy took me to the hospital. My appendix was infected. That's something inside everyone's body when they are born. Sometimes it gets infected and you need surgery. I have a scar from the surgery. I remember my teddy-bear came with me to the hospital and had surgery also. My teddy-bear had a band aid, but no scar. My teddy-bear cried. For a while my tummy hurt. Mommy put medicine on it and kissed it. Then it got better."

> • What shared memory narratives and play may become part of your toddler's autobiographical life story?

Pretend Play About Everyday Events

Experiences of everyday life are typical scenarios for early pretend play. Pretend play themes are introduced by mothers or initiated by toddlers. The scenarios may have rudimentary elements of role-play. For example, you may have seen your toddler pretend to feed a baby doll or toy animal, push a car or truck with people in it, or take a doll or teddy-bear for a walk in a stroller. We can wonder, when toddlers push teddy-bears in a stroller, are they imagining what the teddy-bear feels being pushed in the stroller or are they imagining what it feels like to be a Mommy and push a toddler in a stroller, or some of both?

- What beginning pretend play does your toddler do?
- What pretend play are you introducing to your toddler?

In addition to everyday experiences, other experiences that might be stressful, for example haircuts, taking medicine, visits to the doctor, or a family move to a new home, may also become part of pretend play.

Play with Peers

Toddlers have learned a great deal about relationships from mother–toddler interactions. A foundation for developing friendships with peers has been created. Toddlers have strong social instincts and beginning abilities to initiate and maintain pleasurable interactions with each other. Adults rely on words, toddlers seem to be able to interact, to connect, and to settle disagreements non-verbally in ways we might not even notice. For example, Suzanna crawled next to Tatianna and touched the shape-box Tatianna was manipulating. Tatianna lifted the toy and held it close, communicating, '*it's mine.*' Suzanna remained still. After a moment, Tatianna put the shape-box back on the floor and both girls began to manipulate a different part of the toy. Subtle, non-verbal interactions between the girls seemed to have led to their play together.

Cal took a small truck off the shelf and began to push it on the floor. Adrian tried to grab the truck from Cal. His interest in the toy seemed to have been triggered by watching Cal play with it. The truck had been on the shelf, untouched for the last half hour. When Cal took it off the shelf and began to play with it, the toy had more appeal to Adrian because of his interest in Cal. Cal held on tight. They both yelped and looked towards their mothers for help as they tugged on the truck. Both mothers agreed to help the children: "We have one truck, let's play the turn-taking game: 1, 2, 3, 4, 5, Cal's turn; 1, 2, 3, 4, 5, Adrian's turn." Passing the truck back and forth to each other was more fun for both boys than playing with the truck alone. Their attention shifted to the pleasurable interaction.

Many conflicts between toddlers are triggered by feelings about the possession of a toy. In many ways a toddler's assertion of possession is an assertion of self. In other words, '*It's mine*' has many meanings other than I own it. It can mean,

'*I like it. I want it. I'm playing with it.*' That is to say, the toy represents self-feelings. Mother–toddler interactions that support both a toddler's developing sense of self and social interactions with peers can include designating some toys to be shared and others not. Often mothers and toddlers agree that treasured toys are not to be shared because they are so linked to the sense of self.

- When you bring toys to the playground, which are required to be shared? Which are not?
- When your toddler has a playdate at your home, when do you and your toddler put several toys away to guarantee they will not be touched during the visit?

Mothers have different opinions about how long play visits should last, whether activities should be organized by adults, and whether and how to intervene when the children have conflicts. Mothers' impulses both to protect and to teach their toddlers, and to promote their autonomy, get triggered. Differences of opinion among mothers may be influenced by differences in the needs of the toddlers, ideas about toddlers' social-emotional development, and mothers' childhood memories.

- What memories are triggered by interactions your toddler has with other toddlers?
- What memories are triggered by your interactions with other mothers?

Learning from Each Other, Imitating, and Empathy

Toddlers learn from each other and sometimes imitate each other. They are reactive to each other's emotions; in other words, they are empathic. It seems as though toddlers recognize that another toddler is the same in meaningful ways; maybe it is their similar size and non-verbal communications with each other. They seem to know that they both need caretakers who remain close. Toddlers' interactions with each other have different pleasures and challenges than their interactions with adults and older children.

Apologies

Sometimes toddlers need some time to process angry feelings before apologies are exchanged and accepted, and transitions are made back to friendly interactions. Distinctions may be useful between apologies as social convention and apologies that are expressions of remorse followed by forgiveness. Promoting the development of a child's capacity for remorse may require processing the complexity of the interaction and all the feelings rather than a precipitous apology. On the other hand, the social rituals of apologizing and accepting apologies may contribute to the development of remorse and forgiveness.

Learning

Emergent Steps in Development

Mothers interact with their toddlers not only as the toddlers they are, but also as the children they are becoming. In other words, when mothers see the possible evidence of an emergent step in development, it can be identified and supported. For example, Quince wanted Theo to be interested in books. She had kept several of her own childhood classics and had a few more recently published favorites. Quince was a big reader herself; she had fond memories of being read to by her mother.

Theo was an active toddler and did not sit still long enough to listen to a story. However, during a mother-toddler group when Theo was 18 months, he took a book off the shelf and started to look at the pages. Quince said, "Theo's new activity is reading a book to his special elephant. While cuddling his elephant, he climbs onto the chair next to the bookcase where I always try to read to him. He pretends to read. It only lasts a few moments, but I tell him that it looks like fun, learning how to read."

> • What things do you say to support something your toddler is beginning to do or learn?

Intentions – Pointing to the Future

Christina was trying to teach 15-month-old Melissa not to touch the garbage. But every day they had the same frustrating angry interaction, until Christina realized that Melissa was communicating her intention to touch the garbage – a precursor to being able to stop herself. As Melissa walked towards the garbage, she paused, got her mother's attention, smiled, and dashed towards the garbage. Christina smiled, lifted Melissa gently, and said, "I see you remember there is no touching the garbage. I will help you to stop." Melissa did not protest. Melissa's signal of her intention to her mother was the first step in being able to stop herself. Christina's acknowledgement that Melissa remembered the limit and needed help to stop herself supported her remembering and self-control. Preventing Melissa from touching the garbage reinforced the limit. In a short time, Melissa stopped herself.

> • When does your toddler signal an intention to you?
> • When does preventing your toddler from doing something help your toddler learn to not do it?

Christina also introduced a stop and go game to Melissa. They clapped hands and took turns shouting stop and go. Both Melissa's power of self-control when her mother shouted stop and go, and Melissa's control of her mother when she shouted stop and go delighted Melissa and supported her ability to stop herself.

Learning Codes of Behavior and Setting Limits

Learning accepted codes of behavior – the dos and don'ts of everyday life, is a gradual process. In addition to learning ways to behave, an important part of the process is the development of mental and emotional capacities, including frustration tolerance, impulse control, the ability to manage ambivalence, empathy, and a value system of right and wrong – a conscience. The goal is that toddlers begin to develop standards of behavior for themselves. Your attention to both the external behavior you want your toddler to learn and to your toddler's thoughts and feelings during limit-setting interactions can result in complementary behavioral learning and emotional development.

- What behavioral dos and don'ts have you begun to teach your toddler?
- Which dos and don'ts has your toddler learned?

It may be easier to identify behaviors that have not yet been learned than all those that have. The ones that have been learned may be so incorporated into everyday life that they go unnoticed.

Throughout the first three years, teaching–learning mother–toddler interactions about behavior increasingly evoke feelings of frustration, anger, shame, and fear for both mothers and toddlers. The ongoing repetition of behavioral disapproval and intense feelings that are part of the process can awaken mothers' childhood memories.

- When are teaching-learning interactions with your toddler angry, frightening, or shameful?
- What memories are triggered?

Mother–toddler teaching–learning interactions are part of the process whereby a mother's prevention and disapproval of a behavior become a toddler's self-disapproval and self-control. A mother's approval, support, and validation become part of a toddler's self-approval, standards of behavior, and conscience.

Consistency and Inconsistency

Because of the needed repetition of limit-setting interactions with toddlers, consistency is often emphasized. Inconsistency is also important. Inconsistencies help children to adapt to change and to be responsive to nuance. '*This rule is very important to Mommy; some rules are not so important. I can say anything to Mommy, but not always in front of other people. I can eat French fries with my hands, but not spaghetti.'* These are some examples of inconsistencies that have potential value; the list is long. There are only a few non-negotiable, non-flexible dos and don'ts or ways of being. It takes many slightly varied repetitions to learn all the subtleties and respond accordingly. The totally non-negotiable prohibitions are the dangerous ones, like running into the street, or a personal non-negotiable priority of a parent.

> • What behaviors are you teaching your toddler are never allowed?
> • What behaviors are inconsistently allowed?

Disapproval

When mothers' limit-setting or disapproval of behavior evokes excessive amounts of fear, shame, or anger, self-disapproval may become too harsh. A toddler's frightened crying may indicate the need for loving feelings with Mommy.

Mindy, 17 months, climbed onto the coffee table and lunged towards a bouquet of flowers in a fragile glass vase; her mother got frightened and yelled. Mindy startled, got terrified and, scrambling to get off the table, knocked over the vase and shattered it. Mindy's mother, realizing what had happened and how scared Mindy was, said, "I yelled so loud, you got scared. Breaking the vase was an accident. I got scared too. I am going to say it softly; I know you like to climb, there is no climbing on the coffee table. You can climb onto the sofa." When Mindy's mother described this during a mothers' group, Daphne had a strong reaction. "Saying things like that in the heat of the moment sounds a little fake. Is that really what happened or what you wished happened?"

Pamela, another group-mother remembered the first time 18-month-old Jeremy entered the playroom: "He pointed at the toys, froze, and said 'no touch, no touch.' I was so surprised. I realized that I often tell him, 'no touch,' and he freezes. There are so many things I don't want him to touch. But I don't want him to think he can't touch anything. I changed my frightening no touch rules to gentler, more specific teaching-learning interactions and found ways to say yes. For example, 'yes, flowers are for looking at and smelling, let me help you.'"

The dos and don'ts of everyday life need to be learned in ways that they can be appropriately applied and when there is uncertainty the toddler can check back to Mommy with social referencing.

> • When does your toddler check with you to see if doing something is okay?

Adults typically break some rules: for example, lie to protect someone's feelings. Children need to learn which rules are acceptable to break and in what context, and which rules can never be broken. This is a long, gradual process with much individual variation.

Codes of Behavior and Developmental Goals

After many teaching-learning interactions about behavior, while maintaining feelings of self-worth, toddlers gradually internalize codes of behavior, make them their own, and stop themselves. This process is different from obedience. With obedience, behavior is controlled by submission to authority or to avoid punishment. Most early childhood learning that relates to behavior is about developing mental processes in addition to learning the behavior.

Mothers' Childhood Memories

Memory Themes

You may be able to identify a core theme throughout your various childhood memories. Recognizing the theme during interactions with your toddler can be useful in resolving difficulties and easing stresses. Following, are some examples of themes.

1 Conflict between empathy for your child and behavioral goals.
2 Attachment to your own mother, conflicted with attachment to your toddler.
3 Wishes to provide the best for your toddler, conflicted with the envy of your toddler.
4 Feelings about your wished-for child, conflicted with feelings towards your actual child.
5 Discrepancy between the mother you wish you were and the mother you believe you are.
6 Wishes to protect your own mother, conflicted with getting the comfort you need from her.
7 Attachment with your toddler, conflicted with revived fears of attachment.
8 Conflicts between work and family life.

Childhood Memory Themes: Breastfeeding and Weaning

Weaning from breastfeeding occurs at different ages, for different reasons. Pediatricians, infant mental health professionals, and breastfeeding advocacy organizations have strong opinions. Mothers also have opinions and may have conflicted feelings about when and how they want to wean their babies or toddlers. Memory core themes can provide a way to understand current conflicts.

When Naomi was 10 years old, her mother jumped up from the table to answer the phone, tripped, and spilled a cup of scalding coffee. The coffee blistered Naomi's face, shoulders, and thighs. By the time she was 12 years old, her face had completely healed. One small scar remained on her leg. Naomi remembered, "Worse than the accident and the painful treatments were my mother's frequent rages. They were so scary. Every time my mother yelled at me, I could feel the hot coffee blistering my whole body. There was nothing I could do to stop the yelling. I couldn't wait to grow up, move out, get married, and have a baby." Naomi's vision of motherhood was a remedy for her childhood pain. The actuality of motherhood was different. A core theme for Naomi was feeling unprotected.

While Naomi held 17-month-old Wally tenderly on her lap with his face nuzzled into her breasts during a mother-toddler group, she described her conflict about breastfeeding. "I'm not sure if I want to continue or to stop breastfeeding. Many people think Wally is too old to breastfeed; I'm not sure what I think. I love breastfeeding and I think I'm giving Wally all the attention, love, and security he needs. He's completely safe. I'm giving him all the things I never had when I was a child."

Intertwined with her breastfeeding satisfactions, Naomi described the unrelenting demands of caring for a toddler and typical resentments. "My husband doesn't do any childcare. He never changes a diaper. I do everything. I never have a babysitter. I never see my friends or even talk to them on the phone. Every night I fall into bed at 8:00 completely exhausted."

I asked Naomi what she thought about while breastfeeding. "I know Wally's safe and happy so I can think about other things. I think about friends to call. Sometimes I read, I send emails, things like that." I summarized what Naomi had been saying. "It sounds like breastfeeding is very satisfying for you. While breastfeeding you can feel close to Wally, feel like you are giving him all the love and security he needs, and at the same time you can think about other things." Naomi nodded and I continued, "You don't need to talk to him, play with him, or worry about him. He's completely safe." Naomi cautiously smiled in agreement. I added, "It sounds like the only time you get away from Wally is while you are breastfeeding." Without skipping a beat, Naomi said, "The only break I get is when I'm breastfeeding. I'm with him all the time. Breastfeeding is my only escape."

A new meaning of breastfeeding crystalized for Naomi – a way to escape. The following week, Naomi had begun to wean Wally gradually, had hired a babysitter a few hours a week, and her husband was spending more time with Wally. Naomi explained the changes this way: "I realized that nursing was my way to get away and still be able to feel like the mother I want to be. When Wally was breastfeeding, I believed that he didn't feel and would never feel abandoned, ignored, neglected, or unsafe, as I felt all the time as a child." Naomi's insight about the links between breastfeeding and her painful childhood memories expanded her thinking. Mothers' group discussion promoted her positive feelings about herself as a mother who provided love and safety to her son in many ways in addition to breastfeeding. Gradually, within three months, Wally was no longer nursing.

Conflicts between Work and Family

For Daria, conflicts between work and family life were rooted in childhood memories and had an impact on stressful reunions with and separations from Declan. Daria's devaluation of her mother as a woman, "She never did anything other than take care of me and my siblings," and her over-idealization of her as a mother, "She was always a perfect mother," intensified Daria's conflicts between work and family.

Daria had a full-time, demanding job with some flexibility. When Declan was 16 months, Daria enrolled him in four play activities. Every day Daria left work, battled NYC traffic, gobbled down her lunch on the way to meet Declan and his nanny at music, story-time, baby massage, and gym. Daria was frazzled, her work was suffering, and separations after these 40-minute reunions were becoming increasingly difficult for Declan. Daria was trapped in her conflict until she had an insight, "I just realized, I'm trying to be the perfect mom that I thought my mother was and the perfect executive that my mother never could be." With this insight, Daria was able to find better solutions to integrating work and family life.

Memories of Helplessness

Sometimes, memories of helplessness as a child are related to feelings of helplessness as a mother. Nellie described 14-month-old Lindsay's hitting: "All of a sudden, out of nowhere, Lindsay hits me. You wouldn't believe it because she never hits me in front of other people, she only hits me at home when we are alone. No matter what I do, she won't stop." As Nellie spoke these words, a childhood memory came to mind: "My mother always spanked me; all of a sudden, out of nowhere. She only spanked me at home, never anywhere else. Never in front of anyone. I was so helpless. My father didn't believe me. There was nothing I could do to stop the spankings."

As a child, Nellie was helpless to stop the spankings and unable to be believed. Recognizing her current feelings of helplessness as a reactivated childhood memory, not a current actuality, and feeling believed in the mothers' group, enabled Nellie to stop Lindsay from hitting her.

Memories and Concerns About Spoiling

Mothers' worries about spoiling their toddlers may be related to their own childhood memories. Concerns may be focused on children having their own way or the acquisition of things. Mothers' childhood memories of unmet emotional needs can lead to worries about children being spoiled by having things. The traits that adults do not like in children that fall under the rubric of spoiled are a sense of entitlement, selfishness, and demandingness. These traits are often viewed as the result of overindulgence but may also be acquired by deprivation. In some ways, all toddlers have these traits to varying degrees at various times.

Miranda felt that she was never valued or approved of by her mother: "I don't think my mother ever really liked me. We are very different." Miranda worried that her daughter would be spoiled if she bought her things. Linking Miranda's painful yearnings related to her own unmet emotional needs with her daughter's painful crying for things like ice cream and toys, lessened Miranda's concerns about spoiling and enabled her to make decisions about buying things based on other criteria.

Highlights: 12 to 18 Months

The transition from baby to toddler is defined by the ability to walk and influenced by developing language. Exhilarated curiosity, exploration, and discovery are prominent characteristics of this phase. A passionate self with likes, dislikes, and desires emerges. A toddler's needs to feel understood frequently erupt.

Toddlers can be both wondrous and challenging. Attachment needs, autonomy strivings, and the tensions among them intensify. Mother–toddler interactions can be turbulent; attachment bonds are sturdy. Mothers' childhood memories are awakened and relived. Wishes for a mommy-friend may escalate.

---

11   18 to 24 Months

Mommy-friends

From the time Lilly was born, as Helen pushed her baby carriage around the neighborhood, mothers approached and tried to interest her in joining the neighborhood mothers' co-op. "I was too busy caring for my baby, doing errands for my husband, and household chores to even consider a mothers' group. I quickly brushed them off. I just wanted my maternity leave to end, return to work, and Lilly to start daycare.

"One day, feeling more stressed than usual, I decided to talk with a mother who approached me. We bought containers of tea and sat on a park bench; our babies slept. After hearing about the mothers' exchange of babysitting hours, I decided to join. I needed time away from Lilly. In addition to the babysitting program, once a month there was a parents' meeting. We talked about everything that was going-on, all our questions and worries. The mothers were always so reassuring.

"I quickly discovered important life-and-death information. When Lilly was 18 months, I learned that green poop did not mean she was dying; it meant she ate too much spinach. I stayed in the group for two more years, and when Lilly started nursery school I organized a new mothers' co-op. I never became friends with any of the women in either group. It's really the story of my life. My mother died when I was 2½ years old and my father put me in an orphanage. When I was 3½ years old I got headlice, they shaved my head, and my father took me out of the orphanage to live with a friend of his and her three children. She became a mother to me, and her children were like sisters and a brother. Two years later, my father and I moved to the United States. Before I was 7 years old, I had lost two mothers, three siblings, and my orphanage home."

During early motherhood, Helen's relationships with other mothers were not about friendship, they were about survival. It was a lonely survival with significant loss, as had much of her childhood been.

Mother–Child Interaction

As a toddler explores the world with all its pleasures, uncertainties, and difficulties, secure base mother–toddler interactions gradually become part of a child's sense of self. '*Mommy loves me, I am loveable; Mommy protects me, I am safe; Mommy understands me, I can understand myself.*'

DOI: 10.4324/9781003352549-12

Feeling Understood

Feeling understood helps toddlers understand themselves. It is easy for toddlers to feel understood when they get what they want. But what they want is not always in their best interest and sometimes what they want clashes with what their mothers want. When toddlers do not get what they want, which happens often, feeling understood can be more challenging.

Randi described an interaction with 20-month-old Davina: "She wanted to walk up the slide rather than climb the steps and slide down. She saw her older sister do it and she was determined. As Davina lifted her foot onto the slide, I reached for her hand. She went into total meltdown. She threw herself on the ground and screamed. All I did was try to keep her safe. I understood she wanted to walk up the slide herself, but it was too dangerous to let her do it. This time, instead of trying to convince her that I did the right thing to protect her, I told her I knew she did not want me to help and I understood why she was angry. I couldn't believe it, she stopped crying. I know it won't always help, but this time simply saying I understood helped. I didn't need her to be wrong for me to be right."

> • When is it helpful to tell your toddler that you understand what your toddler wants and how your toddler feels? When is it not helpful?

Thoughts, Feelings, and Behavior

The impulse to criticize or mock what a toddler is thinking or feeling may be triggered. In many ways, from an adult perspective, toddlers can appear irrational while developmentally their thoughts and feelings can make sense.

Lynne was horrified and embarrassed when 22-month-old Max protested sharing his snack at the playground: "I did not say what I felt like saying (you are so selfish, stop acting like a spoiled brat), I thought it would be demeaning and not helpful. Instead, I said, "I know you want all the bananas for yourself, but when we bring bananas to the playground, we share them. Your sippy cup is just for you. I then handed out the bananas to the other children and to Max."

Lynne was confident that in time Max would most likely acquire many of her values. Accepting Max's feelings, offering him a substitute that he did not need to share, and distributing the bananas enabled them to enjoy bananas with their friends and put into action her values about sharing food. Toddlers are gradually learning from their mothers what is shared, what is not shared, and with whom. In the moment changing a toddler's behavior or controlling what happens may be feasible; thoughts and feelings can follow.

> • What values are important to you that you would like your child to have?
> • What interactions are you having with your toddler that are creating a foundation for your toddler to adopt the same values?

Differentiating between Needs and Wishes

Newborns have needs. Babies and toddlers have needs and wishes. There is an important distinction between needs and wishes. Meeting physical and emotional needs is optimal for development. Gratifying all toddler wishes is not practical or possible. As is true throughout life, it is optimal for some wishes to be gratified, some delayed, some satisfied by a substitute, and others renounced. Determining what are a toddler's needs and what are a toddler's wishes can feel complicated.

• When does your toddler's wish seem like a need?

Toddlers seem to grasp the distinction between needs and wishes. They recognize that needs are more urgent. As language emerges, they demand "I need it" far more often than "I want it." Desire is a valuable trait that can be supported even when a wish is not gratified: "You really know what you want."

Gradually, the ability of toddlers to tolerate the frustration of wishes increases. They become better able to delay gratification. They can imagine gratification in the future and therefore are better able to wait. They are better able to accept a substitute; that is, a gratification that has some of the characteristics of what is wanted. Influenced by what mothers treat as needs or wishes, children learn to differentiate between needs and wishes. Mothers also have needs and wishes. Paulette had an insight: "I always say that I need a cup of coffee, but I don't need it, I want it. Wants can be passionate." Your toddler's ideas about needs and wishes will be influenced by what you treat as a need and what you recognize as a wish, both yours and your toddler's.

Mothers' Needs and Wishes

Mothers have needs and wishes that do not include their children. Toddlers begin to learn about their mothers' interests and relationships that they are excluded from. For example, a special hug with Daddy, a passion for work, and exhilaration playing tennis.

Toddlers approaching 2 years may also begin to develop a passionate interest that does not include their mothers. Erik could work on a block construction himself for almost 20 minutes. His mother Madlyn thought something was wrong: "It seems like Erik has an obsession. I'm worried." It turned out that Erik had a new, passionate interest that did not include his mother. Unlike an obsession, a passionate interest is balanced with other interests. It does not intrude or take over, it enriches. After mothers' group discussion, Madlyn realized that her reactions to Erik's block building without her were revived feelings of rejection. Her worries about Erik having an obsession faded. In addition, her ability to satisfy her own needs and wishes that did not include Erik increased.

Internal Conflict

Toddlers' abilities to tolerate ambivalent feelings and resolve internal conflict among wishes in a balanced way also increase during this phase. Sometimes a compromise can help. Elaine was 23 months and wanted playdates with Josh, but did not want him to touch her toys. Games together that did not involve her toys were fun. Before Josh arrived, her mother said, "Josh is coming to visit. Choose a few toys you do not want Josh to touch, and I will put them in the closet. The rest of the toys will be for sharing."

- What internal conflicts does your toddler seem to have?

Gradually, internal conflicts can be managed mentally. Opposing wishes, for example to possess all the toys and to play with a friend, can be reconciled internally.

Shared Wishful Fantasies

Mother–toddler shared wishful fantasies can provide a substitute for the actual fulfillment of a wish: "It would be great to have all the cookies in the world!" Sometimes adding a touch of irony is fun: "Of course, we want Grandma to have some of the cookies so she can give them to us!"

Children catch on quickly to the power and pleasure of wishful thinking. When Jimmy was asked, "If you could make one wish, what would it be?", he answered, "I would wish for one million wishes." Some wishes need to be renounced: "I understand right now you want to marry me, but you are my son and will always be, even when you grow up. You can marry someone else when you grow up."

Mother–toddler window shopping together can include shared wish fulfilling interactions. Mommy's simple words, "It might be fun to have that big jungle gym," can provide momentary shared wish fulfillment.

Elenna was 23 months and wanted a puppy, just like her cousin. Elenna's mother Lydia was definitely not going to get a dog. There was a pet shop in their neighborhood with a large window filled with six playful, adorable puppies. Every day for a week, Elenna and Lydia stood at the window gazing at and talking about the puppies. Elenna called them, "My puppies." They gave names to each one and told Daddy about them. At home Elenna set up a corner of her room with three stuffed animals and a bowl with pretend dog food. With her mother's help she made a cozy bed for the puppies. In a short while, Elenna stopped asking for a dog.

- What wishful fantasies have you and your toddler shared?
- What are the wish-fulfilling elements of your toddler's play?

Sometimes the wish-fulfilling element of a toddler's play is to be like Mommy or Daddy; for example, to pretend to drive a car or go to work. The wish to grow up is deep rooted and strong.

Limits and Contradictions

The limit "Don't do it again" followed by "If you do it again" may reflect a mother's internal conflict about setting the limit. The expectation and plan for her toddler to do something she has just prohibited may influence her toddler to do it again. Preventing her toddler from doing what she has prohibited can reinforce the limit.

During a mothers' group discussion about setting limits, Cassie talked about her frustration with Jud. "I told Jud three times there is no drawing on the table. If you draw on the table one more time, I will take the crayons away. Just as I expected, he did it again." I proposed an alternative to consider: "While taking the crayons away, saying a version of the following might be clearer – There is no drawing on the table. I am not going to let you draw on the table; I will help you stop. You can have the crayons back when you are ready to draw on the paper." Cassie disagreed: "It would not be fair if I didn't tell him before I took the crayons away." I said, "Maybe you think the limit is unfair. Maybe you think it is unfair that you have more power than Jud or you are reminded of unfair limits when you were a little girl. Or it seemed unfair that your mother had more power than you." Cassie felt that many things were unfair to children. "I get to sleep with my husband, Jud sleeps alone. I get to drink wine, Jud doesn't. I guess I am remembering many feelings I had as a child. It is so hard to say no to Jud."

- What are some prohibitions or limits you set that seem unfair?
- How do the limits you set relate to your childhood?
- Which limits that you set are difficult for your child to accept? Why?

Positive Sense of Self and Disapproval

We can assume that when a toddler's behavior is disapproved, feelings of self-worth may momentarily be slightly diminished. We can also assume that mother–toddler attachment with its ongoing security of safety, loving feelings, and expectations of loving feelings returning after disapproval and angry feelings dissolve, protects toddlers from becoming overwhelmed by disapproval.

Disapproval of a specific behavior, rather than a criticism of the total child, helps a toddler maintain a positive sense of self when confronted with disapproval. A toddler's experience in our words might be, '*I am a good lovable person who did the wrong thing.*'

Mothers' Guilt

Many things trigger mothers' feelings of guilt. Since mothers' guilt is so common, though painful, it may serve a useful function. If not excessive, maternal guilt can signal awareness of a toddler's need. On the other hand, maternal guilt can be punishing self-criticism linked to childhood memories.

Ricky had worked hard since getting her MBA and had built a successful business. She loved her work and was eager to keep growing her business. Ricky was worried about 20-month-old Brianna's development. "She just doesn't talk or play like other children her age. Work is so important to me; it pulls me away from her. I feel so guilty. Even when I'm with Brianna, I'm not really with her. I make myself focus on her by telling her what to do so I won't think about work, but something is missing. When I'm at work I'm anxious and guilty about not being with her. Either way, I'm not with her. Brianna's suffering and I'm guilty."

I asked Ricky what it would be like, in moments when Brianna was contentedly playing, to think about something she needed to do at work. A memory was triggered. Ricky said, "I was so angry at my mother who was always working at home, right there behind a closed door. I cried for her, but she would not open the door. When I'm with Brianna, I'm trying so hard not to think about work that I'm not really with her; I'm talking at her and telling her what to do. Maybe I'm trying to not think about how angry I was at my Mom when she was right there, but not with me."

Ricky's efforts to manage her guilt about work were keeping her emotionally distant from Brianna. The entanglement of reactivated anger at her own mother fueled and perpetuated her guilt. With these insights, Ricky's focus shifted from guilty angry attending to Brianna, to emotional connecting. Brianna began to thrive.

- When have your feelings of guilt been useful?
- When have your feelings of guilt been self-punishing and entangled with childhood memories?

Separation and Reunion

Toddlers' distress reactions to separation can reach new heights during this phase of development. Toddlers increasingly struggle with the tensions between their own autonomy strivings and their attachment needs. They have learned from experience that they can get hurt. They have discovered how much they need their mothers. Toddlers this age have more angry interactions with their mothers, which also make separations fraught with fear: fear about losing Mommy's love. The developing expectation that loving feelings return when anger subsides can buffer the impact of angry interactions, but desperate reactions to separation may erupt.

Mother–toddler separations often get more attention than reunions, but both are important. Peggy and 20-month-old Bonnie walk Daddy to the elevator every morning when he leaves for work. He lifts Bonnie to press the button and kisses her. Bonnie giggles. Saying goodbye to Daddy is easy; it is a frequent routine and

Bonnie is staying with her mother. Reunions with Daddy at the end of the day when he returns home are difficult. Peggy explained, "Bonnie and I are happy playing in her room and my husband comes in. He has not seen her all day and arranges his schedule so they can play before dinner, but Bonnie won't play with him. I think the transition is hard for her."

When asked about establishing a reunion routine that might make the transition easier and more joyful for them all, Peggy said, "My mother was always so angry that my father was working all the time. We never had happy reunions. I remember one night my dad came home so late that my mom would not let me play with him. I was so angry at my mother. She was angry at my father and my father was angry at my mother. Everybody was angry. Bonnie needs to know I'm happy to see her Dad. We could run to the door together when he comes home. Bonnie could play with her father while I get dinner ready. Maybe I never did this before because I was stuck in my childhood memories without even knowing it."

Body and Mind Awareness

Diversity

Diversity within families and differences among families have been rapidly increasing during the last three decades. Toddlers' growing awareness of differences and similarities within their family and among people in their community, and what the differences mean, are influenced by many factors.

- What differences and similarities including sex, race, religion, language, and physical traits exist in your family?
- What differences and similarities have been talked about and have not been talked about?
- What differences and similarities do you think your toddler is aware of?

School programs are being developed to address diversities, affinities, exclusions, inclusions, and racism. There is significant controversy, little research, and strong feelings about what to include at each age. One finding is that children are aware of racial differences several years before parents want to talk about them. Children are aware of many things surrounding them before parents feel ready to talk about them.

Toddlers Learn About Differences

During the first three years, that is before children begin school, they learn a great deal explicitly and implicitly about differences and similarities among the people in their family and those around them. They learn from their own observations and from what they are told. Books and videos about different kinds of families, gender and race, pregnancy, donor egg and sperm, surrogacy, and adoption are available for pre-school age children. Some children's books may be useful to decide what you would like to talk about with your toddler.

- What similarities and differences in your family that have not been talked about yet do you imagine will be?
- What differences and similarities has your toddler pointed to or mentioned?
- What is included in your conversations about similarities and differences?

Just as all humans are unique, each family member has traits that are different from the others. Each has some traits that are the same as the others. Identifying similarities among family members highlights familial connectedness whether genetically determined or not. The ways in which individual differences are assimilated into or are alienated from the family culture can be a complex process.

Physical Traits

Olive, who had dark brown hair, was struggling because her daughter had bright red hair. "Where did she come from? She is not at all like me." By the time Olive had her fourth child with red hair, she identified her children as her own in part by the color of their hair. What had been alien had become more than familiar. For Olive, her children having red hair came to mean they were family.

Male or female is the first documented designation of your baby's similarity to or difference from you. When you learned that your baby was a boy or a girl, your reaction may have been influenced by what it means to you, your family, or in the world to be male or female. Your reaction may have been influenced by what it meant to you that your baby was the same sex as you or different.

Facial features, handedness, and eye color similarities and differences in families may be talked about. Specific traits like dimples may be identified. How people feel about the similarities and differences may be talked about less. Some striking similarities and differences may not be talked about at all. Understanding why may be important.

Fredricka was complaining about her mother-in-law: "She keeps repeating, 'Tim looks just like his father.' I think he also looks like me, but I don't say anything. He's 2 years old and ever since he was born, every time we see her, she keeps saying he looks exactly like his dad. I just realized, maybe she's not sure her son really is Tim's father so she keeps saying how much they look alike to reassure herself."

Georgina is an identical twin. Throughout her childhood, differences between her and her sister were important. Georgina explained, "Our differences were used to identify us. I was the smart one; my sister was the pretty one. I was the star athlete; my sister was the cheerleader captain and homecoming queen. She had a birthmark on her eye that our friends relied on to identify us; I wanted one. I was the thin one. When we were teenagers, my sister was hospitalized for anorexia. We wanted to be the same and we wanted to be different. We were very competitive, but it worked out for us. We each found different things we are good at. I frequently point out my sons' differences. They are clearly different; Maybe I don't need to keep telling them."

> • What do the similarities and differences between you and your toddler mean to you?
> • What do differences and similarities in your family mean to your toddler?

The similar and different physical traits, personality characteristics, abilities and disabilities, likes and dislikes within families – those that get talked about and those that do not – have many meanings.

Family Secrets

Every parent may have things in their past or current life that they would prefer never to talk about with their children or want to delay talking about for as long as possible. Some information may be embarrassing. Some things might be private.

Often children are aware when something important that surrounds them is not being talked about. They may experience the feelings but have no way to make sense of them. They may be unable to formulate a question, believe it is not okay to talk about, or have their own explanation that may be more disturbing than knowing the actuality.

> • What do you not want to talk about with your toddler?
> • What do you not want to talk about but you think your toddler is aware of?
> • What difficult topics have you and your toddler talked about?

Choosing what, when, and how potentially disturbing information is given to toddlers can be a challenge. Living with and keeping family secrets can be stressful and intensify disturbing feelings about the information. Providing information prematurely or inappropriately can also create problems. In general, talking about disturbing events that continue to reverberate in the family or currently surround toddlers can provide comfort and build a foundation for open communication.

Learning about potentially stressful information from you – your toddler's secure base, can provide the most comfort. Understanding your own feelings before talking to your toddler can enable you to destigmatize and de-catastrophize the information, formulate it in a way that can be meaningful to a toddler, and answer questions. Beginning conversations about prior marriage, surrogacy, adoption, donor egg and sperm, physical and emotional illness, death, or other life events that affect young children and their families can create relationships that promote adaptation and resilience when faced with life's inevitable difficulties.

Discovery of a Toddler's Mind

A mother-toddler group was meeting for the first time. Darcy described her 22-month-old daughter Millie: "She's just a happy baby. She doesn't understand anything. I don't think she has any thoughts or feelings yet." Darcy's description of Millie was strikingly different from the other mothers' descriptions of their toddlers. Week after week, Darcy was highly motivated to assert Millie's happiness and deny her developing mind; but it was not clear why. It was as though, for Darcy, not having any thoughts or feelings was required to be happy.

Millie had two mothers. Her other mother did not participate in the mothers' group and Darcy rarely talked about her. She was a lawyer at a large firm that Darcy had also worked at before maternity leave. Darcy had given birth to Millie and primarily took care of her. Darcy continued to insist, "Millie doesn't know anything. I'm going away next month. She won't even notice that I'm gone. I don't think she's that aware of anything; she's just a happy baby." I wondered whether Darcy also believed that Millie did not notice that she had two mommies and the other children that she knew had a Mommy and a Daddy.

A few weeks later, when the other women were describing their toddlers' typical oppositional behavior, Darcy's description of Millie slightly but meaningfully changed, "Millie never opposes me. She always wants what I want. She never has her own thoughts or feelings." Darcy was highlighting that Millie had the same thoughts and feelings she had, not that Millie did not have any thoughts or feelings. She indicated how she and Millie were different from the other mothers and children, but implied that she was being influenced by the other mothers. Mothers' group support paved the way for Darcy's self-questioning and interest in what motivated her conviction that Millie was unaware of everything.

Two weeks later Darcy began, "I don't know why I think Millie doesn't know anything and only thinks what I think. Why do I think she's just a baby?" I answered, "That is an important question. Who was the baby in your family?" Darcy quickly remembered, "My self-esteem is from my dad. He always said that I could do anything, be anything, and have anything I wanted. My mother always said that what I wanted didn't count. What I thought didn't matter. I was too young for everything. I was just dismissed." To connect Darcy's childhood memory to her view of Millie, I said, "Maybe your mother saw you as just a baby."

The following week Darcy told us that her view had changed. "Millie knows more than I thought. I realize she's more like the other toddlers. She needs me to tell her more about what's happening and what I think. I can influence her thoughts, but she also has her own thoughts." Darcy was describing the same experience with Millie that she was having with the mothers: Darcy had her own thoughts and was being influenced by their thoughts. She was like the other mothers in some ways, and different in others. Darcy now believed that Millie might miss her while she was away on vacation and planned to FaceTime with her. She realized that she had been treating Millie the way she described her mother treating her.

If Millie was dismissed as "just a baby," Darcy could more easily defer thinking about and talking to Millie about having two mommies. Darcy's awareness that Millie had her own thoughts and feelings and that she could influence what Millie thought made thinking and talking about having two mommies possible. Darcy began to notice Millie's reactions to daddies. They began to talk about the different kinds of families that were portrayed in picture books they began to read and in their everyday lives. Millie's awareness of having two mommies was now clear to Darcy. "I was afraid to talk to Millie about so many things; I was afraid about what she would think and feel. We are much closer now."

Emotion Regulation

Toddlers approaching 2 years have had significant experience regulating emotions. They have had rages, meltdowns, and temper tantrums, and they have recovered. They have felt angry, sad, and terrified, and they have been comforted. They have become out-of-control excited and calmed. They have felt embarrassed and jealous. Toddlers have been helped to identify emotions and re-regulate.

During nighttime dreams, the resources that are available while awake to cope with intense feelings and impulses are not available. While awake, a fierce tiger may lurk under the bed and be feared, but is manageable with Mommy's help; during a dream, it feels like the tiger is going to attack and there is no one to help.

Dreams

Sammy was 19 months. During his nighttime story, his mother Sophie cuddled him in his favorite blanket with little tigers on it. After the story, his father draped the tiger blanket over his head and shoulders, crawled around the room growling, and playfully nibbled at Sammy's toes. Sammy giggled and snuggled close to his mother. His father then swooped Sammy up into his arms, put him into his crib, and said, "Goodnight little tiger." He folded the tiger blanket and hung it on the chair next to Sammy's crib. Sammy protested, but quickly settled down to sleep. Three hours later, Sammy was screaming. Sophie lifted him out of his crib and Sammy cried, "Tigers coming, too many tigers."

Sophie immediately noticed the tiger blanket and remembered the growling and toe nibbling tiger play, Sammy's sleep protest, and his father's words "Goodnight little tiger" – all elements of Sammy's dream. Little tigers, mild protests, and loving play can trigger underlying ferocious feelings and be portrayed in a dream as frightening danger. Talking about dreams with toddlers can be helpful.

- What do you know about your toddler dreaming?
- What do you think is your toddler's sense of dreaming?

Explanations of Dreams

Explanations of dreams that can feel comforting include, dreams are stories you tell yourself while you are sleeping. Dreams can be happy, sad, scary, and sometimes silly stories. Everyone makes up their own dreams. Thoughts and feelings during the day may be hidden in your dreams at night. Your wishes and fears during the day are part of the stories you tell yourself in your dreams. We can talk about dreams. The empowering core of these ideas is that the dreamer creates the dream.

Play

Distinctive characteristics of toddler play are that it is enjoyable, spontaneous, and controlled by the toddler who is absorbed in it. While playing, toddlers learn cognitively, socially, physically, and emotionally. Whether playing with popular educational toys or sticks and stones in the park, toddlers learn about themselves and the world around them through play.

Aggression and Play

Hitting, kicking, and biting are typical for toddlers when they are angry, frustrated, frightened, or overstimulated. They are learning how to inhibit these impulses and instead use words to communicate how they feel, get what they want, resolve conflicts, and defend themselves. Aggressive play provides toddlers the opportunity to satisfy aggressive impulses that are otherwise unacceptable. '*I cannot hit Mommy, but I can hit the pillow.*' In addition to the meanings of aggressive play, there is inherent pleasure in vigorous, assertive physical action.

Kicking a ball, punching a blow-up clown, banging pegs, and a variety of water toys that squirt are forms of aggressive play. Pretend play scenarios can have aggressive themes: for example, crashing cars and fighting animals. Sometimes toddlers become overstimulated or frightened by aggressive play. Mothers have different thresholds for their toddlers' aggressive play. When aggressive play makes mothers feel uncomfortable, they may prohibit play that would benefit their children.

- What kind of aggressive play does your toddler like?
- What kind of aggressive play do you do together?
- What kind of aggressive play is too much for you or your toddler?

Pete was 18 months. When he played with the banging toy, his mother Connie stopped him and said, "too rough." When he attempted to hold on to a toy that was being grabbed by another child, she required him to relinquish it, "Be nice." When Pete wanted to play with a toy that another child wanted at the same time, she insisted that Pete wait. Connie described Pete as, "too aggressive."

During a heated mothers' group discussion about aggression, Connie's impromptu remark provided a way to begin to understand her reactions to Pete's vigorous play and self-assertiveness: "Pete has a huge penis. He never touches it, but someday he will discover it and be psyched. It's not how big it is that matters, it's what you do with it that counts." Connie's comment, which became a frequent refrain, triggered the other mothers' laughter, quips, and related memories.

Connie also described a concern. "In general Pete's too aggressive and I need to control him. But lately when another child approaches him, he just hands over the toy he is playing with. I'm worried; I'm not sure how to help him. I don't want him to be too aggressive, but I don't want him to be too passive. How can I help him?" The answer to Connie's question was embedded in her two separate but linked comments: one about penis size and one about aggression. I asked a surprising question: "I wonder what might be the connection between your reactions to Pete's 'huge' penis, and your view of him as 'too aggressive'?"

Connie and the other mothers in the group wanted to know what I thought. I answered in terms of feelings a "huge" penis might evoke. I said, "Sometimes a penis can seem dangerous and scary." Connie remembered, "I once had sex with a man with a huge penis and it hurt me."

When Connie became aware of her feelings of fear related to Pete's penis, which were based on memories, she became more comfortable with Pete's healthy aggression and he became more self-assertive.

Rough and Tumble

Rough and tumble play may become more vigorous during this phase of development. Its aggressive components may be more obvious. The combination of high-arousal fun, vigorous physicality, and controlled aggression with the safety of a trusted adult contributes to the universality of rough and tumble play and its repetition from one generation to the next.

- How does your toddler respond to rough and tumble play?
- What specifics of rough and tumble play are just right for you and your toddler? Which are too much? Which seem like too little?

Competition, Winning, and Losing

You may have begun to have some interactions with your toddler that include winning and losing games. During first games of competition together, you may have the impulse to either let your toddler win all of the time, some of the time, or never. The reasons for your decisions may be of interest. You may want to teach your toddler about the pleasures of winning or that it is okay to lose. Childhood memories may be activated.

- What kind of competition has your toddler experienced?
- How does your toddler react to winning and to losing?

Toddlers experience various forms of competition: some in play, some in every-day life. Toddlers with siblings may be inundated throughout their daily lives with passionate competitions for space on Mommy's lap, and rivalry for their parents' attention and love. You may believe that competition is an inborn human trait that can be promoted, squelched, or shaped by the environment. Your ideas may include aspects of competition you want to encourage and those you want to eliminate. You may be unsure.

As play with friends increases, various kinds of competition arise, including who goes first, whose choice of book is read, who gets the chocolate cupcake, who gets the strawberry, or all cupcakes may be kept the same in an attempt to avoid competition. Your thoughts about competition, winning, and losing may change as your toddler develops.

Learning

Toddlers are learning constantly. Motivated by intense curiosity, they learn by trial and error, observing and imitating, and teaching–learning interactions. Mothers do a great deal of the teaching, and in a variety of ways monitor their toddler's cognitive, emotional, social, and physical learning.

Comparing Children

One way a mother assesses her toddler's learning and her own teaching is by making comparisons between herself and other mothers, and between her child and other children. Making comparisons is common, may be universal, and can be useful.

Mothers are often self-critical about making comparisons. A mother's comparisons among her own children or between her own and others are potentially valuable ways to monitor baby and toddler development and intervene early when needed. What is disturbing sometimes about making comparisons are the underlying meanings of the comparisons, which often include painful feelings and childhood memories.

During a mother-toddler group, Josephine observed, "Leena is the oldest in the group and she doesn't talk anywhere near as much as the others. I know I shouldn't compare her. My mother always compares me to my cousin. It's awful. But this is different. I am worried about Leena; maybe she should have a speech evaluation."

- When has making comparisons been useful, when not?

Learning by Helping

Children 2 or 3 years old are highly motivated to help with everyday activities. The tasks are of interest, but the feeling '*I am helping Mommy with this important job!*' is central to the experience. For example: helping to put toys away at the end of the day, and washing toys can be fun for toddlers.

Cooking together can become a favorite mother–toddler activity. For toddlers, eating something they have helped to cook can be especially delicious. Simple tasks, for example peeling a hard-boiled egg, or adding several pieces of sliced banana in a special design to a bowl of yogurt or oatmeal can be fun. Helping to cook can increase foods that are liked.

- What activities does your toddler help with?

Body Care

Toddlers begin to participate in their own body care: washing their tummies during baths, hand washing at the sink, a turn at teeth brushing, nose blowing, and maybe shampoo lathering. Your toddler has learned a great deal about peeing and pooping. Most important, your toddler has learned about the body sensations while peeing and pooping, your interest, and your related interactions with each other including words, shared attention, and body care. Your toddler may have begun to signal you that poop is coming. A potty will be the next step.

- What body care does your toddler participate in?
- What interactions do you and your toddler have about poop?
- What interactions do you and your toddler have about pee?

Holding On and Letting Go

As toddlers approach 2 years old, their abilities to hold on and to let go increase. Catching a ball and throwing it, filling and emptying a pail, are games of holding on and letting go. In the same way, toddlers become able to hold on to pee and poop, and to let them go. You might see your toddler discover the power and pleasure of starting and stopping a urine stream or going to a special place to make a poop. These are among the signs of readiness to introduce the potty. Your toddler beginning to announce a poop is coming is a clear sign of readiness. For some toddlers, introducing the potty can promote a leap in readiness to learn about peeing and pooping in the potty.

- What signs of readiness to introduce the potty to your toddler have you seen?

Learning About the Potty

Potties that are on the floor enable toddlers to get on and off without assistance. While seated, their feet are positioned securely on the floor. Feelings of safety and autonomy are both promoted.

Part of the meaning of poop is that it is highly valued, yet it is discarded. It produces a pleasurable body sensation, and a recognizable odor. It is the toddler's poop, it comes out of the toddler's body, but is not to be touched, although sometimes they try. While there are some hazards for babies and toddlers in bathrooms, they are established as safe. A multitude of contradictions are attached to poop and learning about the potty.

> • What do you do to promote feelings of safety for your toddler in the bathroom?

Wynn thought it was the right time to buy a potty for Clara, 22 months. They unwrapped it together and placed it in the bathroom next to the tub. As Wynn was filling the tub with water, she suggested that Clara sit on the potty before her bath. Clara wanted a different first step to learn about her potty. With uncertainty about the new contraption and an assertion of autonomy, she said, "No Mommy! Kitty Cat sit on the potty." Both Wynn and Clara praised Kitty Cat.

Sitting on the potty, holding on to poop and pee, and letting them go into the potty are up to the toddler. The primary motivations are to please you, curiosity, and a sense of mastery. The first step is to feel comfortable on the potty. For Clara, Kitty Cat needed to be comfortable first. Pretend play with dolls or stuffed animals on the potty or with toy figures and toy potties can become part of each phase of learning to use the potty.

Mothers Talk About the Potty

Mothers talk about teaching their toddlers to use the potty. There are books for mothers and books for toddlers. Mothers may have personal priorities. A mother's priorities and approach may be based on professional opinion, a friend's advice, or her own experiences.

The specific interactions of each mother and her toddler that lead to learning to use the potty are unique but share basic principles. Many things contribute to the details: cultural standards, the physiologic rhythms of the toddler, ages and sex of siblings, the toddler's medical history, past and present emotional stresses, and mothers' thoughts and feelings about the process. Ultimately, what will be critical about learning to use the potty are the teaching–learning interactions between mother and toddler. The beginning phase has been described. Following chapters will have examples of the ways in which the process progresses.

Learning to use the potty is a meaningful developmental achievement. The achievement includes the autonomous body control the toddler acquires, the recognition that the potty is the socially agreed upon place for poop and pee, and a decision to do it and become a member of the community of older children and adults who use toilets. Learning to use the potty is a step-by-step collaborative process filled with Mommy's support and congratulations, and a toddler's autonomy and pride.

Transition from Crib to Bed

A main concept related to the transition from crib to bed for both a toddler and the mother is that the feelings of coziness and security that have been established in the crib transfer to the bed. Two main features of the transition are the comfort of knowing that, '*Mommy is close while I am sleeping, and separation from Mommy during sleep is followed by reunion upon awakening.*'

Morning reunion routines when a baby sleeps in a crib require Mommy coming to the baby. When a toddler sleeps in a bed, morning reunions transition to the toddler coming to Mommy. Morning reunion routines help to ensure that when a toddler wakes and gets out of bed, either in the morning, afternoon, or middle of the night, they come directly to Mommy. At whatever exact age between around 1½ and 3 years you decide to have your toddler sleep in a bed, these elements are central. Once the decision about a bed is made, it can be helpful to disassemble the crib in front of your toddler and store it, even if for a short time until another baby uses it. The communication that this is the right time can be clear and a comfort.

The meaning to mothers of their toddlers sleeping in a bed can be significant. The bed can be a symbol of loss: "It's so sad, I no longer have a baby." If the crib is viewed as a physical restraint, fears can be triggered by the freedom of a bed. A toddler's bed can evoke a variety of thoughts, feelings, and memories.

Mothers' Childhood Memories

Memories Related to Poop

Mothers usually do not have childhood memories about learning to use the potty, but they may have related memories. Flora had a vivid teenage memory that she described during a mothers' group. "I was walking home from school with my best friend Patsy and we were hysterical laughing. I had my period and needed to pee. By the time I got home my panties and dress were a mess. Patsy and I were still laughing when we walked in the door; my mother was furious. She thought it was disgusting that we were laughing, 'Look at you; you have blood and pee all over and you are laughing about it.' The more she yelled, the more we laughed. Now I think it's disgusting when Morris poops in the bath. He thinks it's funny and tries to catch the floating poop. I guess dirty and messy can be funny."

- What ideas and memories related to poop influence interactions with your toddler?

Sibling Memories

Sometimes mothers are in conflict about what they think is best for their child and what is best for their relationship with a mommy-friend. Lexington thought that a one-hour playdate was optimal for 20-month-old Seth, but she did not want to appear rejecting of her friend even though after an hour the children's play always turned into fighting.

Mothers' group discussion about Lexington's conflict revealed its connection to childhood fights with her older sister: "If I wanted to play with my sister, everything needed to be her way. She didn't care about what I wanted, but maybe my friend will." Lexington's insight enabled her to come to an agreement with her friend to shorten the playdates.

- What sibling memories stand out for you?
- What interactions with your toddler are connected to sibling memories?

Memories of the Silent Treatment

Skyler described what happened when she prevented Peter, 22 months, from running into the street: "Peter got angry and started to hit me. I held his hands tighter and then he bit me. I was very angry; I grabbed his arm and yelled at him. He started to cry and then wanted me to hold him. I was too angry. I didn't even want to talk to him." At this moment Skyler remembered, "Whenever my mother is angry, she gives me the silent treatment." The link between her memory about her mother's silent treatment and her thought, "I didn't even want to talk to him" was easily recognizable. Skyler noted, "Sometimes I give the silent treatment to my husband and it enrages him. I certainly don't want to do it to Peter."

The idea that children sometimes learn the silent treatment from their own mothers helped to temper Skyler's rage at Peter and helped her to modify her interactions with her husband. Skyler also became curious about how her mother had learned the silent treatment. Skyler's expectations of rupture and repair cycles of loving feelings without the silent treatment helped recovery from angry feelings with Peter to go more smoothly.

Painful childhood memories about the silent treatment from parents and siblings were described by the other group mothers. Vera remembered, "I don't know how I learned to give the silent treatment to my little sister. I was so mean. I just ignored her and pretended I didn't hear her. She cried, but I kept doing it. I still feel guilty about it. When my husband doesn't answer me right away, I get so angry. It feels like he's giving me the silent treatment, but sometimes he's just absorbed in a book. Maybe I'm hypersensitive."

Frightening Memories

As Roberta entered the mother–toddler room she was reprimanding 2-year-old Jade. No sooner had we settled, one by one the children came to their mothers crying because they had been hit by Jade. The hitting happened so unexpectedly it was difficult to anticipate, or to see what had triggered it. Roberta's warnings to Jade had been unsuccessful. The mothers were sympathetic to Roberta, but they were also angry.

Roberta was perplexed by Jade's seemingly unprovoked "aggressive behavior" and frustrated by her own inability to "discipline" her. "I've tried everything: time-outs, no iPad, I even threatened to take her special teddy-bear away. I would never really do that." Roberta was focused on discipline and punishments. Another mother in the group asked, "What do you think is going on?"

To understand more about what might be motivating Jade to hit, I asked Roberta about Jade's play at home. Roberta described the details: "Hide-and-seek is great. I often hide behind a door, and when Jade enters the room I jump out at her and shout 'boo.' She always startles. I played it with my dad. Jade plays tickle torture with her dad. He runs after her, catches her, and tickles her while she squeals." The videos they watched included a selection of cartoons and fairytales often frightening to 2-year-olds.

The following elements of Roberta's description were significant, "She always startles, I played it with my dad, and tickle-torture." A startle is a noticeable indication of hyperarousal, tickle-torture alludes to pain and horror, and 'I played it with my dad' suggests that childhood memories were being relived. I offered the following child development information: "These sound like exciting games that sometimes scare little children." Roberta quickly disagreed and contradicted me: "Jade never gets scared." With mock surprise and disbelief, I challenged Roberta, "Really? Never?"

I had gently confronted Roberta's denial of Jade's fear, and awakened childhood memories that flooded out. "My father wanted a son. He taught me to be tough like he was, not scared like my mother. He taught me to do scary things like climb trees and ride my bike down a steep hill with no hands. We always watched horror movies together. At the amusement park near our house we went on the big roller coaster and sneaked around the haunted house avoiding the moving skeletons and booby traps. My dad always got me past the ticket collectors because he lied about my age."

Recounting memories may have triggered remnants of Roberta's scared feelings. I said, "It seems like appearing not scared and sharing frightening experiences with your father helped you to feel loved and accepted by him. I wonder whether Jade might be feeling some of the same things." This was a new way for Roberta to think about her memories, but it seemed to strike a chord.

The following child development information emphasized an aspect of Jade's experience, of which Roberta had been unaware: "Sometimes children hit when they are frightened. Punishments won't help them to stop hitting if they're scared. Acknowledging scared feelings, feeling protected, and safe might."

As we began to consider the activities and situations that might be frightening to Jade, and other group mothers described their toddlers' fears, a distant memory of Roberta's began to emerge. "I just remembered, when I was a little girl I had a music box with a twirling ballerina. It was kept on a high shelf in my bedroom: it was rarely taken down. I never played with it. It was fragile and delicate. I remember the beautiful music."

At the same time the music box memory was coming into focus, Roberta began to recognize moments when Jade was scared. She began to limit the frightening videos and modified the scary games. She also began to help Jade talk about her scared feelings. By the next week, the hitting had stopped. The joy returned to the group and the warm support among the mothers was restored. The music box memory that had remained in the shadows emerged with all its delicate details. It represented the little girl who on the surface appeared brave and tough but did have frightening feelings that needed to be kept far away, on a high shelf, out of reach, and out of memory.

Highlights: 18 to 24 Months

As toddlers approach their 2-year-old birthdays, many glimmerings of the next year appear: language acquisition accelerates, learning to use the potty has been achieved or continues, play with peers increases. A self with strong wishes, thoughts, feelings, and intentions is seen. Abilities and vulnerabilities emerge. Mother–toddler conflicts intensify. In a mother's words, "For moms whose lives are like drinking from a firehose, mothers talking to each other is lifesaving."

---

12 24 to 30 Months

Mommy-friends

"My sister was my only mommy-friend when Christine was little. Our mother died when I was 14 and I had to take care of my sister. I protected her from my grandmother, who hit me all the time with a belt, or whatever else she could grab. I believed it was making me strong, so I thought it was okay. As soon as we could, my sister and I got good jobs, saved enough money to move to New York, and got married. Our babies were born a few months apart. Since I had experience with babies, my sister called me every day for help. I really helped her. We talked to each other all the time and saw each other as much as we could. She had many questions and I felt confident. I knew about babies and little children. I knew how to connect with them.

"We started dressing our girls alike, and each time I visited her I stopped at a store and bought them matching outfits. We sat on the floor and ate cookies, the girls in their matching outfits. It's like we created a beautiful scene of how life could be. It's wonderful to remember. We never said it out loud, but I realize now that we both agreed we would not raise our children the way we were raised."

Smiling with delight, and a sparkle in her eyes, Felicia described many details about her visits with her sister. It was as though, while sitting in the middle of a group of mothers and their 2-year-olds in New York City, a thousand miles away from her painful childhood, Felicia was experiencing the joy and satisfaction of the better life she had envisioned with her baby and began to create with her sister; her mommy-friend.

Mother–Child Interaction

During this phase of development, toddlers' love and affection blossom. Their kisses and caresses can be exquisitely tender. In moments, evidence of their capacity for empathy is apparent. Toddlers 24 to 30 months have strong opinions and intentions. Their sense of self is strengthening. Angry interactions can escalate. At times toddlers cling close and at others run away. It is a continuing time of extreme contrasts.

- What are the most pleasurable interactions with your 2-year-old?
- What are the most stressful interactions?

DOI: 10.4324/9781003352549-13

Language Development

At this age, mother–toddler interactions become increasingly verbal. At times your toddler's words may be crystal clear and at other times incomprehensible. Other people may find it impossible to understand your toddler. This can be influenced by your toddler's inarticulate speech and by the listener's motivation to understand. At times, you may translate; at other times, not being understood may motivate clearer communication.

- How would you describe your toddler's ability to talk?
- How would you describe your toddler's use of language to identify feelings, communicate wishes, talk about ideas?

Mothers sometimes worry about how frustrating it must be for their toddlers to not be understood. Another interpretation is that even adults who speak the same language struggle to understand each other. Toddlers may be having this experience for the first time, but conversations that include misunderstandings and struggling to be understood occur lifelong. Toddlers are beginning to learn that understanding others and being understood is a process between people talking, listening, misunderstanding, and trying to understand each other.

Separation and Loss

While toddlers have had many experiences with separations and reunions, they are also aware of how small and vulnerable they are. They have had everyday bumps and bruises, maybe some more significant accidents, and may have had experiences of loss: loss of a special toy, death of a person or pet, or the loss of a babysitter, nanny, or friend. Losses can intensify separation reactions. A toddler's grief reaction to a loss may not be easily recognizable.

- What experiences has your toddler had that intensify reactions to separations? How does play about separation help?
- What reactions do you have to separation that make separations from your toddler more difficult?

Intergenerational Loss

Experiences of loss and separation can reverberate for generations. Riley told this intergenerational story about separation: "When my grandmother was 8 years old she traveled with her father, mother, and brother to the United States. When they arrived at Ellis Island, my grandmother was diagnosed with chickenpox and could not enter. She was quarantined alone for ten days in the infirmary. I was horrified to hear this story about an 8-year-old with chickenpox, separated from her family. I imagined how frightening this would be; but my grandmother told me that she was never scared. She said the nurses were very nice and it was fine. I thought my grandmother needed to remember it this way to cope.

"My mother told me that she was always left alone when she was too young and that my grandmother could not understand why my mother always cried. My mother was sent to sleep-away camp every year beginning when she was 6. She cried all the time, and my grandmother would not take her home. My mother did the opposite with me. She never did anything without me. She refused to let me have sleep-overs with friends and would not let me go to sleep-away camp. It seems that my grandmother was traumatized by separation, but has no memory of being afraid. My grandmother left my mother alone prematurely and my mother remembers her fear and anger, and never let me separate from her. I'm not sure what I want to do with Layla. Right now, she's in daycare two days a week. When my husband and I go out for the evening she always has the same babysitter. Separations go easy. I am very different from my mother and my grandmother."

Layla's reflections prompted the mothers' group discussion that followed. Casey said, "My husband and I have Wednesday date-nights and go out several hours on Saturday afternoons. I think it's important for our relationship. Either my mother or the babysitter stay with Xander and Hudson. My husband and I are planning a five-day vacation without the children. My mother will stay with them and the babysitter will help. The children know them both well. If needed we will come home sooner, but I think five days will be fine. Xander is 2½ and Hudson is 5 and they will be together." Eve said, "I go to work every day. That's a lot of time away from Finn. My husband and I go out some evenings, but I'm not ready to take a separate vacation. Vacations are precious family time for us." Payton's descriptions of separations were different: "Murphy has a hard time with separations. Her grandparents don't babysit. I rotate between two women Murphy knows quite well. We go out occasionally, but not on a regular basis."

- How do you decide how much separation is the right amount for you and the right amount for your toddler?

Loss and Grief

Judy announced during a mother-toddler group that Nora, her 30-month-old son Derrick's nanny since his birth, had quit. Judy was angry and felt betrayed. "I have a more than full-time job. I thought Nora loved Derrick. If that's how she really feels, I'm glad to be rid of her; but Derrick is so difficult since she left and the new nanny came. He's so angry and clingy to me. He screams during separations from me and pushes the new nanny away. He hides until I'm screaming in desperation to find him." When Judy was asked what she said to Derrick about Nora leaving, she said, "Nothing. Talking to Derrick about Nora leaving will only make things worse, he's so angry. If he wanted to talk about her he would. Anyway, there's nothing to talk about."

The other mothers suggested to Judy that maybe Derrick's behavior was linked not only to Nora leaving, but also to the fact that nothing had been said. They suggested things she might say if she changed her mind but Judy rejected their suggestions: "I told you, there is nothing to say." I said the following to address both Derrick's and Judy's grief underlying their anger: "It sounds like the thought of Derrick feeling sad about Nora leaving is so painful that you are focusing on angry feelings and angry behavior."

The following week Judy told the mothers' group that Derrick's behavior had become "more difficult." She said, "I decided to talk to Derrick about Nora. I had to try something; he was impossible." Judy told us about their conversation: "'I wonder what you are thinking about Nora. I guess you miss her. We haven't seen her for a long time. She doesn't work here anymore. I probably should have said something sooner, but I was too angry.' Derrick began to sob. I felt so terrible for him. For the first time he was crying in grief like a grown-up. I did not realize that a child could have such intense, real feelings of loss."

The next day Derrick asked his mother if the scrape on Nora's knee was better. The last time Derrick had seen Nora her knee was covered with a large bandage. The injury had occurred when Nora tripped over Derrick's firetruck that had been left in the hall. Derrick's mother reassured him, "Yes, Nora's knee is all better. Nora leaving had nothing to do with that accident. She left for personal grown-up reasons." Children may be vulnerable to thinking bad things are their fault. Talking to Derrick about Nora opened the conversation and helped Derrick to ask about Nora's sore knee.

For a while, Derrick and his mother talked about Nora; the games they had played and the books they had read. Shared memories of love, loss, happiness, sadness, and anger were created together. A distinction between family and non-family was made. Nora leaving her job for grown-up personal reasons was emphasized. Derrick's "impossible difficult behavior" ended. In a short while, they only talked about Nora on occasion.

About six months later, some light was shed on Judy's reaction when Nora quit. Penelope, another woman in the mothers' group, had a dog that was very old, sick, and in pain. Penelope explained, "Over the weekend my husband and I decided it was time for our dog to die. Before my husband and I took Scooter to the vet, we told the children that it was time for Scooter to die; they would never see him again. Grandma and grandpa would stay with them; Daddy and I would be with Scooter when he dies. When we come home, we will have a funeral. The funeral will be a time for us to talk about Scooter, and light a memory candle.

"At the funeral, we told the children that Scooter died peacefully; we were with him when his body stopped working. We all told stories about Scooter and lit the candle. We put Scooter's leash, collar, and bed away. It was very sad, but it was the best goodbye for the family. We cried, laughed, and then had a special snack. The kids, 2½ and 6, were sad but okay."

Judy recalled the loss of her own dog when she was a little girl. "My experience was totally different. I remember going to sleep-away camp for one month when

I was 11; when I came home, my dog was not there. I was never told what happened and it was not okay to ask. I thought maybe she was hit by a car, ran away, or was given away. I guess when Nora left, my memory about my dog and not talking about it was influencing me not talking to Derrick. I didn't think about it then."

Judy's memory and her insight about repeating with Derrick what she remembered her parents having done with her promoted her conviction about the importance of talking about loss.

Underlying Meanings of Behavior

Behavior can be understood in multiple ways. What is observed can be described, what motivated the behavior can be identified, and the feelings that accompany the behavior can be put into words. Helping toddlers to think about the meanings of their own behavior can promote their ability to regulate emotions, enable them to feel understood, promote their capacity for self-understanding, and increase their empathy for others.

Understanding the meaning of a toddler's behavior and putting the meaning into words can be the first step towards influencing the behavior. For example: a toddler who cries when getting a haircut may be reacting to losing a precious part of the body or being touched by a stranger. A toddler hitting may be motivated by anger, fear, or self-protection.

> - When does understanding the underlying meaning of your toddler's behavior influence your response?
> - When does what motivated your toddler's behavior not matter?
> - When does identifying and accepting how your toddler feels help to change the behavior? When does it not?

You may be critical of the underlying thoughts or feelings that motivate your toddler's behavior and, in addition to wanting to change behavior, you may want to change your toddler's thoughts or feelings. Changing someone's thoughts or feelings is different from changing behavior. For example, Georgia had begun to pick her nose. Her mother Dyanna was embarrassed, thought it was disgusting, and wanted Georgia to stop. "I keep telling her it's disgusting, but she keeps doing it." Becky, another mother in the group suggested, "Maybe it feels good to her; she doesn't want to think it's disgusting."

Summer had a similar experience: "Archer loves to go to the playground. We go almost every day. Monday and Tuesday it rained, and yesterday I couldn't go. Archer kept asking and I kept saying, 'don't ask me again'; but what I really meant was, 'I don't like to keep saying no, stop wanting to go.' Finally, I said, 'I know you really like the playground and want to go every day. The playground is so much fun. You are very disappointed that we cannot go today.' I couldn't believe it, but once I acknowledged and accepted his feelings rather than trying to change them, he stopped asking." Dyanna added, "I guess it feels good to Georgia to pick her nose, I did it when I was little, and I was so ashamed. My mother always said that I was disgusting. Maybe I will tell Georgia she can do it in private."

Belle had a different experience trying to influence Gavin's thoughts and feelings. "Last week when Gavin hit Henry, he told me that he did it because Henry was going to try to take his car away. I said, 'You know there is no hitting. I can understand why you thought that Henry wanted to grab the car, it's a great car.'"

- When do you try to change your toddler's thoughts or feelings? What happens?

When trying to change behavior, acknowledging and accepting thoughts and feelings may be helpful. When trying to change thoughts and feelings, acknowledging and accepting existing thoughts and feelings can be essential.

Agreeing to disagree, that is acknowledging your and your toddler's different thoughts and feelings may be a first step. For example, after witnessing a fight between her mother and father, Luna, who was 2½, told her mother, "I don't want to get married." Her mother said, "I think you do not like it when Daddy and I fight. We had a loud, angry disagreement. Now it's over. I like being married."

Parents Fighting in Front of Toddlers

During a mother-toddler group, Penny described a "huge" fight she and her husband had. "We were screaming at each other and said some very mean things. My parents fought all the time. It was awful, I needed to take sides. I wonder if Kelly felt she needed to take sides. I always said I would never fight in front of my children like my parents did; for the moment Kelly was completely out of my mind."

Malinda added, "I never saw my parents fight, then one day they said they were getting divorced. I'm not sure what I think." Malinda's comment triggered a discussion about the rupture and repair cycles in all love relationships: the fighting and the making up, and the ruptures that do not get repaired. We also talked about the different ways couples fight: yelling, mocking, criticizing, physical aggression, and their differing impacts on toddlers. The value of talking with toddlers about parents' fighting and the importance of acknowledging how toddlers feel when their parents fight was agreed. Many childhood memories that included feeling frightened, needing to take sides, and feeling responsible for parents' fights were described.

- When do you fight in front of your toddler?
- How does your toddler react?
- What do you say to your toddler after a fight?

Other situations, in addition to parents fighting, may put children in a position to "take sides." For example, asking "Who do you want to carry you?" can mean "Who do you love more?" When parents ask "Who do you want to read to you?", they may wish to communicate that we both want to read, but sometimes the children feel neither Mommy nor Daddy wants to read. Asking children to choose between Mommy and Daddy can have many meanings and influence children in different ways.

> • When is choosing between Mommy and Daddy useful for your toddler? When is it not?

Dangerous Behavior

Toddlers may do or attempt to do dangerous things. Their ability to assess danger is limited. Sometimes toddlers may do dangerous things to prove to themselves that they will not get hurt. Their motivation to prove they are safe may intensify when they feel threatened. For example, Tucker was 27 months. His mother Valentina explained, "Tucker does so many dangerous things. No matter what I say, he won't stop. Yesterday he kept trying to climb onto the kitchen counter and I kept telling him, 'It's too dangerous; you will break your neck.' As I stopped him, and he wrestled to get free he said, 'Don't worry Mommy, I won't break my neck.' Maybe he was trying to reassure himself." Hazel, another mother in the group, said, "Gianna won't hold my hand when we cross the street. She fights to get away. I tell her she could get hit by a car. I think I get so scared that I frighten her to get her to hold my hand, but it seems to have the opposite effect. She struggles to get free. Maybe I should tell her, I'm keeping her safe by holding her hand."

> • When does your toddler do something dangerous to cope with feeling scared?

Aubrey added, "When I reprimand Cooper, he laughs at me. It seems like he is contemptuous of me, but maybe he laughs because I frighten him. I can't believe he is scared of me. I remember being afraid of my mother, but I was older, and she was witch-like scary."

> • When does your toddler laugh when scared?

It may be difficult to imagine that your toddler could be afraid of you. Recognizing when your toddler is afraid can be useful.

Apologies

Toddlers are continuing to learn about apologies: accepting apologies and making them. Their capacity for remorse is developing. Being self-critical about something they have done is part of the process. One way toddlers learn about apologies and feeling sorry about something they have done is from their mothers. Cecilia described her interaction with Winston: "I was so angry. Winston is almost 2½. He filled the toilet with toilet paper and playdough and tried to flush it. He knows that the toilet is for pee and poop. He's learning to use the potty. The toilet got totally clogged and flooded the bathroom. I yelled at him, grabbed him by the arm, and dragged him to his room. He cried almost in disbelief and said, 'Mommy you hurt me!' He looked terrified. I felt so sorry. My apology was different than when I inadvertently bump into him and say I'm sorry, or when I say I'm sorry you don't like the dinner, you can have fruit and yogurt. This time I said I was wrong. I was angry, but I should not have yelled so loud or grabbed his arm so hard. I think he understood that I knew I was wrong and that I felt sorry."

Delores added, "I can understand why you got so angry, and I think I understand that Winston filling the toilet was related to his learning to use the potty. In a way he was pretending to poop in the toilet by filling it with paper and playdough. It may have been his way of practicing."

For some mothers, apologizing to their children is a frequent communication. For example, during the middle of a mother-toddler group, Viviana said to Griffin, as she restrained him, "I'm sorry but you cannot write on the wall." I commented, "I noticed you apologized to Griffin for telling him that he cannot write on the wall and for stopping him." Viviana explained, "I do always apologize. My mother never apologizes for anything. When I was 12 years old she cut my hair so short. I hated it. She said it would just be a trim and she never apologized for that or for anything. I'm still angry at her. I always apologize for everything; even when it's not my fault. I know I'm doing the right thing stopping Griffin." I said, "It sounds like you are making up for all the apologies that were not made to you and all the apologies you may think you owe."

Many examples followed. Logan added, "The other day Mac stepped on my foot and he said, 'sorry mommy.' I guess he's learning."

- When do you apologize to your toddler?
- When does your toddler apologize?

Body and Mind Awareness

A mother's attention to the underlying meanings of her toddler's behavior can promote her toddler's growing awareness of thoughts and feelings, one's own and those of others. This developmental process, thinking about thinking and feeling, is called reflective functioning or mentalization. A mother's recognition and validation of the thoughts and feelings that motivate her own and her toddler's behavior are entwined with her toddler's developing reflective functioning, a valuable mental process leading to emotion regulation, empathy, and the security of attachments.

Truth-telling

Truth-telling is a value shared in most families. Mothers teach their children the importance of telling the truth and are disapproving when their children have lied. However, sometimes what appears to be a toddler's lie can be understood as the expression of a wish. A question mothers know the answer to may be a perfect set-up for such a "lie."

Greta walked into the kitchen and saw a big puddle on the floor. She asked Lance, "Did you make pee-pee on the floor?" Lance said, "No Mommy." Greta said, "You are lying? There is no lying allowed." Another way to understand Lance's answer to the disapproving accusation is that he wished he had not made pee-pee on the floor because he wanted his mother's approval and was self-disapproving of peeing on the floor.

A distinction between narrative truth and historical truth may be useful in this situation. It was easy to verify that the historical truth was that Lance had urinated on the floor, but his wish that was revealed in his "lie," that is his narrative truth, may have been more important to focus on: "I know you are learning to make pee-pee in the potty. Sometimes people make mistakes." Or, another scenario: "I know you are learning to make pee-pee in the potty, but I think you were angry that I did not let you play with the water, so you made pee-pee on the floor. Pee-pee goes in the potty, even when you are angry." Mothers' disapproval of the behavior is important. Acknowledging and supporting a toddler's motivation to do what Mommy wants and the complexity of thoughts and feelings that motivate behavior can promote learning the behavior, feelings of self-worth, and truth-telling.

Body Likes and Dislikes

A mother's attitudes about her toddler's body can influence her child. Timmy, Pete's brother, who was described earlier, was 29 months and had been pooping in the potty for the last three months. Connie explained why he was still wearing diapers: "Timmy always tells me when he wants to make a poop and I take him to the potty, but he won't pee in the potty. Maybe it's because he has such a small penis compared to his brother Pete. I'm not sure how to help him. Maybe he's embarrassed." At this moment, Timmy approached his mother and said, "Pee-pee Mommy." Connie asked, "Did you make pee-pee in your diaper or do you want to make it in the potty?" Timmy repeated, "Pee-pee Mommy." Connie asked again, "Do you need your diaper changed?" Timmy insisted with more urgency, "Pee-pee Mommy." Finally, Connie took Timmy to the bathroom to change his diaper, which was now wet.

When Connie returned to the mother-toddler group, some of the other mothers described their surprise at her timing and how they drop everything to get their children to the potty fast. One mother said, "I think it's better not to move too fast, it helps them learn to hold it." Responding to Connie's comment about Timmy's "small" penis and remembering her response to her other son Pete's "huge" penis, I said, "It seems like it's hard for you to imagine Timmy might need to make a big pee-pee urgently with such a little penis. I think to Timmy his penis feels big and powerful." At this moment Timmy approached his mother again and said, "Pee-pee Mommy." This time, Connie took him immediately to the potty and he urinated in it. They returned to the group both appearing proud and very pleased. Three weeks later Connie told us, "Timmy is wearing underpants today. My ideas about his penis being little changed. I think when you said his penis feels big and powerful to him and he came right to me, my feelings changed. I actually liked that idea."

Haley added, "After our discussion I realized that my attitude about Gwen's birthmark may make her self-conscious about it. I wish I could get over it; my husband doesn't even notice it. Sometimes it's all I see. I would like to have it removed, but my husband won't agree. I'm not sure what Gwen thinks about it. It's right on the side of her face. Sometimes people ask about it. Sometimes children stare or try to touch it. We have not talked about it with Gwen yet. Maybe we should."

As Haley and her husband began to talk to Gwen about her birthmark, it became less prominent in Haley's mind. She agreed with her husband to wait until Gwen was a teenager to decide with her about cosmetic surgery.

Mothers have things they like and things they do not like about their own bodies and about their toddlers' bodies. Many factors contribute to personal meanings including cultural ideals in ads and films.

- What impact do you think your attitudes about your toddler's body have on your toddler, or will have?

Toddlers are examined, weighed, and measured. In many ways their bodies are evaluated. Toddlers may hear adults criticize their own bodies and talk about diets and surgeries to enhance them. Adult conversations can have an impact on children even when it looks as if they are not paying attention. A main feature of a toddler's body is that it is growing bigger, stronger, and faster.

Emotion Regulation

Life's Big Questions

Toddlers are beginning to grapple with life's big questions. They are aware of natural phenomena that cannot be controlled, are sometimes frightening, and whose explanations are complicated. Day changes into night, thunder booms, big waves noisily crash on the beach, mommies get pregnant and babies are born. Flowers bloom and die. Toddlers begin to wonder about death. There are everyday opportunities to have conversations that lay a foundation for open, truthful information about death. Hearing about disturbing facts of life from their mothers, with all the comfort and security provided, paves the way for resilience when the harsh realities of life are experienced.

During a mother-toddler group about toddlers' emerging ideas about death, Paisley said, "Last week, when Ace was playing in the park, we saw a small dead mouse. Ace said, 'Mommy the little cat is not moving.' Something must have caught his attention. I told him the mouse was dead. I explained that dead means the body stopped working. I think this was a good experience for Ace. I want him to learn about death from me. When we got home, Ace was very happy to see our cat Jingles and told his father that we saw a dead mouse in the park. Ace said, 'The mouse couldn't move, his body stopped working.' Ace repeated to his father what I had told him. I was glad Ace talked about it with his father. When I was growing up, death could never be talked about and it made me very scared."

Talking is a major way in which feelings are processed and worries are soothed. When talking to your toddler about things you believe could be disturbing, knowing your own anxieties and how they are linked to reactivated childhood memories can be useful. An adult perspective can be gained.

The challenge talking to young children about death is to be truthful and at the same time reassuring. It is easier to talk to a toddler about death and for a toddler to process the information in the context of everyday happenings before experiencing a death that creates a personal loss.

Things Mothers Dread Talking About with Their Toddlers

Mothers are often aware of specific topics or events they dread talking about with their children. There may be things they wish their children did not notice and would never know. There is much evidence that children do notice important things around them, especially things that their parents have reactions to, even when their parents try to conceal their reactions. Grandpa may drink too much, and the change in his behavior may be obvious not only to the adults around the dinner table, but also to the toddlers. Having a way to understand what is happening can be a comfort. "I see you noticed Grandpa is acting different. You look scared, but you are okay. Grandpa has a problem when he drinks wine; sometimes he drinks too much. His doctor is helping him."

Play

Play with Peers

Social interactions among toddlers increase. Friendships are created. Both affectionate and aggressive interactions intensify. Specific attractions and clashes between two children can occur.

At times adults may romanticize or sexualize boy–girl or same-sex interactions. For example, "Bart, give your girlfriend a kiss. She wants to marry you." Some adults may find these kinds of comments amusing. They may seem unnoticed by some toddlers, and for others may raise anxiety. Bart corrected his mother and reassured himself when he said, "Mommy that's silly. We are too young to get married."

Languages

There may be inclusion and exclusion dynamics within bilingual and multilingual families. Often a mother speaks her own first language to her baby. For some mothers, one language may be chosen for loving interactions and another for angry ones. Parents may speak one language to each other and a different language with their children. When the primary language spoken at home is different from the community language, there may be tensions around when to speak which. Understanding the meaning of the language chosen in a particular context can be useful.

Antoinette and her mother Camille were in a group with several other bilingual families. Camille spoke exclusively French to 2½-year-old Antoinette. When in English-speaking social situations with other children and adults, this created a bubble around Antoinette and Camille that interfered with Antoinette's social interactions with the other children and adults. Camille recognized this but had been unable to integrate English into their interactions when they were with English-speaking people until she became aware of her sad feelings when she spoke English to Antoinette.

Camille explained, "My mother lives in France and does not speak any English. She felt totally abandoned by me when I moved to New York. When I speak English to Antoinette, I feel so far away from my mother and that I am excluding her. When I speak French to Antoinette, I feel close to her and to my mother. When I speak French to her here, I realize I am leaving all of you out and Antoinette is being isolated from everyone." Each of the women described some of the emotional meanings of talking their first language to their children. Mothers' group discussion and the bonds created helped Camille to expand Antoinette's social interactions in English.

Secret Languages

When adults want to say something in front of children but do not want the children to understand, they may believe spelling words instead of saying them will create privacy. However, a word spelled is another language and toddlers are enormously capable of learning new languages.

Older children may speak secret languages to exclude adults. Toddlers may create generational boundaries in other ways. They may make a place to play under a table that adults are too big to get into.

- When has your toddler created a special place to be with a friend?
- When have you created such a place for your toddler?

Generational boundaries emerge in different ways at each phase of development. Sometimes generational boundaries are blurred or roles are reversed. For example, Clementine remembered, "When I put sunscreen on Ali, I always ask her to put some on my back. It feels so good. It's almost like she's the Mommy. I just remembered that I hated it when my mother put sunscreen on me. Once I got a terrible sunburn and wished I had let my Mother put sunscreen on my back."

Winning and Losing with Peers

Winning and losing games with peers may be beginning. Toddlers with older siblings may have many experiences losing. Winning and losing a game or race with a friend may be different from competition for Mommy's lap but may arouse similar feelings. In general, toddlers are eased into competitive games gradually. Mothers' feelings about winning and losing are communicated to their toddlers and may have an impact. Mothers' ideas about avoiding or seeking competition for their toddlers may be influenced by childhood memories.

Play with Toys – Easy and Difficult

The pleasure of easy, and the challenge and mastery of difficult, the surrender to too difficult, and the boredom of too easy may all be experiences your toddler is beginning to have with toys.

- When does your toddler persist to master a difficult task?
- When does your child give up?
- When does your toddler repeat an easy task?

A toddler's persistence or lack of persistence may be a temperament trait. Sometimes a lack of persistence indicates that the task is beyond the child's ability. The pleasure in the ease or meaning of a task can lead to persistent repetition. Supporting your toddler's ability to persist can generalize to persisting to learn difficult tasks.

Toys and Cultural Change

During the 1950s, toy guns were part of everyday play for many children. In many homes and communities this is no longer the case; gun play has different meanings today from those in the past. It is believed that when children do not have toy guns, they create other kinds of hostile aggressive play. It is also believed that children benefit from actions in play that are otherwise prohibited. Political, economic, and cultural changes influence the manufacturing, marketing, and purchasing of toys. The psychology of development and life experience determine the themes of toddlers' play and the meaning their play has to them.

In the past, distinctions between toys for boys and toys for girls were common: dolls were for girls; trucks and cars were for boys. Tea sets were for girls and cash registers were for boys. Today, the value of a wide range of toys for both boys and girls is appreciated.

The toys that become popular at a particular time in history, within a specific sub-culture, and within each individual family are determined by many factors: developmental, political, economic, and personal. As there are fashion trends, food fads, and music crazes, there are also changing toy favorites. Your childhood memories may influence the choices you make for your toddler.

Picture Books

It is generally agreed that there are age-appropriate objective criteria to evaluate the age suitability of children's books. A mother's personal feelings about a book's content and her concerns that the content will influence or affect her child in ways she does not want may motivate her to edit the written text so it conforms with her own ideas, values, and lifestyle. Adults who strongly disagree with their parents' ideas and values may respond this way to children's books that have ideas with which they disagree. Adults who as children were themselves prematurely exposed, frightened, or in other ways disturbed by ideas in books or in life may be sensitive to this.

- When do you edit a book you are reading to your toddler?
- Do you think your toddler knows that you are avoiding something?

Children need to be protected and they also need to know that different ideas and different ways of living and thinking exist not only in books, but in everyday life. For example, Melody was in a child-friendly restaurant with her husband and 27-month-old son, Chip. "We had ordered, and my husband and I were enjoying a glass of wine; Chip was in a booster seat busy working on a sticker picture. All of a sudden, he slid out of the seat onto the floor and under the table. I lifted him right up and put him back in the booster seat and told him that he needs to sit in his seat. He said no; that boy is under the table playing with his truck. I said, families are different. In our family when we are having dinner, everybody sits at the table, in their seat. I read this in a book. I couldn't believe it, Chip settled into his seat."

Learning

Developing Sense of Humor

At the same time toddlers are beginning to appreciate a joke, sarcasm, and illusion, they are also concrete. For example, Susan and her daughter Jolie were getting ready to go to the park. Susan, as a joke, put Jolie's hat on her own head and said, "I'm ready." The hat was lopsided, half falling off. Jolie laughed, but then said in all seriousness, as she grabbed her hat, "No Mommy. That's my hat. Don't do that."

Jolie both appreciated the joke and at the same time was disturbed by its possible reality and wanted to set the record straight.

- When does your toddler get a joke?
- When is your toddler scared or confused by a joke?
- What jokes do you repeat with your toddler that were learned when you were a little girl?

Actions or words that are designed to be funny and cause laughter are unexpected or silly. Some humor may frighten or humiliate the listener. For example, the curiously common joke, "I've got your nose," can be funny or terrifying and sometimes mocking. A 2-year-old may laugh when grandpa playfully pretends to have severed his grandson's nose and is holding it peeking out between his index and middle fingers. For some toddlers, the adult's affectionate playfulness modulates the horror of the joke and the child giggles; for others, the terror of actually losing a body part, a heightened anxiety at this age, is triggered and the toddler rejects the joke.

Adapting to Mommy

A major task for children is adaptation to the quirks and idiosyncrasies of their own mother. This is a gradual, lifelong process. During a mother-toddler group, through tears of laughter, Christina summarized the conversation. "Listen to us, we are a difficult group of mothers for our 2-year-olds. I'm grumpy until I have my morning coffee. Cynthia needs the bathroom door closed when she's using the toilet and John screams until she opens the door. Sandra yells too much. Patricia can never decide what to wear so she's always late. Myla works all the time. Nicole is a perfect mother who plans to get a divorce."

- What about you does your toddler need to adapt to?
- What have you changed, or will you change, because of its possible impact on your child?

Mothers' Childhood Memories

A New Kind of Peek-a-boo

A new form of peek-a-boo may emerge at this age; your toddler may hide and trigger your panic in an escalating combination of terror and rage. Your toddler may be triggering in you the fear that your toddler experiences when you leave. Your toddler may also be enacting the wish to be found no matter what. This form of peek-a-boo that evokes mothers' genuine feelings of panic is not a game, but can be changed into a game.

Anya described what was happening with Charlie. "He really hides. For a few minutes I can't find him. I actually get panicky and very angry. Maybe it triggers a memory. I just remembered; my mother told me about getting lost in the supermarket when I was 4 years old. It took a while for her to find me, and she was terrified that I had been kidnapped. I don't remember it at all." Natalie, another group mother suggested, "Maybe you can change Charlie's hiding into a fun game. What if you tell Charlie when he wants to play the hiding game to tell you so you can get ready?"

The following week, Anya told us that Charlie now tells her when he wants to play the hiding game, "I don't get panicky anymore. I also tell Charlie that I will always find him. If he hides in a closet, I will find him; if he hides under the bedcovers, I will find him; if he hides behind the curtains, I will find him. I will find him anywhere in the world. He now seems to like hearing this story more than hiding. He asks me to tell it to him many times a day. It's his favorite story."

Aggressive Themes Reactivated

Pretend play scenarios led by mothers can have aggressive themes that at times may overwhelm toddlers. For example, when Tabetha was 2½ years old, she and her mother Elenore had a vast repertoire of pretend play with wild animals. Elenore led the play as her brother had with her. The play always included growling attacks and fighting. Tabetha began to hit playmates. When it was suggested to Elenore that Tabetha's hitting might be related to the play scenarios that might be frightening, Elenore decided to take Tabetha's lead in their play. The play themes shifted to events of everyday life and Tabetha's hitting stopped. Elenore said, "I don't remember being frightened when my brother played these games with me, but once I was bitten by a vicious dog and have been scared of dogs ever since. Maybe that's why I growl when we play and why Tabetha gets so scared."

Memory of a Lisp

Colette and 2-year-old Kenzie were in a mother-toddler group. Kenzie had just completed a speech evaluation. Colette explained, "I'm very worried. Kenzie has a slight hearing loss that might be the reason she is not talking. She may need tubes surgically implanted in her ears. Maybe she will need hearing aids. I know other kids will tease her; they can be so mean." Grasping for reassurance that Kenzie would be okay, some of the other mothers jumped in quickly: "I know many children who needed tubes and they're fine. It's not such a big deal; lots of kids have them." The distress in the room was palpable.

When mothers hear about a child's possible disability, their own anxiety escalates. They may even react as if the disability is contagious. I said, "Colette has raised serious worries that she has. Colette's concerns seem to trigger so much anxiety in everyone and maybe memories. It sounds like you are all trying to reassure yourselves and Colette, but I'm not sure she feels reassured." Colette added, "When I was 10, I had a bad lisp and needed to see a speech therapist. I was so embarrassed, it was awful. I was always teased. The worst part was that my mother was embarrassed and thought I wasn't trying hard enough to talk better. She kept correcting me."

Several of the mothers had related memories, "When I was about 8, I had a weak-eye and needed to wear a patch. Everyone called me Captain Hook." Another mother added, "My 5-year-old stuttered for a while when he was 2. It was very stressful. The doctor tried to reassure me that it would most likely self-correct in about three months, but it did not reassure me. Luckily his stuttering stopped."

Colette's childhood memories about her own lisp had contributed to her reaction of catastrophe and hopelessness to Kenzie's speech delay and hearing loss. Understanding the impact of her memories on her current reaction lessened her despair and promoted her conviction about helping Kenzie whatever the outcome.

> • What childhood memories influence your reactions to your toddler's difficulties?

Grandmothers' Criticisms

A mother's or mother-in-law's criticisms of her daughter's or daughter-in-law's mothering may be triggered by her own memories of early motherhood. Becoming a grandmother can activate feelings of guilt and inadequacy. Criticisms of others may be an attempt to ward off her own self-criticisms.

> **Highlights: 24 to 30 Months**
>
> Two-year-olds are easier to care for than babies and more difficult. They are curious about learning new things and stubborn about sticking to what they know. They can be generous, selfish, delightful, and impossible. They have ambition and dread. They can be exceedingly joyful and heartbreakingly miserable. Two-year-olds are becoming more and more like the rest of humanity.

13 30 to 36 Months

Mommy-friends

"I didn't know what I was doing when Jackson was a baby. I always said that I would not be the kind of mother my mother was, but I had no idea about how to be the kind of mother I wanted to be. I saw a mother in the lobby of our building with her two sons. She was wonderful with them: gentle, patient, and loving. Delilah and I quickly became friends. She had an 8-month-old and a 4-year-old. She was a great mom. I imitated many things she did. Having her as a friend calmed me.

"When Jackson was 2 years and my second son was 4 months, my husband and I became friendly with a two-mommy family. I met them at a music class for mothers and babies. They did everything together. One was Mommy and the other Mama. They were both wonderful mothers, but they were also different kinds of mothers. Now, rather than imitating a mommy-friend, I learned different things from each of them. I think they learned from me also. My boys are now 3 and 5 years; we are still best friends and so are the children."

Andrea, the mother quoted above, tells her mommy-friend stories in a way that highlights some of the major themes of this book: the potential for an expanding sense of self that emerges when a woman becomes a mother; the unique authenticity of each mother; and a mother's ability to be the kind of mother that she wants to be and to have the relationship with her children that she wants.

Mother–Child Interaction

During this phase of development, mother–toddler interactions become more complex in terms of the intermingling of their surface meaning and their underlying meanings. Part of the complexity is, '*Mommy disapproves of my behavior, and Mommy loves me.*'

Mommy-choices, Toddler-choices, Body–Mind Regulation

Identifying mommy-choices and toddler-choices can be useful. For example, bedtime is a mommy-choice – falling asleep is a toddler-choice: that is the toddler's body–mind regulation. Mealtime and the food prepared are mommy-choices – what is eaten and how much are toddler-choices: that is the toddler's body–mind

DOI: 10.4324/9781003352549-14

regulation. Pooping is a toddler-choice: that is, pooping is a body–mind regulation. Pooping in the potty is a mother–toddler, teaching–learning interaction. Mommy provides the potty, the motivation, and the encouragement. The toddler does the pooping. The overarching principle is that toddlers be supported in their awareness of and responsiveness to the signals they get from their own bodies about hunger and satiation, readiness for sleep, and sensations to poop.

When toddlers protest, choices can be useful. For example, "It is bedtime; time to get into your bed. You decide when to fall asleep." Or "It's time for dinner. We have salad, steak, potatoes, broccoli, and fruit tonight. I wonder what you will choose first." While choices will not resolve every conflict, knowing the toddler-choices and mommy-choices can promote body–mind regulations.

- When is giving a choice to your toddler helpful to resolve a conflict between you? When is it not?

Feeling Like a Good Enough Mother

You may have discovered your fluctuating feelings about being a good mother, a bad mother, and what is called a good enough mother. The mother you want to be and the mother you think you are may be becoming increasingly aligned. Angry mother–toddler interactions may have become more intense, but returning to affectionate interactions is expected.

Teaching–learning, mother–toddler interactions may be deeply gratifying at times and painfully frustrating at others. You may be wondering about the role of punishment in teaching your toddler. As has been emphasized throughout this book, the most effective teaching–learning interactions with toddlers do not include punishment. Generating the positive thoughts and feelings that motivate your toddler to adopt your codes of behavior is highlighted. The power of your toddler's attachment to you is the main element of this process. You have a history together of shared memories. Some of your shared memories have been co-constructed into narratives that will become part of your child's autobiographic life story.

Dual Tracking

When Carly was 34 months, her mother Bernadine was telling a mother-toddler group how "angry and fed-up" she was with Carly's difficult behavior. Her words were harsh and conveyed her helplessness. Carly approached her mother in a frozen stare. Bernadine's anger escalated as she continued her diatribe. I interrupted, "I wonder what Carly is feeling about what is happening right now." Bernadine gasped and said, "She looks very scared; she also looks like she wants something from me. Carly, you look scared. I am telling everyone how angry I sometimes feel." Bernadine recognized that her behavior was having an unintended impact on Carly. She identified Carly's feelings and her own and modulated her anger.

The other mothers in the group recognized their own similar experiences. Jocelyn said, "Last night I was so angry at Gabe. It was the fifth time he came out of bed after three stories, a goodnight song, and a backrub. I was exhausted. I literally threw him on his bed. I didn't hurt him, but he was scared. What was going on inside him was totally off my radar. I was not thinking about what might be on his mind keeping him awake. His father has been away for three days. I felt terrible, apologized, and said that I was wrong. I told him that maybe it's harder to feel cozy in bed when Daddy is away. We made a calendar, designating with stickers the days Daddy had been away, and when he was returning. Gabe fell asleep holding the calendar."

- When have you realized that your child is not in the front or the back of your mind, but has fallen off your radar?"

Mothers are usually dual tracking; that is, they are attending to their children while they are focusing on other things like talking on the phone with a friend or cooking dinner. Sometimes they are not dual tracking; they feel passionate about something and are completely focused on it.

Things Difficult to Talk About

You may have had an experience you would prefer never to tell your child. You may wish that your child never knows certain things about you, for example a prior marriage, estrangement from a family member, or a religious conversion. Other topics that you dread talking about with your child may be directly related to your child, for example donor egg or sperm, surrogacy, adoption, or a family genetic disorder.

Advice about what and when to tell children varies. The assumption that children will eventually learn the information and the value of learning important information from parents is generally agreed. Sorting out your own feelings and attitudes before deciding what and when to tell your child will be helpful.

Maintaining privacy and keeping a shameful secret may be different attitudes about the same event, and affect children differently. When potentially disturbing information is learned by children gradually, with age-appropriate details added, the information does not come as a shock, can be destigmatized, and de-catastrophized. It can feel as if, '*I have always known this and it's okay.*' The information gets woven into the love, security, and trust of family life.

- What conversations have you had with your toddler, or will you have, that demonstrate, '*In our family we talk about happy, sad, embarrassing, and scary things?*'

Mommy's Miscarriage

During a mother-toddler group, Aria described her recent miscarriage: "It was very difficult, but I'm okay now. I had told Leah that I was pregnant, Daddy and I were going to have a baby, and she would be the big sister. We've been talking about it for weeks. She sometimes kisses my belly. I have not said anything to Leah about the miscarriage yet, she's not even 3 years old but I think she knows something is going on."

At the beginning of the group Leah had given two dolls to her mother to hold and was absorbed in play across the room. At this moment, she approached her mother and knocked the dolls off her mother's lap onto the floor. I said, "I think Leah is trying to understand what has happened. Maybe it would help to say something to her." Aria said, "Remember I told you that I was going to have a baby. I was wrong. I am sad about that, but I will feel better. I will have a baby another time and will tell you when it is time." Leah picked up the dolls, put one on her mother's lap, one back in the cradle on the shelf, and continued to play.

Exceptional Events

Television and the Internet are ways in which world tragedies come into our homes. News programs with vivid visuals about school shootings, natural disasters, and war are frequently broadcast. Overheard adult conversations may also have an impact even when it appears as if toddlers are not paying attention, or that they do not understand. For example, while Khai was playing with his blocks, his parents were watching the news and were horrified by the destruction caused by a tornado. Suddenly Khai started making a whooshing sound and throwing his blocks around the room. His mother Rochelle realized that Khai was reacting to the devastating images on the TV, as well as to his parents' reactions. Rochelle said, "What you saw on television was a tornado. Daddy and I were surprised. It was very sad and scary. You may have seen the helpers rescuing people. That tornado is not happening now."

When an unusual disturbing event has occurred, using technical language or unfamiliar words to explain it can emphasize that it is a rare occurrence. The use of new words, special words rather than everyday language, highlights the unusualness of the specific event and can create distance from it.

Body and Mind Awareness

Mother–Toddler Differences and Gender

For mothers, gender differences with their toddlers can provide vicarious pleasure and promote their expanded sense of self or can trigger feelings of rivalry, envy, or anxiety. Ariella described, "I just don't know what I would do with a boy. I'm glad I had a girl. I am the youngest of three sisters. I think my father desperately wanted a son. He always wanted to take us to baseball games but I wanted him to take us to the ballet. My oldest sister liked baseball. I think it made her feel close to my father. My middle sister didn't care, she did homework during games. For me, it was as if my girl interests were erased." For Ariella, many likes and dislikes had gender meaning.

- What likes and dislikes do you and your toddler have that seem gender linked?

Mothers can feel gender-different from their daughters. Carla described herself as a woman who rejected female gender stereotypes and found her 3-year-old daughter's exclusive choice of sparkling party-dresses and dolls disturbing, "I do not want Mila to be a girly-girl. She only wants to wear her party shoes and dresses, even to the playground. For Halloween she only wants to wear a princess costume. An airplane pilot would be out of the question. We fight all the time about what she wears and what she plays with. She only plays with dolls."

Suddenly Carla remembered that when she was a little girl her mother had wanted her to wear bows in her hair and uncomfortable dresses with tights. "My mother always wanted me to be a different kind of girl than I wanted to be. She still does. She always says things like get a hairstyle, wear some makeup. You still look like a ragamuffin tomboy. I can't believe it; I'm doing a different version of the same thing with Mila. I'm trying to get her to be more like I am. She's the kind of girl my mother wanted me to be."

With her new awareness of the connection between her interactions with her own mother and with Mila, Carla was able to allow her little girl to be the kind of girl she wanted to be. In addition, Carla began to enjoy her daughter's pleasure in being a girl even though the gender symbols Mila chose were not the same as her own. In time, Mila chose to wear jeans and sneakers to the playground like her mother.

Lola, another mother in the group, said, "I was called a tomboy. I'm not sure what that means today, or if the word still exists. Giselle is like I am but her dad wants her to be more feminine all the time. I think he is sensitive to gender because he just discovered that his sister is gay and, while he is totally accepting, I think he is having a reaction. I think Giselle is fine. She wears jeans to play and dresses to party."

Genevieve added, "I'm worried about Grant; he wants to wear a dress. When he wears an apron to cook with me, he calls it a dress. I think it's because he has an older sister, but I'm not sure. She sometimes puts a dress on him. Maybe I shouldn't let her. I've scheduled a consultation with a child psychologist." Vanessa, another group mother, said, "When I polish my nails, I always put some polish on Jake's toenails. I never buy him sandals and I would never put polish on his fingernails. I don't know why I do this. I've been doing it since he was very little. What do you think?"

- Which gender differences and similarities with your toddler are pleasurable for you? Which are disturbing? Which are you uncertain about?

Toddlers want to do the same things their parents do. They also want to feel emotionally close to them. Sometimes doing the same thing Mommy does seems like a way to feel close. Making a distinction between feeling close and being the same as can be useful. For example, Alec's mother wore red lipstick. When Alec's mother was away for a weekend and Alec missed her, he took her lipstick out of her makeup drawer, and put it mostly on his lips. Wearing lipstick like Mommy was Alec's attempt to feel close to Mommy. Alec's mother decided to Facetime with Alec during breakfast and before his bath every evening while she was away. Alec no longer wanted to wear lipstick.

Beginning Gender Identity

Isabella was 34 months and had very short hair. Both her mother and sister had long hair, her father and brother had short hair. Isabella desperately wanted long hair. She hated being mistaken for a boy and thought long hair would be a sign to the world, '*I am a girl.*' Isabella chose another sign – a sparkling tiara. She insisted on wearing the tiara that had been among the dress-up clothes for Halloween in a neighborhood store. Over the next many months, she acquired a collection of tiaras. Every day she wore a dress and a tiara. Her mother helped her to make it clear to the world that she was a girl. Isabella was no longer mistaken for a boy even though her hair was still short. When her female gender identity was more firmly established, Isabella shed the tiara.

Adaptation to Not Knowing

Darlene and 34-month-old Danny were in a mother-toddler group. Danny was bright and inquisitive. He had become interested in designating who is a boy and who is a girl. He emphasized that his toys were "boy-toys." Darlene was 7 months pregnant and had explained pregnancy and childbirth to Danny. Indicating, with her hands on her belly, Darlene told Danny, "I'm pregnant. That means Daddy and I are going to have a baby. Until the baby is ready to be born, it will stay inside my body in a special place. It will take a long time. When it is time to be born, I will tell you. You will be the big brother." Danny had appeared not too interested in any of these details.

Seemingly completely disconnected to Darlene, she had needed to take Danny to the emergency room because he had put a small toy in his nose and she was not able to remove it. Also seemingly disconnected to Darlene was Danny's nose-picking and sometimes eating what he removed from his nose. In contrast to Danny's apparent body interest as demonstrated by his explorations of his nose, we were told, "Danny never touches his penis."

Danny's body explorations, and thoughts about what is inside and what is outside his body, how things get into the body, out of the body, and back into the body were focused on his nose. However, Danny refused to blow his nose. He did not ask questions and was not interested in what his mother said about bodies, including her pregnancy, boy–girl differences, and blowing noses.

Learning to use the potty, another inside-outside body experience, had gone easily for Danny without much discussion. He was wearing underpants at 28 months. Danny was an avid eater and had slept through the night since he was 7 months. Danny's body functions were quite self-regulated and independent.

The challenge of helping Danny with his quest for answers to the body questions he was grappling with by putting a toy in his nose were addressed with the following child development information: "Sometimes children, rather than needing more information, need help to adapt to what they cannot know or to things that cannot be known. Danny has so many important questions about his body and seems to want to answer those questions himself. Putting the toy in his nose, picking his nose, and eating what he removes may be examples of questions he has and his attempts to answer them himself."

- What is your toddler struggling to understand?
- When would more information help?
- When does your toddler need help being comfortable with not knowing?

It takes a long time to learn about the body. Learning to feel comfortable with what is not known can be important. Play with a pastry decorating tool that included filling the pastry bag with sweet icing, squeezing it out to decorate a cookie, and the pleasure of eating it were useful substitutes for some of Danny's nose explorations.

Treasured Toys

Over time, the external features of a treasured toy change because it has been cuddled, dragged, and dirtied. And while it may look bedraggled and threadbare with missing limbs and other parts to the rest of the world, it is more highly valued by the toddler than ever.

A toddler has endowed a treasured toy with meanings that persist until it is no longer needed because the child's mind has developed and can perform the needed mental functions. These mental functions include: to maintain a positive sense of self, to tolerate frustration, and to regulate angry feelings, fears, and ambivalence. These mental processes throughout life are promoted by the abilities to use language to name emotions, to describe subjective experiences, and to feel understood by others.

At around 3 years of age, toddlers become increasingly capable of these mental functions and the treasured toy is no longer used in the same way. Evidence of these developmental changes can be seen and supported. Anna described, "Since Robbie was born, we have kept his Blanky close; first I did, then he did. When he was a baby, I draped it on him when he nursed. It wasn't a treasured toy yet, but I thought it might become one. When he began to walk, he dragged it around the apartment. He kept it close during meals and he snuggled up in it for his bedtime story. He slept with it every night. I kept it with him when we traveled in the car and on airplanes. When Robbie was about 2 years, every day before leaving the apartment to go to the playground he put the Blanky in his stroller. One day when he was a little over 3 years, as I was loading his scooter onto the stroller, Robbie climbed in. He did not get his Blanky or ask for it. I was not sure if he forgot or decided he didn't need it. I decided not to remind him. It was the beginning of separating from the Blanky."

- If your child has a treasured toy, what changes have you seen in your toddler's use of the toy?
- What do you do to support and expand these changes?
- How do memories of your treasured toy influence you?

Emotion Regulation

A toddler's communications that include exaggerations or what might seem overly dramatic may be a child's way of communicating, '*I feel strongly about this. It is important to me.*'

Leilani explained, "Rosa is just like I was. She has a fake cry. When I tell her it's time to put the iPad away, leave the playground, or no more bedtime stories, she always does her loud, fake cry. I call her the drama queen." I suggested, "Maybe Rosa's feelings sound fake when something is important to her that she knows you won't give to her, and she knows that you don't want her to even want it. I wonder how she would react if you said, 'I understand it is important to you to keep the iPad a few more minutes. It is so interesting to you, but it is time to turn it off. Do you want one more minute to finish what you are doing?' Or at bedtime, 'We have had such a wonderful day together, I understand you want it to go on. Tomorrow we will have another wonderful day'" Toddlers do not need to want what we want in order to do what we want them to do. They can have their own thoughts and feelings, disagree and protest, and still cooperate.

Leilani recognized that she had been ridiculing Rosa by calling her a drama queen and dismissing how she genuinely felt. "Rosa has been doing exactly what I did as a child, and I have been reacting to her exactly the same way that my parents reacted to me. They always said I was a great actor; I was not acting. I could not show them how serious I was."

- When does your toddler seem to be exaggerating or faking an emotion?

Words, Ideas, and Feelings

Most behavioral limits are learned by repeated mother–child interactions. Some behaviors are prohibited, and some are prevented. The prohibition of words, ideas, or feelings as if they were dangerous or bad behavior may interfere with communications and emotion regulation. Strong feelings communicated in an objectionable way, for example by lying on the floor, kicking, and screaming, can be reframed: "I think that means you are very angry at me; it's okay to be angry." In this way, the feelings are acknowledged and validated rather than thoughts and feelings being taboo. Poopy head or stupid may be terms your toddler has heard from a friend or older sibling and is trying them out. "I think you heard someone say those words and you want to see what it feels like to say them and what reaction you get."

Your toddler may have heard you curse and imitate you. If you do not want your toddler to curse, a response might be, "Sometimes I say that word when I have a strong feeling and I am surprised, but in our family I think it is better to use other words we know. You are learning all the words in our language, and you are also learning when to say them. When we are together, I rather we both say ouch that hurts or oops I dropped it!"

- What ideas or feelings has your toddler talked about in a way that you found offensive?
- What ideas or feelings has your child said in words that can be reframed?

Words like shut-up may not be okay around the family dinner table, but in some contexts might be of value to be able to say, to read in books, or to hear in movies. Communicating that you are interested in all of your child's thoughts and feelings can be of value. Home can be a safe place where all experiences, ideas, and feelings can be talked about and understood.

Play

Your toddler may have developed favorite play activities. Play with water is generally appealing at this age and may be related to an interest in peeing. Mud pies and playdough may be particularly engaging or totally rejected because of their connection to poop. Play alone and with others has expanded. Experiences with both winning and losing have increased and reactions to both may have intensified.

Scooters

A cherished possession, having different meaning from other toys, may be a scooter or other riding toy. A toddler's passionate sense of "it's mine" may be related to a scooter's connection to the early mobility of crawling and the exhilaration of walking. The speed of separating and reuniting is accelerated with a scooter. The toddler independently generates the speed and direction of the scooter and embodies the power of attachment and autonomy. When zooming around on a scooter, the sense of self is invigorated. In addition to a treasured toy, a scooter may become a mother–toddler agreed non-shared possession.

- Which of your toddler's possessions are for sharing? Which are not?

Play with Peers

Play with peers has increased: first encounters, forging relationships, and deepening friendships. As in all relationships, ongoing pleasurable interactions among toddlers get disrupted and are repaired. Having some time and space to process a rupture and the feelings evoked may be needed before authentic apologies and forgiveness are possible. The process includes identifying the angry feelings and recognizing what caused them.

> • When are superficial social apologies useful? When are apologies that reflect genuine remorse useful for your toddler?

Trevor and Emerson were almost 3 years and had been having weekly playdates since they were 18 months. Their mothers were good friends. Recently, both Emerson and Trevor were having more squabbles; especially when the visit was in one of their rooms. Both children reacted as if their rooms were being invaded and their toys taken. In a way they were.

The visits were important to both mothers. They agreed that before each visit they would help their child to choose several toys they did not want their friend to play with and they would be put in the closet. Visits were limited to 2 hours. As part of their time together, in addition to play with toys and a snack, their mothers helped the children with an art project. Visits went more smoothly but these changes did not eliminate all conflicts between the children.

During a playdate in Trevor's room, Kendal set out two pieces of paper on a small table with two boxes of crayons, each with five colors. Kendal described the scene during a mothers' group: "I thought we had figured out how to avoid the squabbles. I told Trevor, 'This is your paper and crayons,' and I told Emerson, 'These are yours.' As soon as they opened their boxes of crayons, they both took out a red crayon. Emerson yelled, 'Mine is broken,' and tried to grab Trevor's crayon. Trevor held it tight, hit Emerson, and yelled, 'It's mine.' In two seconds, they were both screaming and hitting each other. I separated them and said, 'I'm going to help you to stop. Let's talk about what happened.' I used the popular, often mocked phrase, 'You both had big feelings.'

"Both children sat back down at the table. It looked like they were sorry about hitting each other and now were ready to draw. After a few minutes of drawing and taking turns with the unbroken red crayon, Emerson broke Trevor's crayon and Trevor drew on Emerson's paper. It was time to put the drawing away.

"When Emerson was leaving, she wanted to take a toy car of Trevor's with her. Trevor said no and Emerson began to cry. Trevor hesitantly offered the car to Emerson, but I told him she can't take his toys. Even though Emerson was sad, it was important for Trevor to know that she was not allowed to take his toys. Sometimes doing what makes him happy is important even if it makes someone else sad. I think I have a problem and always put the other person's happiness above mine. I don't want that for Trevor."

The above story has elements of the ongoing rupture and repair process in toddler relationships and mothers' opportunities to not repeat with their toddlers some of their own problems.

Imitation of Peers

Sometimes toddlers imitate something they see another child do that they are curious about; sometimes the imitations worry mothers because they fear the behavior will be adopted permanently. Avery told a mothers' group about Misa's playdate with Arielle. Both girls were almost 3 years old. "While they were playing, Arielle put her hair into her mouth and began to suck it. This is a nervous habit Arielle has. Her mother firmly tells her to stop. Arielle spits her hair out of her mouth, but in a few seconds it's back in her mouth. I think it's pretty disgusting; her hair is always wet. I am not sure we should continue playdates. I don't want Misa to learn this nervous habit."

- What behaviors are you worried your toddler might learn from other children?
- What behaviors do you want your toddler to learn from others?

Sometimes when toddlers see another child do a self-soothing behavior like suck their hair or their thumb, they may be curious and try it out to see what it feels like. Part of the motivation may be to imagine their friend's experience. Misa may also have had a reaction to the angry interaction between Arielle and her mother.

The following week, Avery described what she said to Misa when she tried sucking her hair, "I think you have seen Arielle suck her hair, I guess it feels good to her. It does not feel good to most people. Maybe she does it to feel better when she has a feeling she does not like. Her mother is trying to help her to stop. I think you are curious about what it feels like and how I would react."

Misa and Arielle continued to have playdates; Arielle continued to suck her hair, Misa did not. Misa may have been influenced by what her mother said. In addition, a self-soothing behavior that is imitated may not have the same pleasure as one that has been originally created.

Learning

Mother–toddler, teaching–learning interactions about the potty increase during this phase of development. The foundation has been laid by the many daily experiences related to poop and pee, including awareness of body sensations, mothers' interest, diaper changing routines, words to describe the process, the introduction of the potty, related play, maturational control, developmental readiness, observations of others, and accumulated world knowledge – everybody poops and pees.

Pooping in the Potty

Jannette, like many mothers, to determine if her daughter Judi's diaper needed to be changed, put her face next to Judi's bottom and inhaled the scent deeply. This routine intimate body interaction on the surface seemed unnoticed by them both. Janette's husband thought it was "weird." On the other hand, Janette thought it was "disgusting" that Judi picked her nose.

Judi was 3 years old and picked her nose frequently with great enthusiasm. Jannette was doing everything she could think of to get Judi to stop. Jannette was also doing everything she could to teach Judi to use the potty. They played with Judi's dolls on the potty and, since Judi pooped every morning after breakfast, Jannette suggested she sit on the potty and hear a story.

Every morning Judi happily agreed to sit on the potty for several minutes while her mother read to her. At the end of the story, she stood up and announced, "No poop coming." However, shortly after Judi got off the potty and her diaper was back on, she pooped. Janette explained, "Judi says that her poop stinks and she won't do it."

Jannette's disgust with Judi's nose-picking and Judi's disgust with her own poop seemed to be connected. The following question was a way to understand more. I asked, "I wonder what the connection might be between Judi picking her nose, something you think is disgusting, and Judi thinking that her poop stinks and it is disgusting?" Jannette was intrigued.

The following child development information included an allusion to Jannette's pleasure smelling Judi's poop in her diaper. I said, "Judi may need to know that her poop smells just the way it is supposed to smell. In some ways toddlers need to know that they are giving a wonderful gift to Mommy when they poop in the potty, and that the special gift from their body is pleasurably received."

Jannette smiled, seeming pleased, excited, and a little self-conscious with the idea that Judi's poop would be given to her as a special gift and would be received with pleasure. Maybe this idea resonated, though she was unaware, with her pleasure in smelling Judi's poop when it was in her diaper. I added, "While poop is valued in the potty, it is also discarded – casually flushed away. It is applauded, but not touched. Both attitudes about poop are held by mothers and communicated to their children in equal measure: poop is not overly valued, and not disparaged."

The following week Jannette told the mothers' group, "I told Judi that her poop smells just right. I dumped some poop from her diaper into the potty so she could see it there. I also told her that it is okay to pick her nose in private. I realized that it was pleasurable to her, and she was asserting her autonomy and control over her body, which may be particularly important to her now while she's learning to use the potty. She now tells me when she needs to poop, and she poops in the potty. I leave it there a few minutes before I flush it. It seems important to her just to know it's there."

The change in Judi's behavior may have been coincidental to the changes in her mother's interactions with her, but Jannette thought that the changes she had made helped Judi to poop in the potty and to stop picking her nose. Maybe Judi's impulse to pick her nose abated as she was able to see her poop in the potty, and though unspoken, for Judi and Jannette to smell Judi's poop together. For Jannette, it was as though the intimate pleasure of smelling Judi's poop in her diaper shifted to the shared pleasure of Judi's poop in the potty.

Pooping and Mommy's Pregnancy

In the middle of a lively group discussion about learning to use the potty, Ajax's mother Elise mentioned, "Ajax is just not into it anymore. I think I'm going to put him back in diapers even though I am going to have a baby next month." Ajax was almost 3½ years and had been using the potty for three months. He wore underpants all the time, but several days earlier had begun to refuse to use the potty. The women were surprised; learning to use the potty had gone smoothly for Ajax, and Elise had been pleased. The mothers asked about Elise's apparent nonchalance about Ajax refusing to use the potty, and her readiness to put him back in diapers. Her response was, "No big deal."

Elise believed Ajax was well prepared for the arrival of his baby sister. She had read many books to him about babies, their crying, and the attention they need. I wondered what Ajax was being told about his mother's pregnancy and what he thought about it. The following child development information added a ripple to our discussion: "Regardless of what information young children have been given about the birth of a sibling, they may have their own theories about who can get pregnant, and how a baby gets in and how it gets out of Mommy's body. When mothers are pregnant, their children Ajax's age, boys as well as girls, may have thoughts and feelings about a baby being inside their own bodies – just like Mommy. Toddlers may think that a baby can get in if they eat something and get out when they poop. These ideas can have an impact on their eating and pooping."

The women remained quiet and curious. Ajax was the oldest in the group; two other children were also in underpants, and another mother was pregnant. I asked Elise about Ajax's reactions to this phase of her pregnancy. Rejecting the connection that I was making between her pregnancy and Ajax refusing to use the potty, Elise asserted, "He's never said anything, we just read books about babies. I don't think he thinks about being pregnant."

The following idea about children's play and being pregnant was my attempt to broaden the discussion: "Sometimes children communicate ideas they have about being pregnant through their play. For example, they may put a pillow or stuffed animal under their shirts or down their pants." Elise said she thought, "It would be weird for Ajax to do that," and then she said, "I want Ajax to feel that the baby is his baby too. That's what I tell him; the baby is your baby too. I don't want him to feel displaced by the baby as I did by my sister."

Elise's reactivated childhood memories about feeling "displaced" by her own sister motivated her to tell Ajax the baby is his baby too. She believed this would prevent him from feeling displaced. I asked Elise whether Ajax could misinterpret "It's your baby too" to mean there is a baby in his tummy too. Elise appeared thoughtful.

The following week, Elise reported, "Ajax played being pregnant for the first time. He stuck out his tummy and said, I have a baby in my tummy." Elise took the opportunity to clarify for him, "The baby is only in Mommy's tummy. You will be the big brother. Only mommies can be pregnant." The next day Ajax resumed pooping in the potty.

It is not clear whether Ajax had played being pregnant before, but his mother had not noticed; whether hearing the mothers talk during the group had been useful to him; or whether Elise communicated something different to Ajax that clarified something in his own mind that enabled him to use play to cope with his worries.

Pretending to be pregnant is different from unprocessed worries about being pregnant. For Elise, the image of seeing Ajax pretending to be pregnant allowed her to differentiate her wish that Ajax not feel displaced by the baby, from a fantasy that he was pregnant. Elise helped Ajax distinguish between having a sister and being pregnant. Ajax's ability to play being pregnant revealed some thoughts that were on his mind of which his mother had been unaware.

Mothers' Childhood Memories

Memory of a Harsh Punishment

For some mothers, harsh punishments as children continue to reverberate. For example, during a group discussion about teaching toddlers to use the potty, Ryleigh described that her almost 3-year-old daughter, Eloise, who had been wearing panties for a month and never wet herself during the day, was still wetting her "beautiful bed" every night. "I'm so angry at her, I yell at her, but it doesn't help. I don't want to yell at her. I feel like punishing her, but I don't want to do that either. I don't know what to do." Ryleigh shamefully confessed, "I just remembered when I was 11 years old, I visited my cousin who lived on a farm. She had a beautiful bed with a pink satin cover and white organza canopy. It was the most beautiful bed that I had ever seen. There was a gasoline pump on the property that the children were not allowed to touch. I filled a watering can with the gasoline and poured it on my cousin's bed. I ruined it. My mother locked me in a shed alone all night. I was terrified."

I linked Ryleigh's memory of the harsh punishment and her own guilt and terror to her current angry yelling at Eloise: "It seems as though fragments of your memory are being repeated with Eloise. There is no gasoline, no pink satin bed cover, and no shed, but there are sheets wet with urine, anger, fear, and helplessness."

This was the beginning of our exploration of Ryleigh's angry and frightening interactions with Eloise. Ryleigh's harshness in response to wet sheets lessened, she helped Eloise get to the potty in the middle of the night, and in a short while Eloise slept through the night and her bed stayed dry.

- What childhood memories do you have about being punished and how do they influence interactions with your toddler?

Fear of Sexual Abuse

A mother-toddler group had been meeting for over two years. The women had shared many intimate details about their toddlers, themselves, and their marriages. Claire mentioned a recent newspaper article about the sexual abuse of a young girl and declared her intention to teach Beverly how to protect herself: "I want to be sure that Beverly will never be sexually abused."

Claire described how she was warning Beverly about potential dangers and teaching her self-protective strategies: "Never talk to strangers, never take candy from strangers, and never get into a car with strangers." Since 3-year-old children are rarely alone with strangers and the parents of a sexually abused child often know the abuser, Claire's rules about strangers seemed not relevant. In addition, frightening warnings can make a 3-year-old feel unsafe and unprotected.

In the middle of enumerating her instructions to Beverly and appearing startled, Claire remembered a kiss when she was 14 years old. "Right there in our living room, my father's friend put his hands on my bottom and kissed me in a way that tickled the inner edges of my lips with his tongue. I never told my parents or anyone. I've not thought about it for years." I wondered what motivated Claire to keep the kiss secret, whether Claire felt unprotected by her parents in other ways when she was unable to protect herself, and whether she had been criticized for typical childhood body pleasures.

The following child development information highlighted parents' protective role. I said, "It is the parents' responsibility to protect their children. Children cannot protect themselves. I wonder when else you felt unprotected." Claire said, "When I was 10 years old, my little brother always spied on me when I was in the bathroom. When I told my parents, they accused me of teasing him and said that I liked the attention." Claire's memory of her parents' accusations and disdain, and her associated feelings about sexually related pleasures, may have motivated her to keep the kiss secret and contributed to her anxiety about Beverly being sexually abused.

I commented on Claire's memory: "Not only do you remember your parents not protecting you, but in addition you remember being blamed for your brother's peeping and being criticized for any excitement or pleasure you got from it." Claire agreed and added that in some ways she thought the kiss was her fault.

Little children cannot protect themselves. They learn to protect themselves when they have been protected by their parents. They also need to feel entitled to say "No" to unwanted touching. In addition, they need to know that their own childhood body pleasures and excitements are recognized and accepted by their parents; for example, running around their room naked. Rather than using frightening hypotheticals, there are many everyday opportunities to support toddlers saying "No" to unwanted touching and many childhood body pleasures to be validated and supported.

There are also situations when children are required to be touched in ways they do not want. Recognizing their discomfort and protests to being touched can be helpful. For example, when being examined by the doctor: "I know you don't like it when the doctor examines you. Do you want me to hold you when you have your check-up?"

- When does your toddler try to avoid being touched? What happens?
- When do you support your child saying no to being touched?
- What are some of the body pleasures your toddler is learning about now?
- Which body pleasures are okay with you? Which are not? Which do you support, with whom, and how?

Claire now recognized that a 3-year-old is not able to protect herself. Beverly was no longer required to do high-five with their neighbor, sit on her uncle's lap, whom she saw rarely, or to be kissed when she did not want to be. In addition, Claire decided to discontinue using the babysitter with whom she had never felt comfortable but had never been quite sure why.

Having Another Child

Ideas about having another baby may have emerged; plans may have been made or a surprise pregnancy may be happening. There may be things you want to do the same and things you want to do differently this time. Alternatively, you may have decided no more children.

Petra described her experience: "My life plan was always to have two children. I was so excited throughout my second pregnancy. My labor was progressing easily, and I was leaving to go to the hospital. Standing at the door, saying goodbye to my 3-year-old, all of a sudden I became teary and thought, why did I do this? My sense of loss in the moment was so intense – I would never again be just Noah's Mommy. A few hours later Noah visited me at the hospital. His dad and I introduced him to Quimby. It was an extraordinary moment."

Highlights: 30 to 36 Months

As your toddler reaches 3 years old, a foundation for the rest of life has been created. The core of the foundation is the accumulation and consolidation of all the mother–baby and mother–toddler interactions that have nurtured your child's development and led to your new understandings of your own childhood memories and to your expanded sense of self.

---

14   Growing Up

The developmental themes from birth to 3 years of age discussed and illustrated throughout this book remain themes for life. At each phase they may look different on the surface, but they are recognizable. Middle childhood, adolescence, young adulthood, mid-life, and later ageing all include new and evolving attachment relationships; separations and losses; body and mind changes; pleasures and emotion regulation challenges; and the awakening of childhood memories. Early childhood lays a foundation for the future and early motherhood prepares us further.

Secure base interactions continue. In many ways throughout life mothers remain a secure base – mothers in actuality, mothers remembered, and mothers imagined. Pleasurable childhood memories reinforce the ongoing meaning of mother as a secure base; painful memories provide potential life-long lessons. Memories of childhood treasured toys reflect the emotional endurance of a secure base.

Some childhood treasured toys have been kept into adulthood. Special blankets, dolls, and soft cuddly toys are carefully stored in memory trunks, or tucked away in closets. Some remain in bedrooms long abandoned, maybe seen on occasion. Others have long vanished. Adult memories of special teddy-bears, blankets, bunnies, and other treasured toys maintain meanings similar to those that the cherished toys themselves had during early childhood. When the memories are recalled, feelings of comfort and pleasure are aroused. Even when the memories include a treasured toy's abrupt loss, or the toy was treasured in the context of threatening and difficult childhood experiences, the pleasurable memory of the object remains and tempers surrounding pain.

Many of the challenges described in this book are typical. Many of the difficulties resolved are dramatic. I have chosen them to make a point: the most practical information about early development and motherhood is sometimes rooted in mothers' own childhood memories. Mothers' reflections about the memories can lead to solutions to typical problems with babies and toddlers that may be surprising or even seem magical.

During the first three years of motherhood, not only does a woman nurture her baby's development, but she herself changes in many ways. She has relived aspects of her own childhood and has grown from the experience. She has had a new and unique love relationship. She has thought about her childhood memories from a

DOI: 10.4324/9781003352549-15

new perspective. Ongoing curiosity about her child's developing mind and her own expanding sense of self are central elements.

I have used the powerful lens of mother–baby and mother–toddler love and attachment, and mothers' childhood memories that are activated, to tell the story of early development and motherhood. Women's friendships during the first three years of motherhood are an integral part of the story. When mothers talk their stories unfold; they meet the challenges and discover magical moments with their babies and toddlers.

Index

Printed in the United States
by Baker & Taylor Publisher Services